# MEGACITY SAGA

*À ma mère*

*qui a su m'inspirer en gardant toujours vivantes mes racines franco-ontariennes*

# MEGACITY SAGA

## Democracy and Citizenship in This Global Age

Julie-Anne Boudreau

BLACK ROSE BOOKS

Montréal/New York
London

Black Rose Books No. DD290
Hardcover ISBN: 1-55164-165-8 (bound)
Paperback ISBN: 1-55164-164-X (pbk.)

**Canadian Cataloguing in Publication Data**

Boudreau, Julie-Anne
The megacity saga : democracy and citizenship in this global age

Includes bibliographical references and index.
Hardcover ISBN: 1-55164-165-8 (bound)
Paperback ISBN: 1-55164-164-X (pbk.)

1. Annexation (Municipal government)--Ontario--Toronto. 2. Citizens for Local Democracy. 3. Democracy--Canada. 4. City planning--Canada. I. Title.

JS1789.2.B68 2000 320.8'59'09713541 C99-901584-2

*Cover design by Associés libres, Montréal*

BLACK ROSE BOOKS

| C.P. 1258 | 2250 Military Road | 99 Wallis Road |
|---|---|---|
| Succ. Place du Parc | Tonawanda, NY | London, E9 5LN |
| Montréal, H2W 2R3 | 14150 | England |
| Canada | USA | UK |

To order books in North America:
(phone) 1-800-565-9523 (fax) 1-800-221-9985
In Europe: (phone) London 44 (0)20 8986-4854 (fax) 44 (0)20 8533-5821

Our Web Site address: http://www.web.net/blackrosebooks

A publication of the Institute of Policy Alternatives of Montréal (IPAM)

Printed in Canada

The Canada Council for the Arts | Le Conseil des Arts du Canada

# TABLE OF CONTENTS

*List of Tables, Maps, Cartoons* ........ *vi*
*Acknowledgments* ........ *vii*
*Prologue* ........ *ix*

CHAPTER 1 ........ 1
Citizens Facing a Megacity Giant

CHAPTER 2 ........ 37
Citizens for Local Democracy Speaks Out!

CHAPTER 3 ........ 84
Within the Belly of a Global Monster

CHAPTER 4 ........ 109
The Living Sponge of the City

CHAPTER 5 ........ 129
From Constitutionalism to the Rights to the City

CHAPTER 6 ........ 154
Performative Citizenship and Citizens for Local Democracy

*Appendix A: Checklist for Local Democracy* ........ 173
*Appendix B: Civic Priorities* ........ 177
*Appendix C: Citizens for Local Democracy Values Statement* ........ 179
*Appendix D: Principles Governing Municipal/Provincial Financial Relationships* ........ 183

BIBLIOGRAPHY ........ 186
INDEX ........ 196

# LIST OF TABLES, MAPS, CARTOONS


*Table 1: Voter Turnouts 1991-1997* ..... 15

*Table 2: November 10, 1997 Electoral Results—Mayor* ..... 21

*Table 3: Occupational Distribution by Local Cities* ..... 44

*Table 4: Provincial Elections, June 3, 1999—Results in the new city and in the GTA, in percent* ..... 66 & 67

*Table 5: Changes in Social Management* ..... 90

*Table 6: Downtown Toronto Provincial Electoral Results 1987-99* ..... 118

*Map 1: The Greater Toronto Area* ..... 3

*Cartoon 1: Voter Stress Syndrome* ..... 20

*Cartoon 2: Name Changes* ..... 87

# ACKNOWLEDGMENTS

This adventure began with my arrival in Toronto. I owe much of the courage and perseverance needed to complete this research to Emmanuel Matte, with whom I first arrived to Toronto. He accompanied me through moments of amazement, curiosity, analysis and discouragement. I thank him sincerely for these and all other moments which brought me where I am today. Roger Keil was the first to bring me to a Citizens for Local Democracy meeting. He was and still is a profoundly thoughtful and supportive advisor and friend. Always a great inspiration, I thank him for introducing me to urban studies and for leading me to discover Los Angeles, where I am completing my doctorate today. Engin Isin gave me his contagious enthusiasm and curiosity for urban politics and issues of identity and citizenship. To him and to Roger, I owe many allusions and ideas, as well as the will to always remain politically active. Janet Conway and Stefan Kipfer are my greatest models for combining doctoral studies and political activity. Their important work in and on Toronto served as building blocks for the following pages. I thank them for their time, their comments, their insights, their passion, and their lifeline contact with the city I had to leave to pursue my studies in California. Matina Karvellas, Samuel Knafo, Grace-Edward Galabuzi, and Scott Redding were my "International Political Economy and urban and local spaces" interlocutors and friends during my studies at York University. We spent numerous hours discussing the latest books by Harvey and others…And should always continue these discussion over red wine. I particularly wish to thank Matina for her continuous hospitality during my trips to Toronto, and for her way to gather friends together for my visits. The Department of Political Science at York University welcomed me for my Master's and provided a warm and stimulating environment. I met incredible friends, professors, and colleagues there. A special thank you also goes to Warren Magnusson, whose encouragement and thoughtful comments helped me finalize this book.

When I arrived in Los Angeles for my doctorate, I found a very different university culture and way of life. Liette Gilbert has been a close friend guiding me through the City of Angels. I owe her countless hours discussing my work under sun, incredible support, insights, and car tours throughout the city! Martha Matsuoka provided thoughtful comments on my work. She helped me understand urban and regional politics in California, and gave me the desire to learn much more about social movements. D. Gregg Doyle helped me with maps and tables and became a good friend. Edward Soja, Michael Storper, Raul Hinojosa-Ojeda, and Raymond Rocco were most patient while I was completing this book, putting my doctoral dissertation on hold for a while…They are precious and challenging advisors.

I cannot close these acknowledgments without mentioning my parents, Lise Routhier Boudreau and Armand Boudreau, who showed me to always believe in the power of curiosity. To the residents of Toronto, to my neighbours, to my friends, and mostly to members of Citizens for Local Democracy, I am grateful for showing me their love for the city which welcomed me. I cannot name here all residents with whom I discussed throughout the Megacity saga. However, I wish to thank them all personally for their insights and beliefs. Although not all of them will agree with my interpretation of the struggle, I wish to thank them for their friendly challenges. Beth Moore Milroy deserves a special mention for her generous comments, at times challenging but always helpful in clarifying many of my arguments. Pauline McAdam and Gail Haines of the City Clerk's Office provided electoral data. I thank them for their generosity of time and resources. Hajo Beeckman of the University of Leuven was conducting research on Toronto during my visit in February 2000. I owe him some contact information and a wonderful trek throughout the Megacity, from Etobicoke, to North York, to Scarborough, to the Habourfront. Geoff Kennedy generously served as my "English grammar inspector." I thank him sincerely for his time and suggestions.

The Fonds pour la formation des chercheurs et l'aide à la recherche du Québec (FCAR) and later the Social Sciences and Humanities Research Council of Canada (SSHRC) helped pay the rent and tuition fees for the past few years. Portions of chapter 1, 2, and 5 were presented at the XIV World Congress of Sociology of the International Sociological Association in Montreal (July 26-August 1, 1998); and at the Annual meetings of the Association of Collegiate Schools of Planning in Pasadena (November 5-8, 1998) and Chicago (October 21-24, 1999). Most of the analysis of middle-class urbanism in chapter 2 builds upon an article published in 1999 in the *International Journal of Urban and Regional Research* as "Megacity Toronto: Struggles Over Differing Aspects of Middle-Class Politics" Volume 23 (4): 771-781.

# PROLOGUE

Toronto the Good. Toronto the Strong. Toronto the Thriving. Toronto the Polite. Toronto the Safe, the Clean, the Green...I was turning these words over in my mind as we stopped at Tim Hortons near Oshawa, for a last stop before entering the city. I wanted to embrace the city, learn its language, hop on its streetcars, "ride the rocket," as they say over there. And I did it all right, commuting one hour back and forth to suburban York University everyday from my downtown apartment. I was entering the city as a stranger...and a few months later I was marching down Yonge Street with thousands of other residents, in the midst of big "No Megacity!" signs. Toronto the Good, Toronto the Strong, Toronto the Thriving...Toronto was shouting! I was used to student demonstrations and street protests in Montreal the Political, Montreal the Sensual, Montreal the Creative. But I did not expect this in Toronto.

They say timing is everything. I arrived in the Toronto of the 1990s, a Toronto of massive mobilization, in the aftermath of the sweeping victory of a neo-conservative government mostly elected outside the metropolis. Toronto was coping with welfare cuts, unemployment, a growth in homelessness. Toronto was resisting the wind of conservatism, partly, stemming out of a discomfort with the metropolis. I arrived in a city in a state of agitation. Building on a three decade long tradition of progressive political activism, downtown Toronto fought for keeping a progressive haven in an increasingly conservative province. I realised that the image of Toronto from Montreal as a city of "Peace, Order, and Good Government" was a misperception. Toronto was Creative and Political. Toronto was inflamed by passionate social activists and radicals, but also by professional mothers, school teachers, civil servants, university professors, computer wizards, pastors—in other words, political mobilization reached every corner of daily.

In October 1996, the six o-clock newscast featured Mel Lastman, then mayor of suburban North York, stunned at the journalist's question: "How would you react if the cities of North York, East York, York,

Scarborough, Etobicoke, Toronto, and Metro Toronto would be amalgamated?" A laughing Mel responded that it was impossible; he asked whether this was serious. Rumours of amalgamation were leaked in the media...It was the beginning of the peak months of the Megacity saga. It was indeed a saga, a historic, quasi-legendary moment in Ontario's political culture. Some moments in a society's life are imbued with political electricity that permeates the everyday fabric. My arrival in Toronto corresponded with these intensely politicised times. And I got carried away in what I would later understand as middle-class urbanism.

Political activity for the urban progressive middle class has been thriving, mostly since the reform movement of the 1970s. Many Torontonians from a middle-class background actively shaped the city's progressive regime over the years. They particularly cherish issues such as access and equity, the quality of life, of education, and the right to have a voice in decision-making. While a change in municipal boundaries usually do not provoke such an emotional reaction among local residents, amalgamation in Toronto captured media attention and political life from December 1996 until the passage of the provincial legislation enacting municipal consolidation on April 21, 1997. Mobilization gradually decreased after that, and political life returned to a more normal course, with its skirmishes among elected officials and more radical activists. While middle-class activism continues to thrive in Toronto, the first four months of 1997 represent a very dynamic moment of insurgency that I like to call the Megacity saga.

This book relates the story of resistance to amalgamation in Toronto. It stresses the importance of these events for social and political life in the rest of Canada. In this age of neoliberalism, the redrawing of boundaries and the reshaping of administrative and political systems of governance seem to obey a single criterion: market efficiency. The Ontario provincial government attempted to reshuffle the governance structure in Toronto without much consideration for the impacts on everyday life in the city, impacts on human relations and identity, impacts on social solidarity and civic life. The Megacity saga demonstrated that people cannot be erased from restructuring processes.

In other words, the politics of everyday life was asserted clearly and loudly by the people we will discover in the following pages, grouped in a movement called Citizens for Local Democracy. By politics of everyday life, I mean focusing on municipal politics on the one hand, and working on the punctual mobilization of a broad base of residents on issues related to their daily life, on the other hand. Warren Magnusson noted that municipalities are located at the juncture of the state and civil society, and thus are particularly well-suited for both institutional and social movement politics.[1] Toronto illustrated his argument quite clearly. Moreover, the Megacity saga highlighted the class component of this interface between municipal politics and social movements, an element often absent from academic analyses.

While municipal amalgamation may seem an arcane or technical issue, citizens of Metro Toronto did not think so. The story of amalgamation in Toronto serves to challenge this perceived triviality and asserts the importance of changing municipal boundaries, fiscal relations, and political responsibilities in this age of globalization. Because neoliberal exigencies are underpinning much of the discourse on globalization, national states have adopted strategies of industrial restructuring and crisis management which have led to the reform of their administrative and territorial structure. This book argues that the Ontario provincial government's decision to amalgamate the former six local municipalities and the metropolitan political structure of Toronto into a single corporation is inscribed in the province's endeavour to position Toronto on the map of the global economy. But also, it is seen as a means to manage the state more efficiently through the devolution of many social services on the shoulders of municipalities. Given Toronto's specific social burden as a metropolis, consolidation of resources within the metropolitan area were essential to bear the burden of the new social responsibilities transferred to the local level.

The province of Ontario had been governed by a conservative government for more than forty years, starting in 1943. It was thus a Tory government that was in place when a two-tiered municipal governance system was implemented in Toronto in 1953, with the Municipality of Metropolitan Toronto and thirteen local municipalities (later consolidated into six local municipalities before being amalgamated into one Megacity in 1998). In the late 1980s and early 1990s, a centre-left interlude in provincial politics with the Liberal and New Democrat governments pushed towards a "social" (rather than conservative and statist) view of metropolitan governance. However, the return of a Tory government in 1995 marked a shift away from this "social" push. When Mike Harris won the 1995 elections, largely due to a widespread reaction against the New Democrat government of Bob Rae and its "social contract," he ended up acting against both the Tory legacy in Ontario and against the centre-Left interlude the province just went through. Indeed, Harris' platform was more in-tuned with neoliberal than conservative statist policies. The Harris government relies heavily on the idea that globalization requires streamlining policies and more government efficiency.

Indeed, globalization prompts the reconfiguration of state power and its administrative-territorial structure. But as Keil puts it, globalization does not lead to the end of states, rather, it "makes states."[2] The state is "re-scaled," "decentred," in such a way that changes in municipal boundaries and political responsibilities become more important than ever. Seen as a neoliberal strategy of adaptation to the forces of globalization, the Toronto amalgamation legislation faced immense resistance from a segment of the population that has controlled Toronto's local institutions at least since the 1970s. The urban progressive middle class was threatened by the disappearance of their major tool for resistance to an increasing provincial-wide discomfort with the metropolis' specific needs. The book starts from the idea that the Toronto Megacity saga was a struggle between the province and the metropolis, the conservatives and the progressives, the urban core and the suburban/exurban constituencies. It was a struggle for the power to define the city, a "class struggle in space," to use Kipfer's phrase.[3]

In this context, territorial restructuring and changes in boundaries are becoming more important than ever. The following pages highlight the importance of these struggles for political leverage and the development of localized identities. With the increasing urbanization of the world economy, urban politics takes on a central role. Urban movements from the 1970s struggled for quality of life against dehumanizing economic development in cities, for public participation in decision-making, and for the right to difference in the city for marginalized groups. Donzelot argues that the urban question is now more a question of the political capacity of cities to create coherence in ever diversified, fragmented, and open societies.[4] Social and economic fragmentation of urban societies are leading to instances of political division reflected on the territorial organization. The issue of local autonomy has a double meaning in the Canadian context. While it could support claims for exclusion, it is also a search for a balance of power between different levels of government. While provinces have complete jurisdiction over municipalities considered "creatures" of the provinces, struggles for local autonomy seek to ensure an appropriate political role for cities in the process of state restructuring.

Important state and economic restructuring waves are flowing through Toronto. Inevitably, this entails cultural and social redefinitions as well. Citizens for Local Democracy initiated a debate on the meaning of democracy. Taken within the context of state re-scaling processes, where different levels of government attempt to adjust the boundaries of their responsibilities to the socio-economic context, rethinking democracy takes a specifically geographical signification. In Toronto, the city has become the point of departure for this redefinition. It is the argument of this book that this entails thinking through the issue of citizenship and membership as well, for many residents of the metropolis do not have citizenship status. What does this mean for membership in society? For political action? The Megacity saga demonstrated citizens' attachment to democratic institutions and processes, but also their willingness to improve them. It opened a window of opportunity for the redefinition of citizenship and democracy, both theoretically and empirically.

### *A Note on the Making of the Book*

When I set out to complete my Master's in Political Science at York University, I wanted to work on the increasing importance of urban politics in the international arena. I had just spent a year with youth in Quebec City working towards the United Nations' Habitat II Summit held in Istanbul in June 1996. But I arrived in Toronto and was completely enthusiastic about the wind of political mobilization sweeping the city on issues related to the importance of urban politics not only in the international arena, but mostly within the state's re-scaling strategies. I wanted to know more about this tradition of middle-class urbanism in Toronto, its impact, its strength, its agenda, its relations with other social movements. In the whirl of the Megacity saga, I could not resist writing my thesis on Toronto, which became a clear illustration of state re-scaling processes, world-city formation, middle-class urbanism, and a live public debate on democracy and citizenship.

I participated actively in these events throughout 1996-97 through various interviews, rallies, and weekly meetings. My main source of information was the very rich e-mail forum list servers. This book is basically a discourse analysis that focuses on story-lines that occurred during the "Megacity saga." I collected thousands of pages of material, from government reports, from newspaper articles, and from the e-mail list servers. Although e-mail material is just beginning to make its way into social research, and although it is considered a grey zone between the public and the private domain, I feel it provides incredibly rich information. This material, by the very nature of its real-time exchanges, calls for an analysis of interactions. At the same time, by its written nature, it necessitates a textual analysis. Despite the interactive nature of e-mail exchanges, it is handicapped from body language, face-to-face interaction, and thus renders participant observation practically impossible. Nevertheless, it provides, on a daily basis, dense data on people's feelings and ideas, and it acts as a fluid and interactive type of archive, usually closer to conversation and interviews than to official documents.

David Harvey explains that discourses constitute "moments" in the social process, in a dialectical relationship with beliefs and values, institutions, material practices, and relations of power:

> Discourses express human thought, fantasy, and desire. They are also institutionally based, materially constrained, experientially grounded manifestations of social and power relations. By the same token, discursive effects suffuse and saturate all other moments within the social process (affecting, for example, beliefs and practices as well as being affected by them).[5]

Discourse analysis seeks to understand why particular vocabulary or rhetorical strategies are used in specific events, and how this usage has the power to construct concepts and categories we use to make sense of the world.[6] However, this kind of link between discourse and power also depends on the legitimization, institutionalization, and routinization (i.e., it has to be constantly reproduced in speech situations) of these concepts and categories. It is at this point that resistance to the dominant discourse can occur. Actors can use story-lines drawing on other discursive categories such as songs, poetry, humour, metaphors, and on grammatical techniques such as using the active voice and personal pronouns.[7] This is what happened during the Megacity saga.

When I came back to Toronto in the summer 1998, I found a city still impregnated by political mobilization. The new amalgamated city had been incorporated on January 1, 1998. A new megacouncil was trying to set foot in City Hall. But the whirl of the Megacity saga seemed to have calmed down a little. Other substantive issues such as homelessness, poverty, access, equity, diversity were occupying the social agenda more prominently. And as the World Cup was raging in the cafes of Little Portugal, the finals between Brazil and France were electrifying the city much better than issues of local autonomy...But when I came back again in February 2000, the city was definitely mobilized. Toronto was preparing its bid for the 2008 Olympics. Bread Not Circuses was active to make sure social issues were considered. Citizens for Local

Democracy was strategizing for the November 2000 municipal elections. Councillor Walker was preparing for depositing a motion to the council for a debate on the secession of Toronto from the province of Ontario.

As I am finishing this manuscript, I cannot help thinking about future projects, as political life always outstrips analysis. But I will leave the reader with the story of the Toronto Megacity saga as it unfolded since 1996. The following pages are mostly narrative, they relate the events through the voice of citizens and residents of Toronto. Some theoretical considerations are sprinkled throughout, but mostly as suggestions for analysis. Chapter 5 is more explicitly theoretical, considering the academic debate on citizenship and democracy. This book was not written with a theoretical outlook, but rather from an archival perspective. Toronto has opened the door to very interesting debates on state restructuring, democracy, and middle-class political mobilization. The story of the Megacity saga highlights these trends very clearly. The book does not intend either to provide a technical impact analysis of amalgamation or to make recommendations on the optimal urban governance structure in this age of globalization.

Rather, the following analysis of amalgamation in Toronto highlights the rationale behind the Harris government's restructuring policies, which are solidly grounded in the neoliberal discourse on globalization. Although many observers were puzzled by the neo-conservative government's rejection of traditional statist policies on the one hand, and its decision to create a huge bureaucratic entity through amalgamation on the other hand, I conclude that amalgamation was in fact very much in-line with the rest of the Tory agenda of the mid-1990s. Toronto and Ontario more generally was infused by negative reactions to this neo-conservative agenda. While some leftist observers and activists dismissed Citizens for Local Democracy because it was very middle-class, the following analysis suggests that it is specifically this middle-class character that makes it very interesting, especially in the context of Toronto's history of progressive middle-class urbanism. After all, Citizens for Local Democracy was able to mobilize a huge number of people of the issue of municipal boundaries...a rather arcane issue for many Canadians! The ultimate failure of the movement to prevent amalgamation and its gradual fading away was of course rooted in the Canadian system of governance which states that ultimately provinces have power over municipalities and can decide their faith. But the Megacity saga also highlights a series of contradictions between differing segments of the middle class: urban/suburban or progressive/conservative.

These contradictions also impact political agendas within the Left, which is divided between old and new conceptions of citizenship and democracy, and between a focus on the democratic process and an emphasis on eradicating inequalities.

This book is but one story on the Megacity saga; it is my story. In some sense, it reflects my personal journey. I remember vividly my arrival in Toronto, my love-and-hate relationship with the city, my everyday experience in learning English, the strong friendships I enjoyed, the numerous puzzling intellectual questions the city inspired me. This is but one story. It is a story that I hope will appeal to citizens and residents of Toronto, but also from other cities in the world. It is a story that I hope will inspire politically-engaged intellectuals and socially-minded policy-makers. We have much to learn from Toronto. I learned much.

*J.A.B.*
*Montreal, March 2000*

## NOTES

1. Warren Magnusson, *The Search for Political Space: Globalization, Social Movements, and the Urban Political Experience* (Toronto: University of Toronto Press, 1996).
2. Roger Keil, "Globalization makes states: perspectives of local governance in the age of the world city," *Review of International Political Economy* 5, no. 4, (1998), 616-646.
3. Stefan Kipfer, "Urban Politics in the 1990s: Notes on Toronto," in *Possible Urban Worlds*, ed. Inura Zurich (Zurich: ETH, 1998), 172-179.
4. Jacques Donzelot, "La nouvelle question urbaine," *Esprit* 258, (novembre 1999), 87-114.
5. David Harvey, *Justice, Nature & the Geography of Difference* (Cambridge and Oxford: Blackwell, 1996), 88.
6. See Maarten A. Hajer, *The Politics of Environmental Discourse* (Oxford: Clarendon Press, 1995); also contribution to the special issue of *Urban Studies* 36, no. 1, (1999). See also the excellent analysis of knowledge production within social movements, using the case of the Toronto Metro Network for Social Justice, by Janet Conway, "Knowledge, Power, Organization: Social Justice Coalitions at a Crossroads," *Community Social Planing Council of Toronto*, Occasional Paper 1, (Fall 1999).
7. M. Richardson, J. Sherman, and M. Gismondi, *Winning back the words: Confronting experts in an environmental public hearing* (Toronto: Garamond Press, 1993), 16-18.

# CHAPTER 1

## CITIZENS FACING A MEGACITY GIANT: STORY OF THE AMALGAMATION OF TORONTO

It had been snowing all day. Big sticky beautiful snow flakes were quietly falling on Toronto. It was mild enough to walk to the meeting. I took Church Street from Wellesley to Queen Street. Covered with snow, I entered the Church. It was packed, humid, and intense. I found a place to sit. What a crowd! There were about 600 or more people there. It is difficult to say. There were many TV cameras from both mainstream and alternative stations. Some people seemed to already know each other. We sang O Canada! I have to admit I was surprised by this opening. The steering committee introduced themselves to the newcomers. "This is a different forum," the young lady said, "to energize and then go back to work in the community." The meeting went on with speeches by John Ralston Saul, John Sewell, other groups such as "People for Education." Organized actions were planned to gather as many letters to the provincial legislature as possible to ask for public hearings. The "Rebellion 1997" was announced. Mayors from the Ottawa region drove down to Toronto on that stormy night to address the crowd and tell us how they were inspired by mobilization efforts in Toronto. The meeting paused with music. "Stop amalgamation, Frankenstein's creation, No assimilation, stop amalgamation!" A bucket circulated in the crowd for donations.

I walked back home that night with a throat burning with excitement, energized and curious about this overwhelming mobilization. Where did it come from? What city was I landing in?

*Background and Context*

Toronto is the most populous city in Canada. The Greater Toronto Area (GTA) comprises about 4.5 million people. This amounts to about 45 percent of the province of Ontario's population, and 15 percent of the population of Canada.[1] The GTA was formerly organized around five regional structures: Halton, Peel, York, Durham, and Metro Toronto. The Municipality of Metropolitan Toronto was established in 1953 in order to equalize service delivery and development costs across what was then the metropolitan area.[2] The designation of the Greater Toronto Area emerged in the 1980s to delimit the new socio-economic boundaries of the region, which now occupies 4,400 $km^2$ or 0.8 percent of Ontario's land.[3] Only the central area of Metro Toronto has been restructured by consolidating its six local municipalities with the upper-tier level of government formerly called the Municipality of Metropolitan Toronto. This restructuring process has thus eliminated the former municipalities of Scarborough, North York, East York, York, Etobicoke, Toronto, as well as the upper-tier metropolitan structure. The question on everyone's mind is why did the provincial government decide to consolidate only the central area leaving aside the newer and prosperous edge cities in Halton, Peel, York, and Durham? The new City of Toronto now has a land area of 622 $km^2$ and a population of about 2.3 million. The Harris Government of Ontario has created a gigantic entity at the centre of the GTA.

Toronto has long been the pride of Canadian urban society. Toronto is polite, civil, calm, and dynamic. Toronto is safe, clean, and green.

> We've been called "the city that works," "New York run by the Swiss" and "the world's newest great city." In 1998, you can also call us "Mega Toronto!"[4]

The Canadian parliamentary political system has created a political culture very different from the United States. The U.S. system is oriented towards a one-to-one relationship between citizens and the state. Canada has opted for a system where citizens' voices are filtered through party lines rather than independent representatives, and through multiple layers of representation (federal, provincial, municipal). Whereas California, for instance, has a system where citizens can initiate laws, put them on the ballot, and have them ratified by the State Legislature, Ontario has developed a much more passive political culture based on the motto of "Peace, Order, and Good Government." Of course, the British flavour of Toronto has been challenged by many waves of immigration. However,

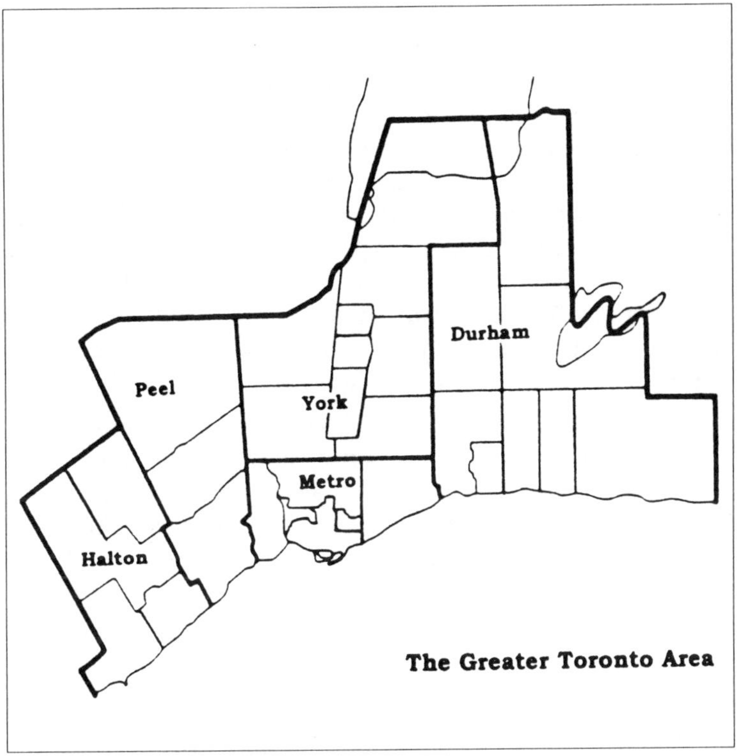


this British image of the city, combined with the North- American model of efficiency remain. But this image and its political culture has been constantly challenged in the past decade. Torontonians were very proud of the distinctiveness of their modernist city in relation to U.S. metropolises. With the shift in orientation from being the core of the Canadian economy to "becoming a global city," the Ontario government initiated a process of municipal restructuring aiming to respond to the changing economic and political context.[5] As Kipfer and Keil note "Rather than an export model of urban reform, Toronto is now considered a poor second behind the shiny new faces of American and European cities and the 'pro-urban' orientations of the latter's senior levels of government."[6] In other words, Toronto's pride in its system of urban governance has given way to a controversial process of restructuring with the goal of carving its place in the club of global cities.

Indeed, by 1996 Toronto was definitively mobilized. Toronto was not exactly a machine that worked well, some rusty bolts and not-so-greasy wheels were uncovered. A wind of political activism struck the city. The actions of the Metro Network for Social Justice (MNSJ) responding to the right-wing climate of the early 1990s, culminated in the "Metro Days of Action" in the fall 1996. Toronto was the stage of a week of forums and activities and a one-day urban strike that froze all important sectors of the city, including the public transit system, much of the commercial, governmental, and even corporate activities.[7] The Metro Days of Action were preceded by a series of demonstrations throughout the province, in London, Hamilton, and Kitchener-Waterloo. For the Metro Days of Action, the old City of Toronto passed a motion that allowed city employees to take a day off work to attend the demonstrations. As stated in *The Globe and Mail*:

> By its advance billing, next week's demonstrations in Toronto by labour groups and their supporters [many of them from a middle-class background] could be one of the most tumultuous protests in Canada's history. Subways could stop running, schools might shut, mail delivery cease, a busy international airport close, government offices grind to a halt, and rail and highway transportation could be disrupted in the country's largest metropolis.[8]

Toronto was also the stage of protests against hospital closings, student protests against tuition fee hikes, a university professor strike against changes in university education, homeless camp-outs organized by the Ontario Coalition Against Poverty, and a growing youth movement referred to as the "squeegee kids." Now Magazine, a weekly cultural left-leaning newspaper in Toronto, published an article on "Citizen insurrection: How to use the timeless art of civil disobedience to upend the Tories."[9] Torontonians were highly politicized before the introduction of municipal restructuring on the public agenda. The former City of Toronto had also been involved in fighting welfare cutbacks and its staff had set up a "Tracking the Impacts Coalition." Organizations such as the Metro Network for Social Justice, the Ontario Coalition Against Poverty, and later Bread Not Circuses, as well as the labour movement, were behind much of this political mobilization. The story of amalgamation and resistance to it is situated against this background. But mostly, it is rooted in Toronto's progressive civic tradition of urban reform developed in the 1970s. Over the years, Toronto has become a site for progressive middle class politics, rooted in downtown middle-class neighbourhoods more than in the labour movement.

As I was walking back home through these middle-class neighbourhoods after the meeting in this downtown church on that snowy January night, I was thinking about the angst against the Harris Government's municipal restructuring policy. People were angry, I thought, because they felt the democratic process had been breached. What I came to realize later, the more I was observing the crowd and the more I was discussing these events with friends, is that changing municipal boundaries in Toronto was not a mundane issue for the people who came to shape municipal institutions into a progressive urban democratic regime. Weeks later, John Sewell came to speak at York University. He urged students to get involved in the resistance movement. I was in fact quite perplexed because York University has a very militant student population. Why were they not interested in such a sweeping mobilized movement? A friend of mine then said to me, "You know, I'd rather spend my time with squeegee kids than with this bunch of middle-class Liberals." Resistance to amalgamation was not important for many of these students, because questions of political representation in state institutions did not resonate to them as a radical movement.

### *"The Big, Bad Megacity Monster"*

Margaret Atwood, the famed Canadian novelist, came to speak to the crowd in the same downtown church on a February Monday night. She delightfully amused the audience by telling the story of "The Big, Bad Megacity Monster" (see an excerpt on page 41). But what is the Megacity? Where does it come from? Toronto's municipal structure has gone through deep transformations since 1995, when Mike Harris and his Progressive Conservative Party (PC) were elected as the Government of the Province of Ontario. The PC won the provincial elections with a "Common Sense Revolution" platform, a decisively right-wing program to replace the New Democratic Party's (NDP) more centre-left ideology, previously in power at Queen's Park, the Ontario Provincial Legislature. The "Common Sense Revolution" did not prioritize municipal reform, but two essential promises made during the 1995 provincial electoral campaign have had significant impact on Toronto's municipal structure. The first promise was to balance the provincial budget, while the second vowed to simultaneously lower provincial income taxes by 30 percent. In order to accomplish these goals, it was estimated that $6 billion needed to be cut out of the $56 billion annual government spending.[10] Among a series of important trimming measures, the PC initiated deep reforms of the education and welfare systems; reforms that meant rethinking the funding relations between the province and the municipalities, as they both shared the cost and implementation responsibilities for education and welfare assistance. In April 1996, the PC government appointed the "Who Does What Panel," chaired by former Toronto mayor David Crombie (1973-78), to "disentangle" provincial and municipal responsibilities. In October 1996, before the Panel had made all its recommendations, the government leaked its special restructuring plan for Toronto.

On December 17, 1996, the government officially stated its plan to eliminate the Metropolitan level of government in Toronto, and its comprising six lower-tiered municipalities (Toronto, Scarborough, York, East York, North York, Etobicoke). These seven city councils were amalgamated into a "Megacity," with a population of 2.4 million.[11] When the Minister of Municipal Affairs and Housing (MMAH), Al Leach, introduced the City of Toronto Act (Bill 103) to the provincial legislature, he stated that the goals of municipal restructuring were to "save money, remove barriers to growth and investment, and help create jobs."[12] The rationale was that the amalgamation of Metropolitan Toronto would save money by eliminating duplication of services in the former two-tiered metropolitan structure; it would eliminate competition between existing municipalities and thus free the way for economic growth; and it would disentangle the complex two-tiered structure, thus increasing accountability to taxpayers.

The first draft of the City of Toronto Act (Bill 103) established the modalities for unification, the composition of the new city council, and the transitional measures. Initially, citizens of Megacity Toronto were to elect forty-four councillors and a mayor. A Board of Trustees was appointed to oversee existing municipal councils' financial operations of $50,000 or more (during the transition period) and review operating and capital budgets. A Transition Team was also appointed by the province to facilitate the organizational transition into the new city and hire necessary staff to ensure continuity in municipal services. The major contention of these two appointed bodies was the impossibility to challenge their decisions and subject them to court review.

Partly responding to enormous public pressures, the government proposed modifications to the Bill on March 27, 1997. The Board of Trustees, which was already in place before Bill 103 was passed into law by the provincial legislature, was declared "illegal" by a court decision. The government thus replaced it with a Financial Advisory Board mandated to act as a watchdog on behalf of taxpayers. Other modifications to the first draft of Bill 103 stated that the new city council would be elected according to the Federal riding system, but the new elected council would have the opportunity to redraw the boundaries for the 2000 elections. Fifty-six councillors and a mayor would be the size of the new council, as opposed to forty-four councillors and a mayor. And finally, neighbourhood committees would no longer be a compulsory element of the municipal structure but could be implemented if the new council decided so. Bill 103 was voted into law on April 21, 1997. The first Megacity elections took place on November 10, 1997 and the new City was incorporated on January 1, 1998.

### *Policy Recommendations on Restructuring in Toronto*

Amalgamation of local municipalities is not a particularly novel idea. It happens regularly, on the grounds that it produces economies of scale and saves money for expensive services such as police or public transit. A big government, less layers of decision-making power, centralisation, less politicians, more control, large scale services…it was the rationale of many governmental institutions in the wealthy years of the welfare state. But in this era of downsizing, ideas of flexibility and market efficiency, fragmentation and multiplication of competitive municipalities has been the norm. Why then had the Tory Government of Ontario chosen the old solution? Amalgamation has not been recommended in any reports on the Toronto region for the past thirty years.[13]

The former centre-Left government of Ontario established a task force on the issue in April 1995. The Greater Toronto Area Task Force was created in the midst of fierce struggles against cutbacks at the Metro Toronto level of government. The provincial government saw the need to "provide direction for the future governance of the Greater Toronto Area, including the potential restructuring of the responsibilities and practices of municipal and provincial governments."[14] When the Metro Toronto Council imposed a series of cutbacks in their programs, a social justice umbrella organization, Metro Network for Social Justice (MNSJ), became very active in Toronto. The city was struck by a huge loss of jobs and a high unemployment rate. Metro Toronto saw the coming-together of communities to fight these cutbacks. Certain segments of the city were already mobilized in municipal politics when the provincial government assigned the Task Force on the future of the GTA (known as the Golden Task Force).

The final Golden report recommended the establishment of an indirectly-elected GTA Regional Council which would strengthen "local municipalities with added powers and the responsibility for delivering a wider range of local services."[15] The report also recommended giving responsibility to local municipalities only for services influenced by local preferences such as roads, public transit, fire, water, and waste management. On the other hand, according to the report, the provincial government should assume responsibility for redistributive services such as welfare, as well as for services that require provincial-wide standards. Metro Toronto's proposal of a "supercity" was rejected by the GTA Task Force. It would have extended the upper-tier governing structure to encompass a large part of the GTA. As a directly-elected government, it would have replaced existing regional structures and provided a wide range of services. The Task Force felt this would have given too much power to Metro and hampered local responsiveness. Rejecting both the GTA Task Force and the Metro Toronto proposals, with Bill 103, and policies on the devolution of social services to local municipalities, the Harris government imposed a very different solution.

A Review Panel on the GTA Task Force Report (known as the Burnham Panel) was appointed to assess the level of consensus. It was determined that a GTA Regional Council would not be viable. When the "Who Does What" panel was appointed in April 1996, its Chair David Crombie was mandated to advise the government on how to eliminate duplication and waste. The panel focused on property tax assessments, transportation and utilities, municipal administration, and emergency and social services. While the panel was working on the disentanglement of services in Ontario, the Minister of Municipal Affairs and Housing, Al Leach, published a "Guide to Municipal Restructuring," which put forward the need to restructure municipal boundaries and urged voluntary amalgamations throughout the province. "It is clear to Ontario taxpayers," wrote Leach, "that maintaining 815 municipalities in the province's current fiscal climate is simply unrealistic."[16] To further his goal of "cleaning up" the "mess" in Ontario's municipal structures, Leach introduced the Better Local Government Act on October 17, 1996. The new policy aimed to reduce the number of local politicians, to simplify municipal election procedures, to get the most benefits for taxpayers in investments, and to better manage liability risks. Following this bill, rumours about the amalgamation of Toronto were leaked to the press.

In October 1996, the Harris government gave the six local mayors thirty days to come up with a restructuring plan for Toronto. Strategically, the mayors knew they needed to propose significant savings to the provincial government in order to avoid forced amalgamation. They estimated savings of $240 million from eliminating the Metro level of government and from a commitment that administrative costs not exceed 10 percent of total spending. They also estimated that $90 to $120 million of transition costs could be absorbed in one year.[17] The report proposed the abolition of Metro Toronto and the creation of a GTA Service Board with weaker powers than the GTA Council proposed by the Golden Report in the previous months, but still in-line with the conventional wisdom.

Leach then released a study conducted by management consultants KPMG (who had three weeks and $100,000 to estimate potential savings) stating that amalgamation would save $300 million a year in Toronto. The report was criticized from the neoliberal right on the grounds that competition between municipalities is more efficient.[18] Nevertheless, this was a prelude to the official introduction of Bill 103 for the First Reading in the Legislature on December 17, 1996, the day following the release of the KPMG report. Despite the absence of amalgamation in the Tory "Common Sense Revolution" platform, and despite silences on amalgamation during the 1995 electoral campaign, the Tory government went ahead with their vision for Toronto, to the despair of many citizens and policy-makers. Inevitably, it raised much opposition.

### *"Sending a Message to King Mike":*[19] *Reactions and Oppositions*

The above headline from the columnist John Barber in *The Globe and Mail* says that the City of Toronto Act was perceived as an outsider's imposition. It came as a surprise and the conclusion that it was the result of the centralising power of Premier Mike Harris was quickly made in the media. Nevertheless, the initial reactions to Bill 103 were polarized.

On the one side, the Metropolitan Toronto Board of Trade was in favour of amalgamation as it claimed it would make the region more attractive to foreign capital.[20] The Urban Development Institute and the Greater Toronto Home Builders' Association endorsed Bill 103 because of its "bureaucratic neatness." As David Hirsh of the latter association said: "We believe that the Megacity will substantively reduce duplication and red tape in the process, thereby unleashing the full potential of our industry to create jobs and wealth as we develop and redevelop the city."[21] A coalition of downtown commercial, media, and law firms has lobbied for amalgamation since the 1970s, when reformists implemented slow growth policies. Consequently, it is not surprising that this business coalition organized around the Board of Trade would support the PC government's Megacity proposal.[22] Moreover, staff at the Metro government level saw in amalgamation a smoother transition than the decentralization of regional services such as policing, water and sewage infrastructure, and public transportation to local municipalities would have been.[23]

On the other side, opposition to amalgamation came from various sources. Certainly the largest and most prominent was Citizens for Local Democracy (C4LD), a group that emerged directly in reaction to this restructuring. Former Toronto reformist mayor John Sewell (1978-80) initiated the movement. Sewell was previously Chair of the province's public housing authority and more recently Chair of the Commission to Reform the Planning Act of Ontario. A lawyer by training, he is also a local public figure, a politician, a policy analyst, and writes a column in the weekly, left-leaning newspaper Now Magazine.[24] Sewell was also the leader of the most important struggle against anti-public housing in the late 1960s. Oppositional in its origins, C4LD was a movement more than an organization. It was led by a steering committee of about fifteen people and had no official membership list. Actions were co-ordinated by the steering committee, but individual initiatives were welcomed. Ideas and actions were conveyed through a strong communication system of newsletters, weekly public meetings, a web page, three e-mail list servers, a telephone tree, and a hotline. C4LD did not have any paid staff and received no government funding; it was entirely financed by individual contributions mostly gathered during the weekly Monday night meetings. These meetings always started with the Canadian national anthem and took place in downtown churches. Information, updates, action co-ordination, and entertainment by prominent artists, academics, and public figures were consistently part of the agenda. Participants came from different backgrounds, but as I discuss later, most of them could be seen as progressive middle-class citizens.

Two main arguments opposing the amalgamation Bill were at the core of C4LD from the beginning: 1) it was a threat for local democracy; and 2) despite the province's constitutional power to impose municipal restructuring, it lost its legitimacy because it was rushed through the legislature without prior public consultations. Indeed, the Canadian constitution states that a provincial legislature may "exclusively make laws in relation to...municipal institutions...civil rights...property rights."[25] However, C4LD argued that Bill 103 (particularly the first draft) breached many democratic principles. Opposition to restructuring drew attention to the impossibility to submit decisions made by the Board of Trustees and the Transition Team to court challenges. Other criticized issues were the restrictions imposed on elected officials in terms of financial decisions, and to the much larger ratio of elected councillors to citizens.

> There is a pattern, a disturbing pattern, a disturbing attitude towards democracy, which has been repeated and repeated by this government. Their attitude is: you win a majority and then you can do whatever you want for four years. An election is reduced, a general election is reduced to a manipulative blank check referendum in a Napoleonic tradition. If you can get them to give you a majority, you can do whatever you want for four years. Even issues which are hardly mentioned during the elections, you have a blank check! You can do it. The truth is, that yes representative democracy is tough, but it's also real. And getting a majority is just the first step in the democratic process.[26]

This excerpt from appraised writer John Ralston Saul's address to that snowy January C4LD Monday night meeting created an important momentum for C4LD, which gained the support of many academics, authors, and public personalities in Toronto. Saul's address was also published in *The Globe and Mail*, which helped publicize C4LD's arguments against the government's restructuring plans.

A month after the introduction of the City of Toronto Act, it became clear that the restructuring of municipal boundaries and of the political system were part of a larger reform. During the week period from 13 to 17 of January 1997, coined as the "mega-week," the provincial government announced a series of "disentanglement" reforms. An advertisement campaign organized by the Harris team was designed to explain the overwhelming changes. "We're moving beyond artificial boundaries of governments and focusing instead on providing people with better services at lower cost," Leach said.[27] The first step was a reduction of the number of school boards in the province from 129 to 66 and the removal of education costs from property taxes. The PC government believed that the education system was too fragmented and that school boards and teachers' unions were working together to keep educational spending high while this investment was not necessarily reflected in student performance levels. In exchange for this relief, municipalities were to be responsible for 50 percent of welfare costs and their full administration. Additionally, the municipal proportion of day care costs were to rise from 20 to 50 percent; while housing, public transit, and public health programs were transferred in totality to municipalities; grants for community policing and libraries were abolished; the provincial share of long-term health care services was reduced from 80 to 50 percent; and finally a province-wide property tax reform based on actual value assessment was announced. Under such measures, it is not surprising that widespread opposition emerged from various sources, including David Crombie, Chair of the "Who Does What Panel" appointed to make recommendations on these issues. Opposition also came from the Metropolitan Toronto Board of Trade, the media, and citizens.[28]

The Association of Municipalities of Ontario unanimously rejected this offloading policy on the grounds that income-redistribution programs should not be paid out of property taxes.[29] This would result in a loss of local control over property taxes because even though social welfare would be funded by locally-raised moneys, the province would still set the standards. Harris rejected the numerous recommendations made by Golden, Crombie, the six local mayors, and many others, and went ahead with his downloading policies as a means to reduce the provincial deficit and to honour his electoral promise to cut income taxes. Even the Metropolitan Toronto Board of Trade rejected the offloading proposal, although 65 percent of its members supported Bill 103, the amalgamation act.[30] The three major newspapers in Toronto also supported Bill 103 but criticized the offloading package.

Citizens for Local Democracy fiercely opposed these reforms, which they saw as part of the same package as the amalgamation bill. Arguments against these restructuring were thus enlarged to concerns about the quality of life in the urban core, the preservation of basic and "progressive" services that developed in Toronto over the years, such as English as a second language programs, multicultural programs, needle exchange programs, women's programs, and so on. Other citizens mobilized around their fear of substantial property tax hikes in downtown residential and small business areas. Hence, opposition to the PC's municipal reforms came from a series of mixed motives that brought people together: democratic principles, concerns about the urban quality of life and the provision of services, and fear of property tax increases.

C4LD defined itself from the outset as a non-partisan movement of concerned citizens. Many of its adherents represent various economic positions of the middle class, they also come from all political parties and ideologies. Coherence rested broadly on a belief in democracy and a certain "middle class" conception of urbanity. The movement was skillfully led by long-term public figures such John Sewell, and activists who were able to attract considerable media attention, as well as the support of most locally elected officials (including then mayor of the City of Toronto Barbara Hall, 1994-97) and not surprisingly the support of the two provincial opposition parties (the Liberal Party and the New Democratic Party).

### *"Today's the Day That We Fight Back": Immediate Aftermath of Bill 103*

Probably the most spontaneous outcome of the Harris Government municipal restructuring plans was the large mobilization it provoked. "It started out so very slick, with the deficit arithmetic," sang Moxi Früvous, a rock group from Toronto, "but today's the day that we fight back." In fact, the group co-ordinated the production of a compact disc with this song and others, as well as speeches and storytelling. The NO mega-CD was released in early March 1997 and was meant as "a protest sing-a-long, an expression of the Toronto artistic community, a political tool, and, of course, a fundraiser for the *citizens for local democracy*."[31]

Citizens for Local Democracy was created immediately after the announcement of the amalgamation plan, to counter the feeling that there was no space to oppose Bill 103, that nothing could be done to stop the Leach and Harris vision of Toronto as a shiny and blooming global city. No referendum to legitimize this major institutional restructuring would be held. A Board of Trustees was appointed to take charge of the cities' financial affairs. Some members of Citizens for Local Democracy literally chased the trustees and unsuccessfully tried to participate in their meetings. Other people distributed newsletters on the subways and in the city's underground malls. The first newsletter headline was "Bill 103 ends local democracy!" Arguments were that "it costs money," "it creates bigger, more distant government," "it doesn't work," "it ushers privatization of services," "it forces two urban lifestyles into one jurisdiction."

On January 29, 1997, the government used its majority to force an end to the Second Reading of Bill 103 in the Legislative Assembly. C4LD immediately launched a campaign to ask citizens to write letters to the clerk of the Legislature asking to speak to the public hearing committee. More than a thousand letters were filed to the clerk. Attendance to the Monday night meetings peaked to about 1200 people. Public hearings started on February 3. The original plan of the government was to force the Third and last Reading of the Bill after fourteen days of hearings, but they were finally extended for five weeks because of the huge number of citizens who asked to be heard. Nevertheless, Leach clearly indicated that he was not prepared to consider major changes in the legislation. The Tory majority on the hearing committee also refused to travel beyond the provincial legislature Queen's Park to suburban City Halls to hold public hearings. Sewell argued that this arrangement would have facilitated participation for all residents, rather than privileging inner-city dwellers.

Whereas municipalities in Ontario rarely organize referendums, opposition to the provincial government's amalgamation plan was strong enough to convince the six local municipalities within Metro Toronto to organize and fund concurrent referendums to ask citizens if they agreed with amalgamation. Leach and Harris said they would not consider the results of this democratic exercise and did everything to delegitimize the process. In early February 1997, up to fifteen meetings a night were held across Metro Toronto, indicating citizen's concern about the issue at stake. On February 15, different organizations, citizens, political parties, mayors, councillors, artists, musicians, marched on Yonge Street, Toronto's central street. The carnavalesque march prominently featured a great symbol of Canadian democracy: William Lyon MacKenzie (1795-1861). MacKenzie, first mayor of Toronto, was a democracy advocate struggling against aristocratic control. The march re-staged MacKenzie's attempted insurrection of 1837 on the same street. Thousands of people attended the protest.

During the weeks preceding the municipal referendums, the Harris government was holding its own series of meetings under the slogan "One Toronto for all of us". At the end of February, Mr. Justice Lloyd Brennan ruled that the Trustees appointments were made "without authority and [were] of no legal effect" until Bill 103 is ratified by the Legislature. It was argued that the Harris government enjoyed no "royal prerogative" to proclaim law in the absence of legislation.[32] Following this court success, a group of citizens announced the possibility of a legal challenge to Bill 103.

On March 3, 1997, the results of the referenda showed an average of 76 percent opposing amalgamation, with a turnout of about 30 percent. Citizens were asked to vote yes or no to the following question: "*Are you in favour of eliminating [insert name of Area Municipality] and all other existing municipalities in Metro Toronto and amalgamating them into a Mega-city?*" Turnouts show that participation was higher in downtown areas (including York and East York) and North York, and lower in the East end and West end suburbs of Etobicoke and Scarborough. The rivalry between North York and downtown Toronto already stimulated important participation rates.

| *Municipality* | *Amalgamated elections Nov. 10, 1997* | *Referendum on amalgamation March 3, 1997* | *Municipal elections 1994* | *Municicpal elections 1991* |
|---|---|---|---|---|
| East York | 50.8% | 41.1% | 35.7% | 33.7% |
| Etobicoke | 46.4% | 19.4% | 39.6% | n/a |
| North York | 51.2% | 40.5% | 31.1% | 28.8% |
| Toronto | 51.2% | 38.6% | 37.0% | 31.0% |
| York | 44.6% | 38.8% | 38.6% | 34.6% |
| Scarborough | 44.5% | 18.5% | 33.2% | 27.8% |
| **Metro Total** | **50.2%** | **31.4%** | **35.9%** | **31.2%** |

**Table 1:** Voter Turnouts 1991-1997
*Source: Toronto City Clerk's Office*

It was the first time a municipal referendum was organized explicitly to challenge a higher level of government. The government reacted to the overwhelming No by arguing that the process was flawed and that people voted against the downloading proposal more than against amalgamation. "The mere fact that we have all those bills out there," said Steve Gilchrist, parliamentary assistant to Al Leach, "makes it more likely that this [vote] is a general concern about the pace and the extent of change rather than opposition to any one issue."[33] Despite the fact that these referendums were not legally binding, the provincial government lost much legitimacy in ignoring them. It was perceived as contempt for the democratic process and the will of the people. On the night of the referendums, about 2000 citizens gathered for a referendum night organized by C4LD, they simply chanted "We said No!, We said No!" In *The Globe and Mail* the next morning, John Barber wrote: "Got that, Mike [Harris]?"[34] The media were very keen on reporting this middle-class upsurge in Toronto. Nevertheless, that same night, the opening of the new restaurant Planet Hollywood in Toronto, attracted 17,000 young people that did not care about the Megacity, they were only enjoying the pleasures of Mega-Hollywood culture.

Nevertheless, encouraged by the support demonstrated by the referendums, Citizens for Local Democracy decided to work on gathering provincial-wide support. The agenda of the movement was broadened to other bills concerning school reform, police reform, hospital closings, environmental reforms, public library reforms, and the downloading of social costs. The e-mail forum was enlarged and people began to post messages from rural Ontario and the Ottawa region. Mayors from different cities drove to Toronto to address the Monday night crowds in downtown churches. Nevertheless, this attempt to mobilize people outside Toronto eventually faded away and C4LD continued to focus on downtown Toronto. The labour movement, and other social movements were more successful in acting in unity with movements outside the metropolis. The provincial major teachers' strike that exploded in the fall of 1997, is a good example of successful middle-class mobilization for social issues directly related to the municipal agenda.

Citizens for Local Democracy began to closely follow the constitutional challenge initiated by the Public School Boards' Association of Alberta (PSBAA) in the name of local democracy in Canada. PSBAA argued that the "implied guarantee of reasonable autonomy for local governments" was eroding in Canada, and asked for a court declaration stating that local governments are an integral part of democratic government. The declaration should also mention that the leadership of local governments should be elected and not appointed, and that these elected leaders should have the right to hire, direct, and fire local staff, as well as to make significant local decisions, particularly to decide how to spend locally-raised revenues.[35] The court challenge in the province of Alberta inspired the Toronto Citizen's Legal Challenge, a separate body formed by five of the six local municipalities and individual citizens. The case was built around two major arguments: 1) the City of Toronto Act (Bill 103) was said to violate the Constitution Act of 1867 because it ignored the convention of reasonable autonomy for local governments; and 2) the City of Toronto Act was considered to do harm to individual citizens according to the Charter of Rights' clauses on freedom of thought, belief, and opinion, as well as freedom of expression and association, and equality before and under the law.[36]

Both arguments were later dismissed during the summer, and it was determined that residents had no constitutional legal rights to the city. Mr. Justice Stephen Borins of the Ontario Court ruled that the province was within its constitutional right to pass Bill 103. The written deposition, however, contained strong language criticizing the provincial actions. Public hearings were "too little too late" and the government should not have dismissed the referendums so easily. Nevertheless, the court decided that these were political rather than constitutional issues.

Just before the Easter break at Queen's Park, the government finally accepted to replace its offloading proposal by an alternative plan negotiated with the Association of Municipalities of Ontario.[37] It proposed a series of minor changes to Bill 103 as well.[38] On April 2, 1997, the Legislative Assembly resumed.

> Megacity madness kicked off at Queen's Park yesterday with prayers, lemon, a card-playing sit-in and a legal challenge.[39]

The opposition parties invented a new delaying tactic. With the help of computerized technology, they filed 12,000 amendments to the Megacity Bill. To follow the procedure, the Assembly had to read and vote on each amendment individually. Queen's Park was open 24 hours a day, for ten consecutive days. Citizens began to sit in the public gallery to support the Liberal and New Democrat representatives in their long hours of work. Each motion was identical, except for the name of the street to which it applied. One could expect such reading to be long and boring, but as a citizen put it:

> There are always lots of minor dramas going on. Like a novel or a movie with many sub-plots. Best entertainment in town and it's free![40]

Breast-feeding mothers, insomniacs, children, many citizens attended the show at Queen's Park. Elected representatives had to be there day and night. They worked on shift schedule to ensure the right number of required representatives in the room at each hour.

One day, Tory members of the government exhausted by their new shift schedule, fell asleep accidentally allowing the passage of an amendment by omitting to say "No." The motion stated that residents of this or that street had to be consulted before any regulations are made under the Megacity act, they also have the right to request public hearings. The Tory representatives forgot to eliminate the motion concerning Cafon Court, a small street in Etobicoke. By their new power to harm any regulations made under the Megacity act, could residents of Cafon Court save Toronto from amalgamation? Speculations, irony, and mockery filled the newspapers for at least two days. Best show in town!

Bill 103 was nevertheless voted into law after the Government stroke out the clause giving residents of Cafon Court powers to change the course of the city. The Tory majority in the Assembly, following the party line, ensured that the City of Toronto Act passed. It was given royal assent on April 21, 1997. The government appointed the Financial

Advisory Board and the Transition Team chaired by Alan Tonks, former Metro Toronto Chairman.

> That's literally the end of democracy, and we've got to stop them from doing it, standing in the road of those trustees, standing in the road of those transition teams, making clear that those kinds of people are not welcome in our society or our city halls.[41]

Sewell told me, a few weeks before when he came to speak at York University, that he predicted the fall of the government if Bill 103 passed. In the end, the government did not resign, but Sewell intended to pursue his crusade in the name of democracy.

Citizens for Local Democracy continued the fight by sending letters to Canadian Prime Minister Jean Chrétien, and to provincial Tory representatives. Elected representatives must be accountable to their constituency, it was argued, not to their leader. The movement launched a campaign to convince Ontario's Lieutenant Governor to withhold assent. It also endeavoured to use the ongoing Federal electoral campaign as a platform to launch a national debate on local democracy.

Another campaign to ask the Governor General to reserve Bill 103 with the authority provided under sections 55 and 90 of the constitution,[42] was launched at the same time as the Citizens' Legal Challenge. The argument was that because Harris did not have an electoral mandate to force amalgamation, because he did not respect democratic procedures and the public opinion, and because he was applying a different set of rules for Toronto in comparison to the rest of the province, the Governor General of Canada was asked to put a hold on this new law.[43]

The Governor General, as the official head of the State, has the authority to use the British Queen's royal powers to repeal a decision of the parliament. This reserve power is very ancient and has been used only in extraordinary circumstances. The Governor General must normally act according to instructions given by the Prime Minister. Regardless of the archaic character of these powers, C4LD argued that a 1937 court decision ruled that just because they have not been used is no barrier to use them now. The campaign was not very successful.

Toronto's hot, humid, and sticky summer months were used to prepare the November 1997 first Megacity municipal elections. C4LD was torn by internal debates about its future role. Gary Morton's dystopian short story, is most appropriate to capture the fearful spirit of the Megacity saga in these first few months:

THE MONSTER OF THE MEGACITY
Gary Morton, 1996

He was the mayor of super-Toronto, king of the beasts. Only it felt like the beast was in his stomach, gnawing at him. The strong, "bah," he spat out a piece of muffin and his face reddened as he smoothed his hair over his bald spot. They were people who could survive in that private sector slum out there—that developers' paradise of homelessness, hunger and unemployment. Survive and keep their health and their sanity. And there sure weren't many of them. What it really was [was] privilege. He had it; there were really only the privileged and the underprivileged. The underprivileged had strength of a sort, but again it was more like that ulcer of his. Democracy used to be a so-good spirit of the voters. But now there was little democracy and a lot of power plays. The people used to protest and riot as a club—the do-good spirit had been replaced by the ulcer. The roaring beast in their bellies that made them move and holler and not think too much. And in some ways that was good because if you did too much thinking about democracy in the megacity, you'd probably succumb to the urge and just throw up.

*"Birth of a City"*

Residents felt the importance of these structural changes in their city. The day following the first Megacity elections the media gorged itself on headlines such as "Birth of a City" (*Toronto Star*), "Lastman makes megacity history" (*The Globe and Mail*), or "The mourning after" (*Now Magazine*).[44] The cartoon of the Toronto Sun depicted a man screaming and running out of the voting booth, and the clerk explaining that it is "voter stress syndrome." Citizens did indeed feel the importance of these elections. The voter turnout, which ranged in the previous elections from 28 to 38 percent, hit 50 percent in many areas across the Megacity (Table 1).

The first Megacity electoral campaign raged in the midst of a province-wide teachers' strike struggling against the government's education reform. I remember my mother telling me: "I really have the impression of being part of an important moment in history," as she was discussing her involvement in the leadership of one of the teachers' union. It was a feverish moment for thousands of teachers taking to the streets to fight for quality education. Many of them were taking to the streets for their first time. In this climate of insurgency, the first Megacity elections were on their way. The new mayor would operate a city with a $6.5 billion budget and a workforce of about 50,000 employees, and Diane Francis, of the right-wing Financial Post (now National Post), stressed the urge for an "experienced CEO."[45]

*Reprinted with permission from the Toronto Star Syndicate*

The *Toronto Star*, for its part, called for a mayor with good management skills, a skillful chairperson to lead a huge council, the city's prime booster, a civic leader, and most importantly, a mayor who will re-appropriate the discourse on community control, citizen participation, and local democracy:

> Those hoping to lead the new city should state how they will guard against those who wish to sabotage amalgamation and return us to

> the inefficient, wasteful system we now have. Community control, citizen participation and local democracy are essential ideas but could be co-opted by anti-amalgamation foes. Candidates who use these code words should explain if they support stripping the new city of real power and investing this power in the planned community councils, thus recreating the six existing municipalities.[46]

Twenty candidates ran for mayoralty. The media only reported on the two frontrunners: Mel Lastman, populist mayor of former North York for twenty-five years, and Barbara Hall, progressive mayor of former Toronto. The other candidates were quite diverse, they ranged from a white supremacist, to a writer, a teacher, a street musician, and a lawyer who advocates for the right to vote in municipal elections for non-citizens.

| | Mel Lastman | Barbara Hall |
|---|---|---|
| **New City of Toronto** | **51.8%** | **46.2%** |
| East York | 39.7% | 58.0% |
| Etobicoke | 52.4% | 45.3% |
| North York | 79.4% | 19.1% |
| Scarborough | 52.6% | 45.0% |
| Toronto | 30.3% | 67.5% |
| York | 47.4% | 50.0% |

**Table 2:** November 10, 1997 Electoral Results—Mayor
*Source: Chief Returning Officer of the City of Toronto*

But in the end, "the flamboyant appliance salesman from the suburbs, whose key promise was to hold the line on property taxes, defeated Barbara Hall, the urbane mayor of the old City of Toronto," wrote John Spears and Gail Swainson in the *Toronto Star*.[47] Mel Lastman made many mistakes during his campaign. He declared that there were no homeless people in North York, while a homeless woman died in a North York service station the same day. What this suggests, is that Mel Lastman, "for all his charm, was not really up to the task of running a huge city with its myriad complex social problems."[48] His campaign offered simple solutions to complex issues, a reassuring, friendly figure in these times of uncertainty and chaos.

> Mel makes his biggest sale: Despite gaffes, polls, he's the Mega Man now.[49]

Barbara Hall, on the other side, ran an excellent campaign according to the mainstream media which depicted her on the night of her defeat as "serene" and "gracious." She stressed consensus and vision. Downtown citizens were clearly behind her, but also York and East York, the two small adjacent cities. She said to her supporting crowd on the night of the defeat that the issue of municipal restructuring captured the agenda and kept people from working on the pressing issues:

> There were thousands of people going out to meetings every night, through the winter and the spring, to talk about amalgamation, instead of talking about how to solve youth unemployment or poverty or homelessness.[50]

In the end, people in Toronto chose assurance over vision. Lastman was mayor of a pro-development suburb for twenty-five years, while Hall was the former mayor of an inner-city that has developed a progressive regime. She was an anti-poverty lawyer, a social worker, and a community organizer. Hall was in power in 1995-97 when the City of Toronto took a strong position against the provincial government's welfare reform.

> Garbage collection said it all about the campaign. Who knew people cared so much about it? I am a profligate producer of garbage and as a resident of the old city, got pickup but once a week and it was plenty. But in Lastman Country, where cars are cars and men are men and there aren't any damn bikes (or Commies either), they got pickup twice a week. It seemed to matter, either as metaphor for what we want out of municipal government (which is apparently municipal services and nothing more) or as a practical expression of what we want (better garbage collection). Hall, with her bigger-than-that view of the world and the city's possible place in it, did not get the garbage issue any better than I did, and it cost her.[51]

I would not go as far as saying that people chose garbage pick-up over solving problems of homelessness, but the urban progressive middle class of downtown Toronto got a clear message from the suburbs. This was not a message of selfishness, but a message of uncertainty in the face of restructuring. John Sewell wrote in Now Magazine that it was the government's strategy to "create crisis and chaos, then hope voters will opt for strong leaders with simple messages, as they have done with such depressing regularity in so many other countries that have slipped slowly and unwittingly into decay and tyranny."[52] It is clear that the misunderstanding between suburban and urban residents is a reality that should be addressed.

As a result of the forced amalgamation, the right-leaning new megacouncil has twice more suburban councillors than their urban counterparts, and less than a quarter of left-leaning representatives.[53] People chose well-known faces and experienced candidates. These elections sealed the municipal restructuring imposed by the provincial government. But Citizens for Local Democracy did not quit the fight.

### *"We're Now into the Era of Cash-Box Politics": The Democratic Process*

C4LD's first reaction to the defeat of many of their preferred candidates was to question the motives behind the Harris government's forced amalgamation. Sewell wrote, "Harris has pushed aside a vision of the humane, caring city. We're now into the era of cash-box politics."[54] Questions were raised about the reliability of the voting lists used for the elections. The electoral process did not function smoothly. Turnouts were larger than expected at many polling stations, which ran out of ballots, thus creating long delays and preventing many people from voting before the closure of the polls. National public television in Toronto did not cover the elections until 9:30, whereas private station CITY-TV turned to full coverage as soon as polls closed, but reported the wrong numbers for a while. The large margin between Hall and Lastman was surprising, as opinion polls predicted a much tighter majority. Mistakes by polling firms might be explained by the fact that they did not take into account the larger proportion of homeowners than tenants voting in municipal elections.

Sewell argued in his article that voters lists were irregular. The province refused to revise the lists to include the 17,000 amendments requested by Toronto from the previous elections, and the further 14,000 amendments coming out of the March referendums.[55]

> Those left off were largely tenants, who favour Hall. In a Third World country, observers might call this election fraud.[56]

Do democracy activists around the world know about this? Certainly not. Who would suspect Canada has irregularities in its elections? But the results remain, and people in Toronto elected a megacouncil with considerable power, a council that governs a city bigger than some Canadian provinces, with about 8 percent of the Canadian population residing within its boundaries. David Lewis Stein suggested that "it is impossible to picture another constitutional conference being held to divide up power in Canada without the mayor of Toronto we have just elected being at the table."[57]

The first megacouncil meeting was held in January 1998. A megacouncil it is, big, confusing, cacophonous:

> It felt like the United Nations. Or the Knesset. Or the Duma. (Russian lower house of Parliament, for those of you who do not read the world news pages.) And at least the huge, cacophonous Italian assembly has the added attraction of former porn star Ilona "Cuddles" Staller as an elected representative to enliven the proceedings. There is no such delightful creature on Toronto's new, humongous, amalgamated city council.[58]

There were much debates about the structure of the new city, particularly the role of community councils. Left-leaning councillor David Miller was appointed head of a special committee to review the Transition Team Report entitled "New City New Opportunities."[59] Various factions viewed the role of community councils quite differently. In discussions leading to the Transition Team Report, both Lastman then mayor of North York and Hall then mayor of Toronto issued reports on their view of governance in the unified city. The difference in tone and vision is quite striking:

> North York: The amalgamation of the seven municipal governments will bring together seven different corporate cultures. Each organization has its strengths and areas for improvement that should be considered in the building of the 'best' new organization.[60]

> Toronto: Now, more than ever, the City of Toronto needs to hear from its communities. It is important that community issues, concerns and ideas are on the table when the Provincial Transition Team makes its recommendations for the decision making processes and structure of the megacity.[61]

The vision stemming out of North York emphasised corporate cultures and efficiency, while the downtown Toronto focused on community participation. North York highlighted its excellence in the provision of high quality services, of a business, non-bureaucratic approach to decision making, of an innovative management system, and of a political structure that supports the professional opinions of staff.[62] The City of Toronto, in contrast, highlighted its tradition of progressive services and programs such as a focus on maintaining a safe and healthy city, an effective public participation, and initiatives aimed at helping alienated groups.[63] As Councillor Miller mentioned, the difficulty in Council stems out of different political cultures among suburban and urban councillors. Council is still unstable and establishing a unified political culture for the new city is not an easy task. With the redrawing of ward boundaries for the 2000 elections and the diminution of the number of councillors, Council is once again destabilised.[64]

In the end, the Transition Team Report recommended a governance structure where "citizens know their participation is meaningful."[65] The report is filled with language of democracy and citizen involvement. The report recommends that community councils should "listen to the community, monitor its well-being, and bring community priorities and concerns forward to City Council."[66] On the issue of neighbourhood committees—which would be built more from the ground up—the Transition Team recommended not taking action at this moment. The Megacity Council adopted in October 1998 the recommendations of the Miller special committee concerning community councils. They have a mandate over local planning, development control, local transportation, local recreation, and neighbourhood matters. Alongside with six other committees (Policy and Finance, Administration, Planning and Transportation, Economic Development and Parks, Works, Community Services), the six community councils are accountable directly to City Council and the mayor. They play an advisory role and can conduct hearings on behalf of City Council. They are composed of city councillors elected in the area and are not an additional layer of government. Basically, they are a top-down local body. Council passed with a very close vote a motion to ask the province to change the legislation in order to give final decision power to community councils, rather than a mere advisory role. However, the mayor was opposed to this and ultimately the province did not act on this motion. There was a fear that final decision-making powers would simply recreate the old local municipality structure.[67]

Undoubtedly, this mere advisory role for community council, stripped of budgeting powers, did not satisfy many local activists who were pushing for a sort of recreation of the former six local municipality structure. The Transition Team rejected this idea from the onset, and clearly recommended not to take action on what was called neighbourhood committees. These could have taken the form of citizens' assemblies or town hall meetings or coalitions of residents' associations.

Nevertheless, an experiment of citizens assemblies has been established in one downtown Toronto ward, with the full endorsement of the two elected councillors, Chris Korwin-Kuczynski and David Miller. The founding meeting was held on November 5, 1997. Three assemblies were planned for 1998. The Citizens' Assembly is a voluntary organization made up of residents "who are looking for ways to preserve and enhance citizen participation and promote local democracy in the new City of Toronto." The goals of the assemblies are to improve communication between individuals and community groups, to promote regular communication between residents and councillors, and "to support and initiate community projects which increase citizens participation and community self-government."[68] Despite the exhaustion of volunteer resident organizers, the Citizens' Assembly still exists in Parkdale-High Park. They were set up out of the momentum created by anti-amalgamation mobilization. As Councillor Miller said, residents felt they needed to use the energy of coalition against amalgamation in a positive way when the new city was incorporated.[69] The Assembly was directly involved in influencing Miller's special committee on the evaluation of the Transition Team report, and was quite vocal on structural issues for the organization of the new city. Assembly meetings usually attract about 100 residents and entertain strong ties with city councillors, who are invited to report on issues to the assembly. The agenda is completely set by residents who attend the meeting, not only the organizing committee. Councillors interact with residents and then use this precious feedback at City Council meetings. The Citizens' Assembly is a self-appointed body; it does not pretend to represent all residents of the area.

During the debate on neighbourhood committees in Miller's special committee, there was resistance to formalise the Citizens' Assembly structure as it would have stripped it of its grassroots nature and created problems with establishing proper mechanisms for representation. Some councillors were pushing for creating mechanisms within the city structure to support the growth of Citizens' Assemblies. But it was defeated, mostly by suburban councillors who felt threatened by such a grassroots political culture. Well-established ratepayers' associations were also opposed as it would have undermined their legitimacy to "represent" the area.[70] But Miller ventured to say that perhaps with the reduction of the number of councillors in 2000, it will create a vacuum where Citizens' Assemblies will become more meaningful for councillors who will have less time to sit on committees and thus will have to rely on the work of residents to provide them with feedback.[71]

In addition to the governance structure, the council established a number of Task Forces on issues such as homelessness, the environment, children and youth. Interestingly as well, on March 4, 1998, the megacouncil created a Task Force on Community Access and Equity, which established the need for public consultation in order to make recommendations to the megacouncil on how to "ensure the voices of the City's diverse communities continue to be heard."[72] Participants in C4LD played a role in these consultations, but many activists quickly became disillusioned by the process. As Kipfer writes:

> The "equity agenda" in the new Toronto is a largely symbolic affair, defined as it is by fashionable declarations of support for the 'diversity' and 'uniqueness' of Toronto as an immigrant city. Indeed, predominant notions of diversity and multiculturalism have become tools to promote the competitiveness of the global city of business. Multiculturalism is reduced to colourful festivals and tasteful food while the meaning of diversity is limited to a lifestyle choice and a marketing strategy to sell Toronto's Olympic bid and capture the youth market in designer clothing.[73]

Nevertheless, on December 15, 1999, the Council adopted the recommendations of the Task Force and established five community advisory committees on aboriginal affairs, disability issues, status of women, race and ethnic relations, and lesbian, gay, bisexual, and transgendered issues. For many activists this was simply a watered-down version of their recommendation to setting up a special standing committee of Council, an equality commission within the bureaucracy, and an arms-length equity council.[74]

### *Megacity Toronto: Transition and Growing Pains*

> They argued, of course, because they're local politicians and that's what we pay them to do. They also made decisions—quite a lot of decisions, actually—about street parties and Blue Boxes and the homeless and whether to land the Olympics and how to land the Olympics and what to do about property taxes and how to spend the money in that fire-breathing dragon of an amalgamated budget. They even made decisions on how to make decisions. They decided to put off other decisions. They schemed, hyped, postured, dissembled and backstabbed. They coalesced into blocks, only to

> regroup into more expedient alliances. They took shots. They buried the hatchet. And then they cast their votes –over and over and over again, thereby creating out of all this talk, the raw material of politics, what the incumbents and editorial writers will later refer to as "the record." That is: the birth of the megacity.[75]

The new city structure established, the megacouncil was on its way to "build a new city." The feeling of starting anew, the nervousness of city staff amidst the changing structure, the marketing hype of the Olympic bid. Megacity Toronto was carving its place as a new city, with growing pains and transitional saga. Interesting episodes are the Lastman/Harris skirmish around revenue-neutrality, the property tax reform, and ideas about secession.

In the Spring 1997, the provincial government's Fair Property Tax Act was introduced. The basis of the property tax reform is a re-assessment of the market value of homes as of June 1996. The new system fixes residential taxes at approximately 1.26 percent of the property's market value, to be reassessed every three years. Given that many properties in the former City of Toronto have not been reassessed for over forty years, the reform means a huge increase. Astonishing tax fluctuation stories filled the media with figures where small retail stores would be consumed by tax hikes of up to 10,000 percent while bank towers would pocket million-dollar refunds.[78] New mayor Mel Lastman screamed when Ontario Finance Minister Ernie Eves announced in December 1997 that the province's promise of a revenue-neutral transition in financial responsibilities between the province and municipalities, would fail in Toronto. The new Megacity would have a deficit of $163.5 million ($84.1 million from increased responsibilities and $79.4 million from the loss of provincial grants).[76] This would mean Lastman would not be able to keep his promise of a three-year property tax freeze in Mega-Toronto. The new mayor called Harris a liar… And the circus continues! The province finally offered the Megacity a two-year $200 million interest-free loan and a one-time $50 million grant to ease the transition.[77] Despite the fact that the rest of the province was offered grants to relieve the downloading transition, Toronto will have to repay the loan. Nevertheless, Lastman was now able to honour his election promise to freeze taxes.

Citizens for Local Democracy was part of the opposition movement. They marched with inner-city small business owners under the banner "Citizens and Merchants Unite!". However, participants in the movement expressed concerns. They did not want to join a protest that could be confused with right-wing "no taxes" ideology, or divert attention from the plight of the small and marginalized in the city:

> When you're canvassing for a No vote on Megacity, please don't say people should vote No because their property taxes will go up; if you say this, you're reinforcing the Tories' premise that the most important thing is always to have lower taxes.[79]

> I do not want to join any "protest" (like a Tax Revolt) that could be taken over, or otherwise confused with any initiative promoted by (i) "Tax-fighter" Mike Harris; or (ii) the interests of the owners and/or major occupants of the Bay Street (et al) towers in downtown Toronto.[80]

To avoid such confusion, the struggle was defined by some C4LD members as a struggle for independence and security for "the small people." Property, C4LD argued, is sometimes the only security people have, guaranteeing their independence. The struggle was also made in the name of tenants' rights. Tenants would be severely touched by rent increases. As C4LD member Michael J. Murphy explained:

> ...this means that about 6,000 to 12,000 tenants will be looking for other accommodations in the very near future. Of the 6,000 to 12,000, about 35% can afford to "make the leap into home ownership," according to the recent statistics from the Canada Mortgage and Housing Corporation, and these people will most likely wind up in condominiums. The remainder will most likely wind up on the street.[81]

Another argument used to resist the Fair Property Tax Act was that property taxes should stay under local control and should not serve to finance welfare programs. Taxes generally serve three purposes: financing of services, redistribution, and encouragement of socially desirable behaviour. According to C4LD member Robert Cooke, inner cities should not pay more taxes because service costs are lower due to density. Redistribution is best accomplished through income tax, not property taxes. Finally, by punishing inner-cities with higher taxes because real-estate market values are higher, the government encourages suburban lifestyle, business-flight, and car-dependency.[82] The Fair Property Tax Act nevertheless came into effect, and the new Council had to find ways to mitigate its devastating effects on downtown commercial and industrial sectors. Given the urgency of the situation, Lastman asked

Harris for a three-year cap on commercial and industrial property tax to 2.5 percent (up or down). And the Council ultimately decided on a seven and a half year phase-in period.

Jumping ahead in the more recent period, Fall 1999 came with another interesting episode. Mayor Lastman declared in Florida that Toronto should be its own province. He later pulled back from his statement, but it had already unleashed waves of ironic and also serious comments back in Toronto. Most observers knew that constitutionally, the creation of a new city-province would virtually be impossible. But well-respected urban analyst Jane Jacobs had already toyed with the idea.[83] A *Toronto Star* editorial pointed to the fact that with a population larger than that of Newfoundland, Prince Edward Island, Nova Scotia, New Brunswick, Manitoba, and Saskatchewan combined, Toronto still cannot collect sales, gas, or tobacco taxes.[84] Proposals varied from the creation of a Province of Southern Ontario to the creation of a new designation of city-states that could also include Montreal and Vancouver.

Main arguments in support of such a special designation relied on the imbalance of power between urban regions and mainly rural provinces, as well as the importance of the urban regional economy in the global world. Gwyn criticized the Canadian and Ontario governments for not having come to terms with Canada's urban economy, a reality that has replaced mines, forests, fishing, farms, and hydro-electricity: "the source of national wealth, now coming from our minds and imagination, rather than from the ground. Our cities now are Canada."[85] *Toronto Star* economics editor David Crane explored the city-state system in Germany. To compete in the world, it was argued that Toronto needs the same resource and power as other global cities such as London, Paris, or Berlin. And Richard Gwyn noted that "a quarter-century ago, native self-government was obviously impossible. Today, it's happening."[86] And of course, references to the special status of Quebec within the confederation were explicit in many instances, from Sewell to Gwyn:

> Toronto is now a city-state, rather than just a city. Watch it, and perhaps Vancouver and Montreal will also "do a Quebec." That province has gained special status without a comma of the Constitution being changed.[87]

While discussions on secession in Toronto are received with an ironic smile, there is substantial work initiated towards the goal of "self-government" or municipal autonomy. As the Local Self Government Bulletin No. 3 indicates, "the Toronto debate goes beyond asking for autonomy and respect, and raises the question of the kinds of power which should be exercised by a big city."[88] John Sewell maintains an e-mail list and a web site on self-government in Canada, with links to other provinces such as Alberta and Newfoundland (www.localselfgovt.com). The web site was created and funded by Sewell and Alan Broadbent (President of Avana Capital Corporation in Toronto). The advisory committee includes distinguished members such as the President of The Canadian Urban Institute, John Farrow, Professor of Political Science Andrew Sancton (University of Western Ontario), and Professor Beth Moore Milroy of the School of Urban and Regional Planning at Ryerson University.

Moreover, a Committee for the Province of Toronto was formed as a "community group committed to achieving Provincial Status for Toronto under Canada's Constitution." They supported a notice of motion to City Council. The notice of motion was presented by Councillor Walker on December 9, 1999 and was officially deposited in February 2000. It builds on the wide opposition to amalgamation in 1997 and the wide discontentment with downloading policies to demand to the City of Toronto to 1) "hold a public referendum as part of the 2000 municipal election to determine public support for proceeding with separation from the Province;" and 2) "develop an extensive communications package outlining the argument (financial, social) for and against separation and a plan to provoke full participation and debate on the part of the citizens prior to the referendum."[89] The Committee for the Province of Toronto argues that:

> It is time to take this forward step so that we can take control of our own destiny. Without the broader base of taxing power of a province, independent from Ontario, we will never become the truly great city that we could be. Provincehood for Toronto would put an end to this or any future Ontario government ever again plundering the economy of Toronto to curry favour in the rest of the Province.
>
> Torontonians have shown they have the ability to lead. We have the rights inherent in a free and democratic Canada. We have the right to create Canada's newest province, the Province of Toronto.[90]

### *"One Vision, One City, One Plan": Building the New City*

More than a year after the incorporation of the new city, Toronto is now embarked in a process of "city-building" and a grandiose visioning process. The City launched the process leading to the new Official Plan by pushing a visioning exercise involving hundreds of appointed decision-makers, community leaders, politicians, bureaucrats, developers, business interests, planners, university presidents, editors of major newspapers, heads of media institutions, leaders of trade unions and from the non-profit sector. The new Official Plan is seen as more than a mere document dealing with zoning and development. As the City's official newsletter puts it:

> The amalgamation establishing the new City of Toronto has made it possible to set out a new vision and shape the city's future in ways that will enhance the best of what it has. It has made new ideas possible.[91]

The focus is on "renewal," "reinvestment," and public-private partnerships. The process may seem as a direct continuation of the reform language of the 1970s. Council's vision for the city highlights Toronto as a "caring and friendly city," a "clean, green and sustainable city," a "dynamic city," and a place with a "quality of life."[92] However, as Kipfer and Keil remind us, the key focus is competitiveness and entrepreneurialism.[93] Combined with the 2008 Olympic bid and the waterfront regeneration, the new Official Plan is inserted in the overall strategy of marketing the new city as a rising global city. A promotional booklet on Toronto emphasizes these "new opportunities":

> Toronto's age reflects its attitude—young and enterprising. An accessible, responsive and newly amalgamated city, Toronto's economy is booming...People call us determined, competitive, dynamic. Others call us Toronto. Feel free to call us HOME![94]

And the story continues. Toronto has been transformed in the past few years. Transformed not only by institutional and territorial restructuring, globalization, and demographic changes, but transformed also by a strong wind of political agency. People sense the importance of the moment.

## NOTES

1. Engin Isin and Joanne Wolfson, *The Making of the Toronto Megacity: An Introduction*, Working Paper no. 21 (Toronto: Urban Studies Programme, York University, 1999), 54; Tourism Toronto, *Toronto 1998 Visitors Guide* (Toronto: Tourism Toronto, 1998), 4.
2. Stefan Kipfer and Roger Keil, "Still Planning to be Different? Toronto at the turn of the millennium" *DISP* 140 (2000), 28-36.
3. Isin and Wolfson, *The Making of the Toronto Megacity*, 54.
4. Tourism Toronto, *Toronto 1998 Visitors Guide*, 4.
5. Graham Todd, "Megacity: Globalization and Governance in Toronto," *Studies in Political Economy* 56 (1998), 193-216.
6. Kipfer and Keil, "Still Planning to be Different?"

7. Martin Mittelstaedt, "Shutdown of Toronto would make history," *Globe and Mail* (October 19, 1996), A1, A4.
8. Ibid.
9. Glenn Cooly, "Citizen Insurrection: How to Use the Timeless Art of Civil Disobedience to Upend the Tories," *Now Magazine* (February 8-14, 1996), 16-20.
10. Isin and Wolfson, *The Making of the Toronto Megacity*, 59.
11. Given the strength of the word, the media quickly embraced the term "Megacity." Opponents to the bill also used the term widely, for it denotes all at once gigantism, boosterism, remoteness from the people, etc. Government officials and documents never used the term however, they preferred slogans like "One City for All of Us" or "unified city." Technically, it is an inappropriate term, as megacities commonly refer to cities of over 10 million of population. But since it has been widely accepted in Toronto and Ontario to define the new city, I will continue using it.
12. Al Leach, *Statement to the Legislature by The Honourable Al Leach, Minister Of Municipal Affairs and Housing On Who Does What* (www.mmah.gov.ca/inthnews/backgrnd/970113e.htm, January 13, 1996).
13. Isin and Wolfson, *The Making of the Toronto Megacity*, 2.
14. Greater Toronto Area Task Force, *Report of the GTA Task Force* (Toronto: Publications Ontario, 1996), 17. For interesting background and analysis of governance restructuring in Toronto, see Frances Frisken, "Planning and Servicing the Greater Toronto Area: The interplay of provincial and municipal interests," in *Metropolitan Governance: American/ Canadian Intergovernmental Perspectives*, eds. David Rothblatt and Andrew Sancton (1993).
15. Greater Toronto Area Task Force, 221
16. Al Leach, "A Note From the Minister, Municipal Affairs and Housing," in *A Guide to Municipal Restructuring*, ed. Ministry of Municipal Affairs and Housing (Toronto: Publications Ontario, August 1996).
17. Frank Faubert, Barbara Hall, Doug Holyday, Mel Lastman, Frances Nunziata, and Michael Prue, *Change For the Better: A vision for the future of our communities, A framework for restructuring local government* (www.city.toronto.on.ca/3wrd/change.htm, 1997). If he could have read the future, Mel Lastman, the soon-to-be Megacity mayor, would have erased these numbers from the report, as Harris brought them back to light when the province created a $163.5 million deficit on the new Megacity by transferring many services.
18. Wendell Cox Consultancy, *Local and Regional Governance in the Greater Toronto Area: A Review of Alternatives* (www.city.toronto.on.ca/3wrd/cox.htm, January 10, 1997).
19. John Barber, "Sending a message to King Mike," *Globe and Mail* (March 4, 1997), A10.
20. M. Grange, "Amalgamation follows Tories' philosophy," *Globe and Mail* (December 18, 1996).
21. Colin Vaughan, "Developers support megacity for bureaucratic neatness," *Globe and Mail* (February 24, 1997).
22. Graham Todd, "Megacity," 206.
23. Isin and Wolfson, *The Making of the Toronto Megacity*, 63.
24. Sewell now writes for Eye, the other Toronto weekly cultural newpaper.
25. Canada, *Constitution Act of 1982*, section 92 (8).
26. John Ralston Saul, Address to the Monday night meeting, January 27, 1997, recorded *on no mega-cd [no—megacity]* (Toronto: Protest Boy Records, 1997). A slightly different written version of the argument can also be found in John Ralston

Saul, "John Ralston Saul: On false populism and the Harris Tories," *Globe and Mail* (January 30, 1997).

27. Leach, *Statement to the Legislature.*
28. Ijeoma Ross, "Neighbours rally to fight amalgamation in Metro Toronto," *Globe and Mail* (February 1, 1997), A6.
29. In designating the "disentanglement" reforms, the terms "downloading" or "offloading" were more commonly employed than the term "devolution." This choice of vocabulary reflects the emphasis put on funding relations between the provincial and the municipal levels of government, rather than on the actual provision of services and the decision-making powers associated with the design of these services. The PC government shuffled the financial costs of certain services down to the municipal level of government without decentralizing the power to design many of these services and their standards.
30. Ijeoma Ross, "Business favours megacity, poll finds," *Globe and Mail* (March 3, 1997), A3.
31. Jian Ghomeshi, *no mega-cd [no—megacity]* (Toronto: Protest Boy Record, 1997), emphasis is original.
32. John Barber, "Experts joining throng of megacity bashers," *Globe and Mail* (February 26, 1997), A2.
33. M. Campbell, I. Ross, G. Abbate, and M. Grange, "Metro voters reject amalgamation," *Globe and Mail* (March 4, 1997), A10.
34. John Barber, "Sending a message to King Mike," A10.
35. John Sewell, *Local Government and the future of Canada,* presentation to the Municipal Governance Institute, Vancouver (Posted on C4LD list server, June 20, 1997).
36. It was alleged that the Megacity council created a ratio population/representative too large to assure decent access and protection; that the large size of the new council prevented face-to-face debates; and that it would be dominated by party politics and standardized solutions because of the large bureaucracy involved.
37. The province took only 50 percent of the costs of education off property taxes; it continues to pay 80 percent of the costs of welfare assistance and child care, and the total costs of long-term care facilities. See Isin and Wolfson, *The Making of the Toronto Megacity*, 67.
38. The new city council would comprise fifty-seven members instead of forty-four; the powers of the Board of Trustees and the Transition Team were limited. The former became the Financial Advisory Board and could not veto the decisions of elected officials anymore, but only ask for reconsideration if disagreement occurred. The Transition Team's powers were reduced to recommendations that the new council could accept or reject. The new ward division and the structure of the "community councils" were to be determined by the new elected council. See Legislative Assembly, *The City of Toronto Act: Third Reading* (Toronto: Publications Ontario, 1997). The size of the Council was later reduced again to forty-four for the 2000 elections. See Ministry of Municipal Affairs and Housing, *Fewer Politicians, Lower Taxes ...More to do in the City of Toronto*, Press Release (December 2, 1999).
39. Lisa Wright, "Tension builds at Legislature," *Toronto Star* (April 2, 1997).
40. Posted on the C4LD list server, April 6, 1997.
41. John Sewell, reported in J. Rusk and I. Ross, "Tories' megacity bill now law," *Globe and Mail* (April 22, 1997), A3.
42. Section 55 of the Canadian Constitution: "Where a Bill passed by the House of the Parliament is presented to the Governor General for the Queen's Assent, he shall declare, according to his Discretion, but subject to the Provisions of this Act and to

Her Majesty's Instructions, either that he assents thereto in the Queen's Name, or that he withholds the Queen's Assent, or that he reserves the Bill for the Signification of the Queen's Pleasure." Section 90 of the Canadian Constitution: "The following provisions of this Act respecting the Parliament of Canada—namely, the Provisions relating to Appropriation and Tax Bills, the Disallowance of Acts, and the Significance of Pleasure on the Bills reserved—shall extend and apply to the Legislatures of the several Provinces as if those Provisions were here re-enacted and made application in Terms to the respective Provinces and the Legislatures therefore, with the Substitution of the Lieutenant Governor of the Province for the Governor General, of the Governor General for the Queen and for a Secretary of State, of One Year for Two Years, and of the Province for Canada." See Canada, *Constitution Act of 1982.*

43. Sample letter to the Governor General posted on the C4LD list server (April 12, 1997).
44. *Toronto Star*, "Birth of a City," *Toronto Star* (November 11, 1997), B1; Globe and Mail, "Lastman makes megacity history," *Globe and Mail* (November 11, 1997), A1; John Sewell, "The mourning after," *Now Magazine* (November 13-19, 1997), 16.
45. Diane Francis, "Megacity needs an experienced CEO," Article printed on a flyer supporting Mel Lastman for his electoral campaign.
46. *Toronto Star* Editorial, "What Toronto needs from new mayor," *Toronto Star* (October 12, 1997), F2.
47. John Spears and Gail Swainson, "Lastman leads new unified city," *Toronto Star* (November 11, 1997), A1.
48. Timothy Appleby, "Hall accepts her defeat with grace," *Globe and Mail* (November 11, 1997), A13.
49. Robert Benzie, "Mel makes his biggest sale," *Toronto Sun* (November 11, 1997), 5.
50. Barbara Hall, reported in Appleby, "Hall accepts her defeat with grace," A13.
51. Christie Blatchford, "In the end, voters put their wallets first," *Toronto Sun* (November 11, 1997), 5.
52. Sewell, "The mourning after," 16
53. David Lewis Stein, "Lastman faces wild ride with left-leaning council," *Toronto Star* (November 11, 1997), B1, B4.
54. Sewell, "The mourning after," 16
55. Ibid.
56. Ibid.
57. Stein, "Lastman faces wild ride," B4.
58. Rosie DiManno, "Binoculars in order for this council," *Toronto Star* (January 7, 1998), B1.
59. Transition Team, *New City New Opportunities* (Toronto, December 1997).
60. W. A. Liczyk, *Building a New City: A Blueprint for the Political and Administrative and Organization Structure* (City of North York, June 27, 1997), 4.
61. City of Toronto, *Community Consultation: Options for Decision Making in the Megacity* (City of Toronto, June 1997), 27.
62. Liczyk, *Building a New City*, 4.
63. City of Toronto, *Community Consultation*, 8.
64. Phone conversation with Councillor David Miller (February 25, 2000).
65. Transition Team, *New City New Opportunities*, 97.
66. Ibid., 101.
67. Phone conversation with Councillor David Miller (February 25, 2000).

68. Citizens' Assembly Ward 19, *What Is The Citizens' Assembly?* (webhome.idirect.com/~burp/what.htm).
69. Phone conversation with Councillor David Miller (February 25, 2000).
70. Ibid.
71. Ibid.
72. Task Force on Community Access and Equity, *Consultation Guide* (City of Toronto, June 1998).
73. Stefan Kipfer, "Whose City Is It? Global Politics in the Mega-City," *Cityscope*, Newsletter of the Community Social Planning Council of Toronto (Winter 1999-2000), 17.
74. Community Social Planning Council of Toronto, "An Act for the new Millenium?" *Sound Bite* 15 (January 18, 2000), 1.
75. John Lorinc, "Making of the Megacity: An Epic Tale of a Political Founding," *Toronto Life* 32, no. 17 (November 1998), 110.
76. These figures were later revised to $151 million.
77. Lorinc, "Making of the Megacity"
78. Ibid.
79. Debbie Fields, Foodshare, Address to the Monday night meeting (February 17, 1997).
80. Sally D. Gibson, posted on the C4LD list server (February 14, 1998).
81. Michael J. Murphy, posted on the C4LD list server (March 13, 1998).
82. Robert Cooke, posted on the C4LD list server (February 16, 1998).
83. Jane Jacobs, *Deputation to the Standing Committee on General Government conducting hearings on The City of Toronto Act—Bill 103* (February 3, 1997).
84. *Toronto Star* Editorial, "There's method in Mel's madness," *Toronto Star* (November 24, 1999).
85. Richard Gwyn, "Lastman catches attention on city-state," *Toronto Star* (November 26, 1999).
86. Ibid.
87. Ibid. See also, John Sewell, "Welcome to the Year of the Slingshot," *Eye* (December 30, 1999).
88. John Sewell, *Local Self Government—Bulletin no. 3* (www.localselfgovt.com, January 2000).
89. Michael Walker, *Secession of the City of Toronto from the Province of Ontario: "Let the People Decide,"* Notice of Motion (Toronto City Council, December 15-16, 1999).
90. Committee for the Province of Toronto, www.interlog.com/~cjazz/prov-t.htm.
91. City of Toronto, "Facing Up to the City's Future Challenges," *Toronto Plan* 2 (October 1999), 1.
92. City of Toronto, *Toronto City Council's Strategic Plan—Part 1* (Toronto: Strategic & Corporate Policy Division, Chief Administrator's Office, City of Toronto, November 1999), 1.
93. Kipfer and Keil, "Still Planning to be Different?"
94. MovingTo, "Toronto Spells Home," *Moving To and Around: The Greater Toronto Area* 26, no. 4 (1999-2000), 6.

CHAPTER 2

# CITIZENS FOR LOCAL DEMOCRACY SPEAK OUT!

We are a gentle, angry people,
And we are singing, singing for our lives
We are a gentle, angry people,
And we are singing, singing for our lives
We are a democratic people, We are young and old together
We are a land of many colours, We are a peaceful, caring people.

—*Song entitled "Gentle Angry People"*
*Words adapted from Holly Near and Ronnie Gilbert, "Lifeline"*
*Citizens for Local Democracy web site, 1998*

People of Toronto resisted. They resisted the sweeping changes the Ontario Tory government rushed through the Legislature. These restructuring plans responded to the requirements of neoliberalism. They are seriously threatening the progressive regime of Toronto. The Ontario government's Common Sense Revolution harmed the poor and the marginalized, people that are not always organized to resist. But in Toronto, the government hit a forceful opposition: the urban progressive middle class. Middle class people are not necessarily better organized than the poor and the marginalized, but they have more resources. Resources like money, resources like cultural and political skills, education, positions in the state apparatus or in key sectors of the professional world. The middle class is composed of experts and leaders. It captures media attention. Most of all, the middle class exhibits a sense of ownership in a society where it feels it has the right to fix norms and conventions; a society it shapes to its image and to which it identifies. Only a slight portion of the middle class calls itself "activist," be they environmentalists, advocates of the marginalized, feminists, or human rights advocates. Most people in the middle class consider they suffer elites' decisions; they are part of the "respectable" silent majority. Some middle class people are "professionally" progressive as social workers, care givers, academics, human rights lawyers, or civil servants.

These Torontonians are indeed a "gentle angry people," to quote from the anti-Megacity song. They resisted the loss of their world, their progressive daily world, the society they believed in, the society they cared for. This chapter is a tale of resistance, of brilliance and errors, of hopes and closures. The story of promising moments and of missed opportunities. This tale was reconstructed out of thousands of pages of newsletters, of e-mail messages, of deputation, brochures, of poems and songs, of newspaper articles, of conversations, and of personal souvenirs of rallies, meetings, anxiety, excitement, experience, and fieldnotes. It looks at Toronto which is indeed "everywhere the eye can see: one vast expanse of urban, cosmopolitan...megalopolis," as Rosie DiManno, city columnist at the *Toronto Star* writes, "with a sum greater than its parts; a hybrid, a mutant, a mongrel, a kit 'n' caboodle."[1]

### *Citizens for Local Democracy Organized Resistance*

Citizens for Local Democracy (C4LD) was formed in reaction to the Progressive Conservative political agenda, specifically in reaction to Bill 103, the City of Toronto Act. C4LD's actions in the name of local democracy pushed away concerns about efficiency and fiscal neatness and swept Toronto with concerns about urbanity, quality of life, and public participation. It brought the issues dear to the progressive middle class to the forefront of public debates and sought to change the suburban political agenda put forth by Mike Harris and the Tories.

In a city where 54 percent of the population will be non-white by the year 2000[2] and where racism persists; in a city where homelessness is more and more criminalized; in a city where local councils have been removed further from citizens; in a city where property taxes are skyrocketing; in a city where welfare benefits are shrinking; in a city where hospitals are closed down; in a city where rent control is endangered and where affordable housing is diminishing; such sweeping social and political transformations are most likely to create social protest. A survey of 1,200 adults residing in the Greater Toronto Area conducted by the Ekos Research Associates and commissioned by the Toronto Star in August 1997, indicates the "resurgence of a social agenda."

Respondents ranked the fight against child poverty, the opening of new hostels for the homeless, or adding day-care services over hiring police, tax reductions, and environmental issues. Sixty-seven percent said they are concerned about the growing gap between the rich and the poor.[3] The survey demonstrates new interest in a social agenda, after many years of obsession with fiscal crisis (and this was before budget surpluses were announced by the government for 1999).

Citizens for Local Democracy is a movement born in this context. As mentioned before, it is a movement, rather than a formal organization.[4] It was formed as an informal grouping acting along the lines of individual or small group initiatives that are encouraged and strategically analyzed by a steering committee of ten to fifteen people. Tarrow's distinction on the types of movement organizations is helpful to understand the role and power of Citizens for Local Democracy.[5] Although C4LD did not have a formal hierarchical organization (but it had some "invisible" hierarchies), it nevertheless began its action by what Tarrow calls the "organization of collective action at the point of contact with opponents," in this case the Harris government. C4LD mobilized the informal social network of the urban progressive middle class to build an amazing expression of local activism in Toronto. The other step in movement organization is called the "connective structure" to refer to the links between "leaders and followers, centre and periphery, and different parts of the movement sector, permitting co-ordination and aggregation between movement organizations and allowing movements to persist even when formal organization is lacking."[6] Without such degree of organization, Citizens for Local Democracy's mobilization peaked in the struggle against amalgamation and related reforms, but gradually dispersed its energies afterwards.

During this peak period, C4LD's steering committee organized open Monday night meetings and defined the overall strategy of action. There were no "assigned" positions, although someone was in charge of money, someone chaired the meetings, and the others gradually took upon specific responsibilities such as writing the newsletter, managing the electronic outreach strategy, or media outreach. The steering committee was originally composed of John Sewell and the people who organized the first meeting on December 11, 1996, as well as those who gradually volunteered. After the initial months of struggle, Citizens for Local Democracy elected some new people on the steering committee. The movement did not keep a membership list although it maintained a phone tree to keep people updated and remind them of the next meeting. The movement established a particularly effective communication system. It distributed about thirty different newsletters all over the Megacity. It facilitated three e-mail lists, one for notice and information sharing, one for discussion and debate, and one to distribute media reports (these lists were discontinued after 1998). There were about 220 persons on these lists according to an in-house on-line survey in October 1997. About 28 percent of the people on the lists attended the Monday night meetings, 32 percent had not attended any meetings at the time of the on-line survey, and 25 percent had attended five or less. People said the lists' greatest success were in providing information, connecting people with the same civic commitment, and developing a sense of local community, as well as engaging work and task groups.[7] The movement also created a very well done and incredibly rich web page (www. c4ld.org).

Particularly in the first five months of the struggle to defeat Bill 103, many groups gravitated around the movement. C4LD saw its role as a catalyst to attract much energy and mobilize for resistance. "The key to a successful group is making sure it does things," is written in a document on ideas for organization posted on the web site, "Yes, the group is a forum for discussion, but it also must do things, such as: send letters to city council; organize a campaign to pressure MPPs by letter or in person, get speakers on the list for various hearings, get the message out widely to the whole community." In other words, the prime goal of the Monday night meetings was to "generate energy" and "create a sense of community," because

> …warm bodies can't be ignored, in a politician's office, at a meeting asking to speak, and so forth. Undoubtedly, it is often not easy to be forward, but the purpose of the group is to give people a voice, and being forward is often the only way this can happen.[8]

C4LD was able to activate this latent energy, to give individuals confidence in their power to act, to learn how to create an "activist" momentum. These meetings were very successful and indeed very energetic! In peak times, there were more than a thousand people gathering in a downtown church in the midst of the cold months of winter. On the referendum night, about 2000 people got together at Massey Hall, a downtown theatre. In September 1997, after the adoption of Bill 103 on April 21, a few hundred people still attended the C4LD meetings. There were speakers to provide new information, updates from the steering committee, organization of action (newsletter distribution, phone blitz, rallies, etc.), a bucket passing around to collect money because the movement was self-financed, and entertainment (singers, storytellers, etc.). C4LD was particularly successful in having well-known speakers: John Ralston Saul, the respected philosopher and writer, Margaret Atwood, the successful Canadian novelist, Jane Jacobs, the world-wide renowned urbanist. C4LD wrote in a document about ideas for organization destined to help other people form similar meetings, "There need to be enough information, laughter, and activity at every meeting to ensure people want to come back to the next meeting."[9] And many people came back. They came because they were worried about what was happening to their city, because they were curious, because they liked the atmosphere, the warmth, and the energy.

THE BIG, BAD MEGACITY MONSTER

A Story by Margaret Atwood

Monday night meeting, February 24, 1997

And then, he got elected. And then he proceeded to do the exact opposite of what he'd said he would do. He invited the Big, Bad Megacity Monster to come into the City of Toronto and mush everybody up into one homogeneous glob. All the better to eat them up. And the people saw that the housing values would go down, down, down. And the taxes would go up, up, up…until they went right up to the sky! And the people would have less and less money, and those that could afford to would move out. And those that were left would be expected to pay for everything, but they wouldn't be able to. And this made the people very, very upset. And they jumped up and down and waved signs and made speeches in saying: "He lied to us!" He lied to us; the Big Blue Harris lied to us! Say, can this be common sense, or is it common nonsense? He screwed our taxes and our rents, and caused a huge unholy fuss. He wants to take this ill-planned law and shove it down Toronto's craw. Oh! Big Blue Harris, think it through. Pause and consider, and keep in view the needs of citizens, not just you.

*People in Citizens for Local Democracy*

People active in the movement came from various backgrounds and for different motives. As a participant describes:

> Our ages range from 10 to 79. We come from every part of Metro…we are still in school, work shifts and/or nights, retired, semi-retired, self-employed, underemployed, unemployed, and fully employed. A number of people had taken time off regular day jobs, and several others were on off-days or work in the evening. All of us had rearranged already-busy schedules in order to be present. Most, but not all, of us have a long history of involvement in public issues. These include the environment, planning, transportation, community services, government finance, education, poverty, health, the arts, housing, equity, and spouse abuse. We are individuals who share a commitment to truly participatory and inclusive democracy.[10]

In the mainstream media, they were also described in their diversity:

> Along with a couple of men with their grey hair in ponytails and a handful of people dressed in their weather gear of bicycle couriers, the audiences ran the gamut from school students to senior citizens, from immigrants [very few] to old-money families, from New Democrats to members of the Progressive Conservative Party.[11]

Many of these people were active in the reformist years of the 1970s when a coalition of conservative-leaning and left-radical "reformists" won the municipal elections in a context where ideas of city planning were shifting towards more sensitivity to community needs (thanks to the influence of Jane Jacobs who had already settled in Toronto). It was a context in which young middle class people adopted non-conformist/bohemian lifestyles, while middle class homeowners begun to move out of suburbia to resettle downtown.[12] After the struggle against the Spadina Expressway, which would have gone through Toronto's central and "bohemian" neighbourhoods, the reformist coalition had a clear mandate to preserve a dense urban fabric against suburban infrastructure and developers' interests. This was an important step towards the politicization of planning in the urban core of Toronto, towards the praise of the city's mixed and safe spaces, and towards progressive middle class urbanism.

These 1970s middle class reformists now constitute an important contingent of C4LD. Their spokesperson, John Sewell, was mayor in the

1970s and very active in the Spadina Expressway battle. In the 1990s, C4LD participants were particularly sensitive to urban and material issues related to the quality of life, the education of their children, public services, human rights, democratic participation, access and equity, and environmental and land use regulations. An analysis of Citizens for Local Democracy's agenda, arguments, and actions will highlight below the continuity with the reformist years and the huge efforts deployed to save this Left-liberal progressive regime in Toronto.[13]

A thorough analysis of the background of people in Citizens for Local Democracy is nevertheless difficult to achieve. C4LD was a movement, and consequently neither membership listings or data is available on the class background of its adherents. However, given its evident location mostly in the downtown core, it is reasonable to assume that a majority of its participants worked in sectors such as art, culture, recreation, social science, education, government service, and religion, which are highly concentrated in the older City of Toronto (see Table 3).[14]

These were sectors directly attacked by the PC government from the beginning of its mandate. Other occupations requiring higher education, such as health, and natural and applied sciences, are also prominent in the old City of Toronto.

I am not implying that C4LD's membership comes only from an urban middle-class background. Yet it is noticeable when attending the meetings that a large component of the group does. Moreover, an examination of the type of activities undertaken by the movement, the values conveyed in its many statements, the way the meetings were conducted, illustrates that C4LD was operating within the terrain of action proper to the urban progressive middle class developed in Toronto. Municipal institutions were crucial tools controlled by the progressive urban middle class to advance its leftist agenda. Participants in C4LD perceived themselves as "ordinary and good citizens" rather than "angry radicals." They saw themselves as part of the social majority adhering to democratic principles. And this explains the fierce struggle against the disappearance of their municipal institutional tool.

Overall, Citizens for Local Democracy could be qualified as a coalition for democracy, concerned with the flourishing of an urban progressive regime in Toronto. In this sense, the movement had limited goals and did not pretend to be a revolutionary group. In contrast with some other social movements, C4LD was not labour-based, nor was it based on a specific personal identity such as the gay and lesbian

| | Toronto | East York | York | Etobi-coke | Scarbo-rough | North York | Metro Toronto |
|---|---|---|---|---|---|---|---|
| Occupations in art, culture, recreation and sport | 55.2 | 4.5 | 4.1 | 8.8 | 12.0 | 15.4 | 100.0 |
| Occupations in social science, education, government service and religion | 54.3 | 5.8 | 6.7 | 14.1 | 18.1 | 1.0 | 100.0 |
| Management occupations | 35.2 | 4.6 | 4.2 | 13.6 | 18.4 | 24.0 | 100.0 |
| Health occupations | 31.4 | 4.8 | 5.2 | 12.0 | 21.7 | 24.8 | 100.0 |
| Sales and service occupations | 30.1 | 4.7 | 6.5 | 13.0 | 22.4 | 23.4 | 100.0 |
| Natural and applied sciences and related occupations | 29.2 | 4.5 | 4.0 | 12.8 | 25.0 | 24.5 | 100.0 |
| Business, finance and administrative occupations | 27.0 | 4.9 | 5.0 | 13.9 | 25.6 | 23.6 | 100.0 |
| Occupations unique to primary industry | 25.5 | 5.3 | 7.5 | 18.0 | 23.1 | 20.6 | 100.0 |
| Trades, transport and equipment operators and related occupations | 21.8 | 4.1 | 8.2 | 16.6 | 24.8 | 24.5 | 100.0 |
| Occupations unique to processing, manufacturing and utilities | 20.6 | 3.1 | 7.6 | 16.0 | 27.4 | 25.3 | 100.0 |
| **Total share of employment** | **22.8** | **30.9** | **4.6** | **22.1** | **5.9** | **13.7** | **100.0** |
| Average household income $ | 56,014 | 49,754 | 43,192 | 56,871 | 51,033 | 55,532 | 52,066 |
| Median household income $ | 38,243 | 39,171 | 34,038 | 45,121 | 43,544 | 41,252 | 40,228 |

**Table 3:** Occupational Distribution of Local Cities, in percent
*Source: Census 1996, Statistics Canada*

movement or ethnic movements. C4LD was concerned with the urban quality of life and with political participation. It was not against the system but rather seeking to better it. It was a coalition spanning across the political spectrum, from homeowners associations to tenants' rights groups, from human rights activists to parents' associations, from environmentalists to feminists. This diversity of ideas characterizes what Eder labelled "middle-class radicalism," underscoring the crucial role of the middle class in social movements. I would add more specifically "middle-class urbanism," to underscore the urban character of many of the struggles.[15]

### *Middle-Class Urbanism*

Despite a long tradition of middle-class urbanism in Canada, the middle class has long carried a negative connotation in theories of social transformation because of its ambiguous position between capital and labour, for its individualism and its absence of class consciousness. It gained some theoretical value in the 1970s, mainly because of the work of Bourdieu on taste in the middle class and theories of new social movements.[16] With the decline of what Eder calls the "industrial protest culture," the middle class now "has a central role in the restructuring of class relationships" and in the mobilization of a new protest culture.[17] Middle class people are important actors in new social movements, from the peace movement, to feminism, to environmentalism. In this sense, middle class people can be very radical. Their class position does not determine the type of political action they undertake. However, movements operating mostly within the middle-class "action space," tend less to adopt wide-sweeping anti-system agendas and instead focus more on reform than revolution. As we will see below, Citizens for Local Democracy, like most movements structured around urban struggles in Canada, operated within the "middle-class action space." This did not preclude the organization of radical actions. However, it created some tensions within the movement on the degree of radicalism able to sustain the consensus across political views.

Defining the middle class as playing "a central role" in the mobilization of a "new protest culture," as Eder does, ignores the wide variety of political ideologies and values among people classified as "middle class." There are progressive and conservative middle class people, there are politically active and politically apathetic middle class people. These differing aspects were at the core of the struggles against municipal restructuring in Toronto. There are increasing gaps in income levels between the lower and the upper middle class. There are other major axes of identification and political consciousness cutting across the middle class, such as gender, race, and ethnicity. These debates are not new. The difficulty for the purposes of social scientific enquiry remains in identifying who is part of what segment of the middle class. A myriad of indicators can be devised, to the point that one wonders what utility the concept of middle class still has. Interestingly however, the Megacity saga in Toronto provides an opportunity to study the middle class in a politicized and spatialized framework. Understanding the middle class and its polarized segments is central to the analysis of municipal restructuring in Toronto. It sheds light on the choice of action undertaken by Citizens for Local Democracy, its value statements, its agenda, and the outcome of its incredible level of mobilization between 1997 and 1999.

Eder holds that the concept of middle class has two important explanatory virtues. Firstly, it helps identifying the reservoir of potential mobilization. The "social opportunity structure" of the middle class, that is the set of conditions distributing the chances to act (occupational differentiation, educational differentiation, income differentiation, lifestyle differentiation, etc.), will logically motivate collective action on different issues than the more traditional industrial issues of the working class. Secondly, the concept of middle class sheds light on the "new field of social conflict" centred on quality of life and identity issues more than industrial issues.[18] The increasing role of the middle class in defining the boundaries of these new issues creates what Eder calls the "cultural opportunity structure." It is important to note that the concept of middle class can only explain mobilization if one understands the category not only as determined by objective variables such as income or education, but mostly as a subjective concepts to which one adheres. These "cultural affinities" convey values in what Eder calls the "middle-class action space." These affinities are developed through interactions and communication and create the context of collective action. An analysis of the middle class, therefore, entails gathering two sets of data. The first one is a traditional demographic analysis of the class origins of the participants in the movement. The second is a discourse analysis of the protest culture, of the values, interests, and norms conveyed by the movement. As I already mentioned, given the nature of Citizens for Local Democracy, specific demographic data is very difficult to find. Henceforth, I will turn to a discourse analysis below. But before this, let me dwell a little more on the notion of middle-class urbanism in Toronto.

Citizens for Local Democracy and its allies fought for the preservation of "middle class urbanism" in Toronto. By this I mean that they fought for the preservation of a progressive urban regime based on democratic principles and a certain conception of urbanity emphasizing quality of life. As mentioned before, the first two arguments around which the oppositional movement mobilized were: 1) the threat of local democracy; and 2) the lack of legitimacy in the provincial government's process. These are two priorities of a well-functioning democracy. The particularity of the old City of Toronto was that its progressive middle class had developed a progressive political regime. It had institutionalized middle-class ideas of good urban life for all. With amalgamation, the balance shifted between these ideas in the downtown core and more conservative suburban values, pitting one segment of the middle class against another. A few words from the eloquent text by John Lorinc, entitled "Making the megacity: an epic tale of a political founding" captures the image of the progressive urban politician very well. In describing Megacity councillor David Miller (representing the urban district of High Park), Lorinc writes:

> He's a tall, good-looking guy, slightly stooped, with a faint trace of an English accent. In many ways, he is exactly what you'd expect in a local politician from High Park: young, urban, progressive, but in an unmistakably middle-class way. You could drop him into the Danforth or the Beaches [two charming areas East of downtown] and never know the difference.[19]

In contrast, Lorinc describes suburban mayor Lastman:

> Regardless of what you think of his style, his politics or even his famous hair plugs, you have to admit it was an amazing run, during which he went on a building spree to transform an unremarkable suburb into an unremarkable suburb with a high-rise downtown and a do-me attitude a la New York.[20]

The case of Toronto highlights not only the spatialized nature of differing political, cultural, and social values within the middle class, but Kipfer qualified the politicized climate of the 1990s in Toronto as a "class struggle in space." As he puts it:

> Symbolically, the new right urban politics builds on and promotes resentful and racialized images which associate the urban with categories of immigration, crime, drug-abuse, welfare-dependency, deviance and oppositional behaviour and counterpose these images

> of the 'inner city' to representations of 'normal' and 'productive' life in ex-urban neighbourhoods.[21]

This spatialized symbolic dichotomy between the urban and the suburban, the poor and the middle class, is not unique to Toronto. However, the internal dichotomy within the middle class between its urban and its suburban segments was particularly prominent in the struggles over municipal restructuring.[22] While the suburban middle class identified the urban middle class as oppositional and radical, the urban middle class stereotyped its suburban counterparts as conservative for the "love of their lawn." This misunderstanding was evident from the very beginning of Citizens for Local Democracy, whose activity focused on downtown Toronto (with some pockets in the older suburbs). It became clearer with the defeat of urban former mayor Barbara Hall by suburban Mel Lastman during the first Megacity elections in November 1997. The defeat of the urban progressive middle class in these struggles is further accentuated by the size of the new council, in which downtown representatives constitute only a minority.

There are two levels to this urban/suburban middle class split. Firstly, the Megacity elections illustrated the misunderstanding between the urban core and its older suburban rings (the postwar suburbs) within the new amalgamated city. According to Engin Isin, the election of suburban Mel Lastman as the new Megacity Mayor was misinterpreted by the urban progressive middle class. As Isin says, Lastman's promise to freeze property taxes,

> ...was heard loud and clear by the groups that surround the city. Not because these groups are well-off suburbanites "who liked their lawns," as the city elite would like to think of them, but because they were groups made up of immigrants, refugees, the working poor, non-unionised and low income service workers and tradesmen, who felt the most adverse impacts of the declining real wages in Ontario in the last decade. It is these groups that, perhaps, the old City of Toronto's new [progressive middle] class never understood.[23]

Adding to this dichotomy, the outer/newer ex-urbs of the Greater Toronto Area (known as the '905' region in reference to its different telephone area code) were decisively more conservative than the older ring and the urban centre.[24] One of the major contentious issue between this outer ex-urban middle class and its urban counterpart was the pooling of tax revenues across the Greater Toronto Area to help support services in the new Megacity of Toronto. Politically, the PC could not include the whole

Greater Toronto Area in its restructuring of municipal boundaries without losing its support in the 905 region. Although taxes are always a sensitive issue for voters in Toronto and elsewhere, it is important to note that the urban/suburban middle class split has a long history that goes beyond the tax issue. It is perhaps best illustrated by the Spadina Expressway battle in the 1970s.

The concept of middle class provides very interesting hints in the analysis of the Megacity saga. It helps understand why Citizens for Local Democracy was able to create such an amazing mobilization moment in Toronto, building on the reservoir of progressive middle class people in the old city. It also highlights reasons for the movement's failure to attract more radical activists and marginalized people. This expression of local activism in Toronto is in fact very much in-tune with the development of a "protest culture" that is not labour-based and more focused on quality of life issues than the more traditional industrial issues of work conditions and income redistribution. Interestingly, focusing on the quality of life seems to lead to a spatial differentiation between the values of urbanity and suburbanity. Finally, the concept of middle-class urbanism sheds light on the non-revolutionary character of Citizens for Local Democracy. In contrast with other social movements that are clearly anti-system, C4LD rather sought to preserve its control over urban institutions and its belief in the democratic process. In the end, it is probably the threat against the urban progressive middle class in the face of an uncompromising Tory government, which led a gentle angry people to use more and more radical means of action. And we saw angry teachers, small business owners, mothers, professionals, intellectuals on the street; angry grannies in the public gallery of the Legislative Assembly; angry Liberals in the newspaper...and so on.

### *A Discourse Analysis of Citizens for Local Democracy's Middle-Class Urbanism*

To better understand these actions, let us look at Citizens for Local Democracy's "action space," that is, the cultural context of its action. Beyond the strategic goal of defeating Bill 103 and the restructuring package of the Harris government, some of the most stringent concerns of people in C4LD are characteristic of middle-class urbanism and liberal democracy. A recurring argument against amalgamation was the fear of losing on the quality of life defined according to the preferences of local communities. In the first newsletter distributed by C4LD, the argument is spelled out clearly:

> Local democracy and a high quality of life are two sides of the same coin…If local councils are dismantled, the different approaches they have taken to respond to local wishes will surely soon be dismantled as well. The high quality of life in Toronto neighbourhoods will decline if the province abolishes responsive local councils.[25]

Another important issue characteristic of middle-class urbanism is the quality of education for children. Given that the Harris government introduced school reform bills that preoccupied C4LD adherents greatly, the movement was very active in the struggle against Bill 104 reforming the school board structure, as well as supporting the province-wide teachers' strike against Bill 160 that transformed the education system profoundly. In the early days of the Monday night meetings, a speaker clearly spelled out this concern and its relationship with municipal restructuring:

> What this government is trying to do to the schools is at least as bad as what they are doing to our cities. If we don't save our schools, they will set us back for decades…We need to send the message loud and clear that schools are not a business, with "clients" and so on. Schools are public services.[26]

C4LD participants were generally very concerned to save the quality of social services developed in Toronto, in other words, to preserve the urban progressive regime. One of the greatest fears was that amalgamation would increase competition among social service beneficiaries for the scarcer resources available in what was becoming a neoliberal urban regime:

> Toronto works because it is a community of communities. In a megacity people will face competition for all the services required, and for racial minorities, the intolerance level will peak. People will be less understanding of the issues of human rights and these communities will be subjected to more hatred and racism because of the competition for services.[27]

> What are the stakes for me? Let me tell you a little about myself. I am a middle class person living in a nice house in a nice neighbourhood in a 28 year old marriage. Pretty straight, eh? But I am also one of those citizens who would be prepared to pay higher taxes if it meant that the services that have been available to the people of Metropolitan Toronto could be salvaged. In other words,

> I don't want this government's tax break if it means that everything I was raised with will no longer exist—not for me, and not for my children. So there are my politics on the table.[28]

Faithful to Left-liberal political principles, C4LD participants held human rights and democratic principles dearly to the forefront of their values:

> It is also necessary to work out the fundamental principles of democratic government, as in the Universal Declaration of Human Rights. Petty arguments on who should receive money and who should not must give way to a proper definition of the human species which differs from others mainly in its symbol using capabilities, and from there a recognition of the fundamental rights of the human species to exercise its human qualities, and to achieve its full human potential.[29]

Within the action space delimited by the old City of Toronto's progressive regime, C4LD people have tried to ensure access and equity for all. Many people collaborated with the Task Force on Community Access and Equity established by the Megacity Council to "discuss the best ways to ensure the voices of the City's diverse communities continue to be heard." [30] Using the language of the Charter of Rights, a participant posted a very interesting comment on the e-mail forum, pinpointing the socio-spatial and political peculiarity of Toronto in relation to its surrounding suburban area and to the rest of the province of Ontario:

> Statscan [Statistics Canada] says [that] almost all of Ontario's visible minorities live in Toronto. [A citizen] tried, without much success, to prove during the legal challenge that Toronto was being discriminated against on the basis of its disproportionate population of four specific groups given special rights under the constitution. Now that we have the data, it is time to start the accusations: The Toronto Tax is Racist…By the way, this is not just rhetoric on my part. I really do believe that the Tories abuse of Toronto is, in part, motivated by multiculturalist racism.[31]

The issue of social equity was indeed deeply important for C4LD people. Other people on the forum e-mail list expressed impatience in the face of continued studies and reports on homelessness instead of action and funding. Gary Morton, a "citizen-writer," constantly reported the actions of the Ontario Coalition Against Poverty. Others expressed concern about women issues or racism. C4LD was also very involved in the fight against hospital closures, particularly the Women's College Hospital and the Wellesley Hospital (which was located in the heart of the gay neighbourhood and provided quality care for people living with AIDS). The movement was also very active in the coalition Bread Not Circuses, raising social concerns about Toronto's bid for the 2008 Olympics.

Some disagreement often arose on the e-mail forum about these concerns. This prompted very interesting debates, with opinions representing the gamut of political ideas. But at the core, C4LD was able to produce a Checklist for Local Democracy, some Principles governing municipal/provincial financial relationships, a Statement of Civic Priorities, and a Value Statement to build a basic consensus of the cultural context of their action (see appendix A, B, C, and D for the full text of these documents). When looking at these documents used as tools to guide political action, urban progressive middle class values are to be found. They usually cross different ideologies, from liberalism, to conservatism, to social democracy, to radicalism. And this is what makes them so useful as rallying point for political action. This capacity for coalition-building is what makes middle class activism so important.

Perhaps one of the most important statements designed as a tool for political action in the early days of Citizens for Local Democracy is the Checklist for Local Democracy adopted on March 21, 1997, in the midst of the struggle against Bill 103. It is concerned with rights of municipalities against provincial unilateral restructuring. It mostly transposes individual rights to municipal entities. The Checklist compares the Harris government's actions in designing Bill 103 with these democratic principles. It illustrates C4LD's action space, its ways of thinking shaped by the liberal language of rights, a language particularly dear to the progressive middle class concerned with access and equity. Coupled with the "Principles governing municipal/provincial financial relationships," the Checklist for Local Democracy provides an illustration of both the belief in democratic principles and process, and the will to strengthen the institutionalization of an urban progressive regime.

At the onset, it is important to underscore that C4LD did not use the term "liberal democracy" per se. Nevertheless, its statements illustrate a belief in political liberalism, which obviously should not be confused with a belief in economic neoliberalism prevalent on the Right. To the contrary, political liberalism generally refers to representative democracy and pluralism. If we take the first statement, C4LD emphasizes the principles of representation, accountability and consent at the core of political liberalism. A democracy is a government by the people, first and foremost. The democratic process of elections are crafted to operationalize this

CHECKLIST FOR LOCAL DEMOCRACY (EXCERPT)[32]

1. Municipal governments are *elected by and accountable to* their local citizens, therefore changes to the structure of municipal governments should require the *consent* of their citizens.

2. Municipal government responsibilities are the *exclusive authority* of locally elected councils and cannot be suspended or assumed by provincial appointees.

3. Municipal governments, through their locally elected councils, have the exclusive authority to determine their *internal administrative structures* including the hiring, management and firing of staff and the manner of delivering services under their responsibility.

4. Municipal governments, through their locally elected councils, have the exclusive authority to decide *how to spend locally generated tax revenues.*

5. Local governments have the authority and duty to manage public services and affairs under their responsibility and *within their jurisdiction.*

6. The process for reviewing or developing proposals to restructure municipal government should *involve citizens* in a meaningful way. It should begin with a full and independent study of the problems with current structures, the opportunities restructuring presents, and the impacts of the different restructuring options.

7. These studies and any restructuring proposals should be *publicized* and made widely available to all citizens throughout the municipalities affected. A meaningful *public consultation process* should be undertaken to facilitate citizen debate and input. Any restructuring proposals should include a recommended process for public consultation and decision making on the details of the finally agreed-upon structure, such as ward systems and boundaries, council size, etc.

8. Restructuring proposals should ensure the protection of reserve funds for local citizens, the protection of the *financial interests of the citizens*, and ensure that *levels of service do not deteriorate*.

9. All organs of local democracy are subject to the *rule of law* and the supervision of the courts.

popular sovereignty and protect it. The principle of popular sovereignty relies on basic democratic rights in the tradition of representative democracies: freedom of thought, belief, opinion, expression and association, as well as guarantees of equality before and under the law (as enshrined in the Charter of Rights). These are the necessary rights to make democracy work and obtain the "general consent" of the population. C4LD apply these principles to "local citizens" to emphasise the local nature of these rights.

Interestingly, the statement also implies a "transfer" of these individual rights to local institutions. In the second and fifth statements, the local level of government is protected with "moral authority" and "legal rights" (see Appendix C). In this sense, C4LD recalls the double sovereignty principle in liberal democracies, that is 1) autonomy of sovereign and equal states and 2) autonomy of sovereign and equal individuals. Autonomy is defined as a principle of determination which is free from the use of political power and coercive relations. Autonomy has traditionally been applied to individual citizens through the language of rights. It has protected citizens' rightful share of the process of governance.[33] In Canada, the principle has historically been further applied to a particularly detailed jurisdictional division of powers between the central and the provincial governments. Citizens for Local Democracy extends this principle to local governments by affirming the "exclusive authority" of locally elected representatives within their jurisdiction. In this sense, C4LD's action space is based on a double principle of autonomy. On the one hand, each jurisdiction, particularly municipalities, has the right and should develop the capacity to make autonomous decisions.[34] On the other hand, individual citizens have the right to autonomous decision through their accountable municipal elected representative.

The local jurisdiction is considered of primary importance for a healthy democracy because it is closer to local needs, and because it is well-suited for encouraging public participation. In the Checklist, statements 6 and 7 reaffirm the centrality of the democratic process. It determines the means by which the democratic process is to be operationalized: access to public participation and information through local institutions. In the nineteenth century, Alexis de Tocqueville and John Stuart Mill hoped that municipalities would become the main source of vitality in democracies, particularly in implementing efficient public administration, citizen participation, and an appropriate separation of powers. Citizens for Local Democracy believes firmly in these local functions.

Statements 3, 4, and 8, as well as most of the document entitled "Principles governing municipal/provincial financial relationships," are more specific on the operationalization of popular sovereignty. To some degree the focus on the administrative structure of municipalities, particularly on service delivery, indicates an instrumentalist view of local democracy. In this sense, the grand ideas of Tocqueville and Mill about the local as the field to educate the citizenry to democracy, are reinforced by C4LD's concern about the preservation of an urban progressive regime. Public participation and active citizenship are sought in order to sustain this regime. But participation is difficult to nourish without visible outcomes in people's daily life. Issues about the quality of urban life (service delivery, property taxes, poverty, etc.) are thus central. The link between quality of life issues and public participation at the local level resides in the principle of self-determination, in which each community has the right to determine its preferences. Moreover, the Checklist refers directly to the classical liberal principle of "no taxes without representation," which is literally applied at the municipal level. Municipalities, according to C4LD, should be considered a legitimate level of government, not a "creature of the province."[35]

Proper checks and balances is another very important liberal democratic principle. C4LD abides to this idea in the last statement on the division between the executive, legislative, and judicial bodies of the state. But most importantly, the Checklist and the "Principles governing municipal/provincial financial relationships" affirm the need for a balance between different levels of government, in this case the provincial and the local. Under the British colonial rule, cities were gradually incorporated in a process that put them under the "protection" (or discipline) of the national and provincial governments.[36] By insisting on their autonomy, C4LD advocates for the "rights" of cities as entities, but also as a means to ensure individual rights of participation.

In sum, this Checklist for Local Democracy emphasises an ordered conception of democracy that is grounded in the liberal language of rights, representative democracy, participation in the "formal" realm of politics, and well-defined jurisdictional boundaries. This conception of democracy is instrumentalist in the sense that it focuses on outcomes, the delivery of good and efficient public services.[37] It is also procedural, that is it emphasizes fair process such as general consent, available information, and citizen participation.

The Statement on Civic Priorities adopted on September 15, 1997 was crafted as a preparatory document for the November 1997 first

Megacity elections. It reaffirms three basic principles to which electoral candidates must abide for the sake of local democracy.

STATEMENT ON CIVIC PRIORITIES (EXCERPT)[38]

Citizens for Local Democracy affirms these three principles:

1. The new city must include at the *local level strong, effective, and democratic decision-making structures* similar to the six existing city councils.

2. Those elected must be people who have shown they *want to involve citizens* and communities in decision-making at City Hall. They *must be people who were against the idea of forced amalgamation in the first place*, people who agree decisions should be made public by elected (not appointed) officials, on the basis of supporting evidence and justification that is publicly debated and evaluated before decisions are made.

3. Those elected must implement programs which *will better share money, power and resources among all people living in the new city, programs which respect local values and resist the effects of globalization.*

The document continues with proposed policy actions to be undertaken in the new Megacity. These should guarantee a local democratic decision-making structure by strengthening the community council to virtually recreate the former six local municipalities. This would also ensure local control over municipal institutions such as community health facilities, libraries and cultural centres. Also prominent in this statement is the desire to maintain the level and quality of services in the new city, to avoid neoliberal privatization, and to maintain municipal staff workers' rights and salaries. Along with measures designed to ensure a fair property tax system, these concerns are clearly linked with the desire to maintain control over a progressive urban regime. It is a civic priority, C4LD affirms, to dedicate "special attention to eradicate homelessness, creating more affordable housing, ending the plight of poor children, stopping workfare and other programs which stigmatize the poor, and meeting challenges facing immigrants." Economic justice, resource redistribution across the new city while respecting community preferences, are seen as the only way to "resist the effects of globalization" (see full text in Appendix A).

These concerns are synthesized again in Citizens for Local Democracy's March 9, 1998 Values Statement. Two months after the first megacouncil meeting, C4LD adopted a value statement designed to find a common ground with other groups who share these values and would be interested in fighting the Tory government. The statement highlights the impacts of the conservative government restructuring on everyday life. "This is what we hear from our neighbours...What do you hear?" says the statement. Reduction in health care and education services, unemployment, lack of housing, "the government's been changing everything at once, no matter what we say. What happened to discussion and public debate?" The statement calls for other people, from all community backgrounds and ideological convictions, to "work together to build public policy that meets our needs." Outreach is done in the perspective of influencing politicians.

CITIZENS FOR LOCAL DEMOCRACY VALUES STATEMENT (EXCERPT)[39]

In *our* Ontario, we want politicians to work for

- compassion and respect among people
- fairness and anti-discrimination
- safe and healthy homes, workplaces and communities
- diverse and inclusive communities
- adequate food and shelter
- accessible education and health care
- strong public services under public control
- public libraries, recreation and arts
- accessible children's services

These values are legitimate and are certainly shared by people of all classes and backgrounds. What makes this statement part of the middle class action space is its strong emphasis on action by political pressures in order to influence public policy, rather than calling for alternative lifestyle, civil disobedience, metropolitan strikes, or communal solidarity. "What policies make communities safe and strong? How can communities be involved in democratic decision-making? How can we ensure that all communities have appropriate services that meet their needs? How can we reduce the gap between rich and poor? How can we protect the natural environment? How can we elect a government that will act on the values that we stand for?" These are the questions posed by Citizens for Local Democracy. In "its" Ontario, the movement underscores that democracy means popular control over decision-making. With access to information, appropriate time and resources, and accountability of elected representatives to their constituencies, "democratic decision-making works." Ontario needs strong public services to "build strong communities." Believing in democracy means working for equity, basic rights for all, and C4LD adds the availability of public services because "We are more than just consumers." Finally, another common value is the belief that "a strong economy shares resources and opportunities, and protects the natural environment." (See full text in appendix B.)

Based on this analysis, Citizens for Local Democracy operates within the space of progressive middle-class urbanism. Its wide-ranging core values based on liberal democratic principles and the quality of life are good rallying points for political mobilization across ideological boundaries. Middle-class urbanism, in the end, holds a central role in social transformation. The case of Toronto illustrates the importance of these movements, and will hopefully change the negative connotation the concept of middle-class has for theorists and activists alike.

### *From Discourse to Action*

Citizens for Local Democracy was very creative and undertook some radical actions and other actions closer to more traditional lobbying techniques. Interestingly, this creative tension is personalized in John Sewell himself. Sewell is a highly-coloured character with an impressive experience of urban politics, both as an activist and as an elected official, using radical techniques in formal realms, and more formal techniques in informal realms. Sewell is an amalgamation of liberalism and radicalism. His leadership benefitted the C4LD, and this tension between radical activism and lobbying was a major strength of the movement as both types of activist cultures are interdependent. The most important accomplishment was to open a space to talk about democracy and urban life in Ontario. C4LD has opened a window of opportunity, it has swept to the background concerns about competitiveness, streamlining, and global city formation. People wanted to discuss the impacts of these restructuring on the quality of everyday life, and on democratic participation.

Citizens for Local Democracy formed a middle class action space in which it mobilized large segments of the population, from all allegiances and backgrounds, each with their own agenda but meeting on the core values of a well-intentioned Western society. By energizing people on these values, C4LD was able to create a promising moment in Toronto. As Jane Jacobs said, "This is not an apathetic city. This is not a lethargic city. This is not a docile city. But everything takes so much effort…We have lots of very talented people in Toronto and lots of people who love Toronto. Everyone who loves their city and who tries to stop bad things from happening has an impact on their city."[40]

There is no need to be a long-time activist, in other words, to act on everyday life and on the city, one simply needs to love it and try to stop those "bad things," which are disrespectful of the core values of access and equity. This is the message sent by C4LD, Jane Jacobs and many others. This is the message sent by the urban progressive middle class. And it implies bringing together some people who are not always comfortable with the label of "angry radicals." As John Sewell puts it: "There was never much pressure for individuals to do things they did not think appropriate—everyone could operate at a level they felt comfortable at."[41]

The overall strategy of C4LD was to work on two fronts: 1) to influence the policy-making process by using all channels of participation in the state, in the formal realm of politics; and 2) to work in civil society, outside the official channels of participation, in the informal realm of politics. These two fronts were interacting and thus produced a dynamic and creative set of actions. For instance, C4LD used formal channels of participation with methods that stretched the rules of procedure to their limits, thus redefining these channels with a culture closer to everyday city life. Let me illustrate the extent of C4LD's creative and effective dynamism with a selection of episodes during the peak months of the Megacity saga.

### *Entering Queen's Park: Public Hearings and the Public Gallery*

> As with so many others speaking at these hearings, this is the first time I've exercised this democratic right and, while it is an intimidating experience, I guess this government is to be recognized for creating a climate where citizens have been compelled to ask themselves what democracy means to them—and to act accordingly.[42]

Throughout the saga, citizens spoke as loudly and creatively as they could in the provincial legislature at Queen's Park. The movement's active participation in the public hearings on Bill 103, which began on February 3, 1997, illustrates a very creative use of the formal channels of democratic participation. Through different discursive strategies and through the "politics of presence," C4LD tried to force the government to listen, in a process that was qualified as "not worth the loss of time," before it even started. Indeed, Minister of Housing and Municipal Affairs, Al Leach, made it clear that he would not consider major changes to Bill 103. Leach stated to *The Globe and Mail* that unless there was new information the government was unaware of, they will pursue with their agenda.[43] Leach knew the vast majority of the speakers were against amalgamation, and that most of them were part of C4LD. Each citizen presenting to the hearing committee did some careful research and gave good arguments, sometimes in a very personal manner. C4LD encouraged citizens to write letters to the clerk of the provincial legislature asking to speak to the hearing committee. It also provided alternative information on the Bill, as well as guidelines for speakers that helped citizens prepare their presentation.

> When I received the Clerk's response to my request to speak here, I discovered that the Assembly has a heraldic device that appears on its letterhead, and that the device includes a motto. It says: AUDI ALTERAM PARTEM. That means HEAR THE OTHER SIDE. And not only *hear*, because AUDI means *listen to, learn from, heed*. This is the motto of democracy. Because the "other side" does not mean only the opposition parties: it means all those who hold different views, even if they are a minority. Democracies do not trample the rights of minorities; if they do so, they are not democracies in our modern sense.[44]

Citizens for Local Democracy encouraged people to attend the hearings even if they were not speaking. The tiny hearing room was always filled with citizens. This is what I would call the "politics of presence."[45] Filling up Queen's Park served to make the point that people cannot be erased from Bill 103 or any other law. It has put pressure on elected representatives, it has also redefined the boundaries of the formal public sphere. But because the audience had to keep quiet and avoid raising signs and posters during the hearings, many of them dressed in yellow, the colour chosen to represent the No side during the referendum campaigns. In this way, they were redefining the space of the room and the meaning of the hearings. C4LD was there, always there. It focused on visibility, presence, and warm bodies, to remind politicians, administrators, and journalists, that such broad-sweeping municipal restructuring could not ignore the people of the city. The strategies chosen by C4LD do not exactly correspond to what Ann Phillips calls the politics of presence, that is the necessity to provide special representation rights for marginalized groups in order to give them access to channels of participation, because no one can adequately represent others. C4LD made no particular efforts to include "invisible voices." Nevertheless, it demonstrated much creativity in representing citizens.

The hearing room, and later the public gallery were quite interestingly used in an informal manner, challenging official conventions. The whole process of filling-up the gallery has educated citizens on how the Legislature works. On June 17, 1997, when the Harris government introduced a Bill to modify the House rules that restricted debates and inputs from the opposition parties, C4LD led a group of citizens to shout down at government members demanding to be heard, from the public gallery. One man got arrested for raising a sign, and in the end all the citizens were arrested and put out of the gallery.

Chris Stockwell, the Speaker of the Legislative Assembly, was depicted by the press as a truly patient man with a good nature as he did his best to accommodate the flow of people coming to the public gallery. He had set up an overflow room with television monitors, "providing coffee and refreshments for the protesters" and he arranged "to have an official from the clerk's office on hand in each room to explain procedural matters."[46] Stockwell was invited by Sewell to speak at one of the Monday night meetings to explain the Legislature's rules governing spectators and the parliamentary rules governing the debate.

The movement was very successful in encouraging citizens to activate their right to participate, to learn citizenship by experiencing it. The problem was that appealing to such a clear symbol of citizenship, many people who do not hold the citizenship status felt uncomfortable in getting involved in the struggle against amalgamation.[47] In the end, nevertheless, this was the story of a redefinition of the formal process for the purpose of ensuring citizen voices. Citizens declared so, many times during the hearings:

> In other words, I want a voice.
>
> Bill 103 is taking away that voice. More insidious still, it takes away our elected voices. You have already heard, I am sure, other citizens

> decrying the lack of democracy in your naming trustees to oversee local monies spent before even passing this legislation. In naming a transition team; i.e., an appointed group of individuals, you are effectively superceding our elected representatives. We eagerly await Lloyd Axworthy's [Canadian Minister of Foreign Affairs] stiff note of protest to the Ontario government. This type of "Hong Konging" is undemocratic to the point of benevolent dictatorship.[48]

The public hearings were a story of citizens investing Queen's Park with their everyday life concerns, figures of speech, and dynamism. Many speakers did not respect the traditional serious, disembodied, un-passionate, rational discourse expected in such situations. For instance, a lady submitted a written presentation to the committee and began her speech by saying that she would not read that presentation because it would use up her allowed ten minutes. Instead, she asked the Chair for permission to sing with fellow members of a group called the Raging Grannies. They all sat in front of the committee, wearing hats with nice flowers. It created a commotion in the tiny room. The Chair protested that they were not allowed to wear proxies identifying their allegiance. The grannies did not listen, hats with flowers are not proxies…and they began to sing to the tune of "Mr. Sandman, send me a dream":

> Mr. Harris! Give us a break!
> Won't you admit now
> You've made a mistake?
> It is not too late
> To stop Bill 103
> Say "Goodbye"
> To Megacity!

And the Tory committee members stopped writing, sleeping, or daydreaming. They listened. Other citizens appealed to the very nature of conservatism and reminded the Tories what conservatism has always been in Canada:

> These Tories are not Conservatives. They are authoritarian who would make the old Central Planners of regimes-past proud. The fascists, dictators and communists, present and past, had no regard for its citizens. Their prime concern was holding on to power.[49]

> I call upon the Progressive Conservative members to remember that conservatism is more than a philosophy of the marketplace; it is also about nurturing our communities. It is more about decentralizing

> than centralizing. It's about compromise rather than confrontation.[50]

In all his disturbing creativity, John Sewell skillfully used another interesting discursive strategy. He appealed to the Tory members on the committee as citizens, as fellow human beings with a conscience and respectable values:

> Something has gone dreadfully wrong for your leaders to ask you to be so unreasonable, so dictatorial, so revolutionary. Would your children or grandchildren think you wise to support such action? Or the members of your church? Of course not.
>
> How can you as individuals be part of this destruction of democracy? Not one of you ran for office on the platform that you would dispense with elected officials at another level of government because you thought dictatorship was better. Of course, you didn't.
>
> Each of you has a strong personal value system, one that is rooted in the idea of democracy. We want to hear from each of you personally reaffirming that value, and denouncing these pernicious sections [of Bill 103]. Tell your leaders that they are wrong, and that as individuals you will not countenance legislation which puts our cities in the control of those who have all the characteristics of dictators in communist countries.[51]

Sewell has an amazing ability to resort to moral outrage, using strong language with traces of cold war indignation. I believe he embodies much of what Eder calls middle-class radicalism. His deputation, and most of his public speeches and newspaper articles, were a masterpiece of synthesis. Indeed, Eder holds that middle-class radicalism can take three forms: 1) protest based on moral indignation; 2) political pressure groups relying on expertise and public relations; and 3) social movements which are lifeworld-oriented and offer alternatives to labour activism.[52] Sewell constantly used these three tactics. He offered very carefully-researched policy analyses; he was a public relation expert; he shaped his discourse with moral overtones; and he constantly referred to urban quality of life and social activism. His outrage was contagious.

> It is not easy for me to be here today. I am completely unused to doing anything like this. My life is filled with grandchildren, lectures, hobbies, and travel, and frankly as the young say—this is not my idea of a fun thing to do.

> I have always voted considering the best information I could gather, and I have always voted, but never have I been politically active. However I am here to speak before this committee because I believe it to be very important to talk to you.
>
> I believe in democracy. I love Toronto.[53]

Many citizens came out as actively outraged and voiced their fear of losing their lifeworld. While one citizen described how she envisions the effects of Bill 103 as "the change of Toronto, a place to live, the meeting place on the lake where people of all cultures and economic status have equal say in the management of their city…to Toronto, the Megacity Corporation where all inhabitants must contribute to the individual profit of a few," others carried on with a plea to "think of the effect on places people love, think of people like me and Liliana and Nathan choosing to leave, or choosing to stay while neighbours move away and taxes go up and shopkeepers go bankrupt and services decline and the place we now love becomes a memory."[54]

> The issue of democracy is for me the single most important one in this debate. I want those who make decisions about the fabric of me and my neighbours' everyday life to be accessible and accountable. I and every person I know care very deeply about the ability of our community to make its own choices about maintaining its artistic life, as well as its libraries, its museums, its parks, and all the other facilities that are the oxygen that keeps this city alive. Democracy on the local level is the lifeblood that carries that oxygen. Bill 103 would strip this city and the five others in Metro of the ability to make those choices. It would drain the lifeblood of local democracy from this region, and oxygen starvation would not take long to set in.[55]

The appearance of the well-known urbanist Jane Jacobs before the committee opened the door to a reflection on identity, differences and the importance of details as the "essence" of the city. Each municipality has its particularities that will be lost in the Megacity. For instance, a citizen mentioned that the City of Toronto was the only city in Metro Toronto that tries to provide housing to the very poor and the homeless. In contrast, the City of North York defined "family" in a very restrictive manner, thus prohibiting rooming and shared accommodations by limiting the number of people allowed to live in a house. This of course discouraged poor people to live in North York.[56] In his presentation, Councillor Joe Mihvec of York said that the number of angry phone calls he received concerning Bill 103 illustrates "how deeply people across Metro feel about their sense of place."[57] Indeed, many deputations reaffirmed Toronto residents' belief in their urban progressive regime:

> In Toronto, with its accessible political system, I found, like other immigrants before me, that everyone can get involved in building a mutually beneficial future. Toronto is a special place—a meeting place for diverse cultures—and its political system has been the key.[58]

> Over the years, living in Toronto, I learned to appreciate the accessibility of municipal government. I never realized how much until Mike Harris and Al Leach launched this mega disaster, this attempt to globalize Toronto at the expense of its citizens. Bill 103 threatens the closest thing we have to democracy.[59]

> Those of us who object to this impending juggernaut rolling over us have been accused of being old fogies, stuck in the old ways, unwilling to accept change. That's the usual definition of Tories, or Conservatives, isn't it? We do not see ourselves as conservatives, actually though we do tend to see some of you as you have described yourselves—revolutionaries. Revolutionaries unfortunately, to the point of anarchy, and while we are not conservatives, we are not anarchists either. What we are is conservationists, and we are terribly concerned about what this bill do to all those regulatory functions that are designed to protect us, to protect the environment, that respond to human need, human peril, human desire for fulfillment.[60]

C4LD emphasized public access to the corridors of power and to accountable representatives, but also to reliable information, and always to public consultation and citizen input in defining the public agenda. John Sewell's electoral campaign as a candidate for the 1999 provincial elections put these issues to the forefront and denounced the Harris government's strategies to "shut down public debate."[61]

### *Investing Democracy: Megacity, Provincial, and Federal Elections*

This is the story of determined citizens investing their knowledge and time to use formal venues of public participation to the maximum of their potential. It is a story with less media visibility than glamorous yellow t-shirts in Queen's Park. But it is a story about carefully designed political strategies to give a more transparent meaning to democratic elections.

| **New Metro Toronto Districts** | C4LD Endorsements | Independent | New Democratic Party (NDP) | Liberal Party (LIB) | Progressive Conservative Party (PC) |
|---|---|---|---|---|---|
| Beaches-East York | NDP | | 45.93 | 21.75 | 29.78 |
| Broadview-Greenwood | NDP | | 46.92 | 24.69 | 24.70 |
| Davenport | NDP | | 31.76 | 49.72 | 15.83 |
| Don Valley East | LIB | | 4.38 | 50.50 | 43.19 |
| Don Valley West | LIB | | 4.69 | 43.62 | 50.52 |
| Etobicoke Centre | LIB | | 2.78 | 40.37 | 54.12 |
| Etobicoke-Lakeshore | NDP | | 14.72 | 35.85 | 46.98 |
| Etobicoke-North | NDP | | 23.92 | 38.27 | 34.03 |
| Eglinton-Lawrence | LIB | | 4.31 | 56.78 | 35.25 |
| Parkdale-High Park | LIB | | 11.78 | 54.92 | 30.17 |
| Scarborough-Agincourt | LIB | | 3.58 | 50.70 | 43.15 |
| Scarborough Centre | NDP | | 19.91 | 34.53 | 43.12 |
| Scarborough East | LIB | | 40.88 | 6.83 | 49.50 |
| Scarborough-Rouge River | LIB | | 6.10 | 57.27 | 34.44 |
| Scarborough-Southwest | NDP | | 23.22 | 33.66 | 39.76 |
| St. Paul's | LIB | | 7.13 | 50.57 | 40.39 |
| Toronto Centre Rosedale | Independent (Sewell) | 19.33 | 8.80 | 38.9 | 29.88 |
| Trinity-Spadina | NDP | | 47.89 | 27.48 | 20.50 |
| Willowdale | LIB | | 4.26 | 42.28 | 50.52 |
| York Centre | LIB | | 10.7 | 61.09 | 26.43 |
| York South-Weston | LIB | | 20.99 | 53.39 | 21.91 |
| York West | LIB | | 12.99 | 63.32 | 19.57 |

| New Metro Toronto Districts | C4LD Endorsements | Independent | New Democratic Party (NDP) | Liberal Party (LIB) | Progressive Conservative Party (PC) |
|---|---|---|---|---|---|
| **Other Districts in the GTA** | | | | | |
| Bramalea-Gore-Malton-Springdale | | | 5.9 | 38.81 | 49.38 |
| Brampton Centre | | | 14.23 | 28.00 | 57.77 |
| Brampton West- | | | 6.33 | 37.23 | 55.87 |
| Burlington | | | 4.68 | 30.71 | 62.74 |
| Durham | | | 9.26 | 32.12 | 57.07 |
| Halton | | | 5.18 | 27.01 | 64.95 |
| Markham | | | 3.79 | 30.61 | 62.08 |
| Mississauga Centre | | | 5.03 | 40.26 | 51.63 |
| Mississauga East | | | 7.24 | 38.99 | 51.58 |
| Mississauga South | | | 5.88 | 31.48 | 61.77 |
| Mississauga West | | | 3.84 | 38.03 | 57.31 |
| Oak Ridges | | | 3.86 | 34.35 | 59.99 |
| Oakville | | | 3.72 | 32.75 | 61.90 |
| Oshawa | | | 22.62 | 29.02 | 46.75 |
| Pickering-Ajax-Uxbridge | | | 5.71 | 34.28 | 58.19 |
| Thornhill | | | 3.54 | 47.36 | 48.21 |
| Vaughan-King-Aurora | | | 2.92 | 40.17 | 54.7 |
| Wentworth-Burlington | | | 8.44 | 33.50 | 58.07 |
| Whitby-Ajax | | | 8.15 | 34.00 | 57.85 |
| York North | | | 4.67 | 32.89 | 61.81 |

**Table 4:** Provincial Elections, June 3, 1999—Results in the new city and in the GTA, in percent

*Source: www.electionsontario.on.ca., www.c4ld.org*

Citizens for Local Democracy constantly encouraged people to set up meetings with their provincial representative, to e-mail, phone, and fax them ideas, opinions. The rationale behind this "powerfaxing" and these massive lobbying tactics is that representatives are supposed to be accountable to their constituents, not to their party. C4LD was set to convince individual representatives to vote against Bill 103, despite the strict party line system in place in Canada.

C4LD was a non-partisan movement that mobilized a wide array of people across political ideologies from Conservatives to Liberals to New Democrats, to Greens, to anarchists, to Marxists, and so on. It was non-partisan, but certainly not ignorant of party politics. In fact, C4LD skillfully toyed with parties, either as allies with Liberals and New Democrats during the filibuster and the municipal referendums, or as possible venues to get the Tories out in the 1999 provincial elections. C4LD's strategy during the last provincial elections was to encourage strategic voting by carefully analyzing voting patterns in the previous three elections in each riding in the Megacity and determining whether to endorse a Liberal or a New Democrat candidates. The second step of this strategy was of course to convince voters to cast a strategic vote according to these endorsements. Other ideas of infiltration in the Conservative Party by becoming a member were floating around. Everything to get the Tories out! C4LD mostly fought the rigidity of party lines that prevents representatives from being accountable to their constituency. This was the central theme of John Sewell's candidacy as an independent for the 1999 provincial elections. In the end, Mike Harris and the Progressive Conservative won a second mandate with a platform entitled: Blueprint: Mike Harris' Plan To Keep Ontario On The Right Track. The results strikingly confirmed the "class struggle in space" between the new amalgamated city and the Greater Toronto Area.

Results show that the 905 area is resolutely Tory, and that the Tories did less well in the amalgamated city as they did in 1995 (with only 7 out of 22 seats rather than 16 out of 30 in 1995). Some may argue that the Tory 1999 victory illustrates that resistance to amalgamation and political mobilization since 1995 in Toronto was nothing very significant. However, it seems to me the 1999 results rather show a clear tension between the exurbs, where the Tories won every single seat, and the urban core, where they did less well than in 1995. Their more difficult victory in the urban core could reasonably be attributed to citizens resentment. Importantly as well, C4LD's endorsements were successful in 12 ridings out of 22. The issue of endorsement created important tensions within the anti-Tory movement more broadly and within C4LD, which ultimately lost key participants following debates on the issue of endorsements.

Indeed, dissension occurred when it was decided by a very close vote within the Steering Committee to make endorsements in every riding. Some of the leading members on the issue of endorsements disagreed with this decision because in four specific ridings, endorsements were unnecessary given that the PC would never be elected there.[62] For members like Joey Schwartz and Gord Garland, who had done most of the statistical work to propose endorsements and secured the support of trade unions, a C4LD endorsement in these ridings would be perceived as a partisan support for the Liberal Party, and it would dilute C4LD resources unnecessarily. Schwartz concluded that because of this split in the movement, the loss of the most knowledgeable members on the issue of endorsements, and the dilution of resources, C4LD played a minor role in the 1999 provincial elections.[63]

But we are getting ahead of ourselves. Citizens for Local Democracy was very active in both the 1997 Federal elections and the first Megacity elections in November of the same year. The Federal elections were used as a platform to launch a national discussion of local democracy. "The issues are local in nature, but they are national in scope. Across the country, local democracy is under attack," says the May 1997 Newsletter.[64]

The movement attended many All Candidates meetings and tried to push candidates to talk about their vision of local democracy. They were constantly asked to avoid the Megacity issue since it was considered a local, not a national issue. However, on May 16, the Federal New Democratic Party held a press conference outside City Hall against the backdrop of a big yellow No Megacity! sign. Four Federal candidates from downtown Toronto, Olivia Chow (Trinity-Spadina), David MacDonald (Toronto Centre-Rosedale), Jack Layton (Broadview-Greenwood), and Mel Watkins (Beaches-East York), declared their support for local democracy and the importance of discussing the issue at the national level. Citizens for Local Democracy often referred to Alexa McDonough's deputation to the hearing committee on Bill 103 as an example of the importance of local democracy nationally. McDonough was the national New Democratic Party leader. She came to speak to the hearing committee about the experience of amalgamation in Halifax, her home town.

The noise the movement made throughout the Megacity saga drew large turnouts for the November Megacity elections. Faithful to its mission to disseminate information for good public participation, C4LD decided to assess all Megacity candidates' performance on local democracy. The movement was incredibly effective at producing "report cards" for all candidates, in which their positions on different issues, their past voting record and little juicy details on their background were analyzed and rated according to C4LD's values and principles.

The movement also denounced anomalies in the electoral lists for the Megacity elections.

*Keeping an Eye on the System: Manufacturing Dissent*

"Watching" and putting under public scrutiny minute actions undertaken by the enemy was one of C4LD's main strategy. This provided people with valuable alternative information. The group undertook all kinds of "watches": Tory Watch, Leachwatch, MPP watch, Council Watch, Media Watch, all of which were part of a broad "democracy watchdog" initiative. The objective was, of course, to share information and organize collective action, but also to discredit the enemy by unveiling past moves, votes, affiliations, and even salaries. The Megacouncil Watch also plays the important role of having "a visible presence at council and Committee Meetings."[65] Watching and presence, information and analysis, organization and reaction, mobilization and pressure, C4LD played a crucial role of "troublemaking" in the formal realm of politics.

This story is thus a wink to Edward Herman and Noam Chomsky's *Manufacturing Consent*.[66] Citizens for Local Democracy was one of these high-tech socio-political movements, a web-wizard movement, but also a movement well-rooted in real life, in crowded churches every Monday, in the public gallery, on the streets, on the television screen, and written black and white in the mainstream and alternative media. Information was a real strength of C4LD's action in the informal realm of politics. C4LD mobilized energies and skills to produce alternative information through these "watches," and through policy analyses, and the development of historical and technical backgrounders and guidelines for entering the formal channels of participation. The movement developed excellent means to disseminate this information, to initiate debates and discussions, to attract mainstream media attention, and to influence the definition of the public agenda. Against the government's polished image of Toronto as a great global city, C4LD presented the image of a Toronto being harmed by tyranny. A member sent a note to all major newspapers in North America and to CNN, explaining what Mike Harris was doing as an "anti-democratic despot," in the hope of tarnishing his polished and rational image.[67] C4LD's web page was considered a success in using the Internet as a tool for political mobilization. Members of the group widely used the editorial pages of the mainstream media to publish their opinions. C4LD fought the three major newspapers in Toronto for supporting amalgamation. This led to a boycotting campaign of the *Toronto Star* because it has a more progressive tradition and citizens felt betrayed. For instance the February 15, 1997 editorial said:

> The anti-amalgamation rhetoric is pretty reckless. No claim seems too outlandish, no hyperbole too outrageous. The critics care not so much to inform, but foment dissent, stir up anger, confuse, befuddle, scaremonger and defeat Bill 103—by whatever means necessary.[68]

But John Sewell responded: "We will prevail because we have three important things on our side. Weight of community. Strength of democracy. Power of citizenship."[69] One member even sent a complaint to Ontario Press Council arguing the media violated the right of free expression in the coverage of the Megacity elections by covering only two mayoral candidates and ignoring the other eighteen candidates. "They keep information on candidates from us and we are not informed and can't vote properly," the letter says, "Perhaps state funding of citizens groups so that they could deliver fair information on candidates would be better than our current system of a Corporate Press that masquerades as a Free Press."[70] C4LD attracted much interest in the mainstream media, where the movement was negatively portrayed. *The Globe and Mail* editorial on April 23, 1997 argues that the Megacity Bill was "obsessed over by John Sewell and his band of urban guerilleros" and that Bill 103 is not the Tory government's most important initiative. What is most significant is the property tax reform, the downloading of services and the creation of a regional service board. An outraged Sewell responded that *The Globe and Mail* should recognize the thousands of people "who have taken their duties as citizens seriously," which is "to fight for democracy because that's the only way the vast bulk of us get to have some control over the issues that affect our lives," because the only thing "the powerful focus on is money."[71]

The Megacity saga brought enthusiasm to Toronto's civic space. The media were keen to report on "ordinary citizens" taking up what were usually seen as radical, activist-labelled actions. However, this focus on civic space, citizenship and democracy, bothered most editorialists who used military vocabulary (urban guerilleros, Megacity fighters) to describe the upsurge of political activity, at the expense of economic tranquillity.

*Taking over the Streets: Chanting for the Spaces of Civil Society*

> [applause] In life, I was William Lyon MacKenzie, the first Mayor of Toronto, [applause] and one of the leaders of the revolt of 1837! [applause] And so I am in death...be not afraid I come not to haunt you, it's others I have come to haunt, [applause] but not you. You I come to support and encourage, for hopefully, in recounting some of my struggles for responsible government a century and a half ago, I can fortify you in your belief of the rightness of your actions and encourage you in the struggle which you must wage to preserve the democratic principles and institutions which I and my fellow reformers fought so hard for and paid so dearly to create [applause] and which you must now defend against the desecration of what looks like the latest incarnation of the oppressors of my time: the Family Compact [Anglican-dominated small group who thought it was running Ontario]! [applause] My God! They're back [laughs], but I suppose today we couldn't call them the Family Compact, they would be something like the Corporate Family Compact, or perhaps the Family Corporate Compact, or perhaps just the Corporate Compact. [laughs][72]

It was a sunny day. The calendar indicated February 15, 1997. But it felt more like a timeless day lost between 1837, 1969, and 1997. There were thousands of people marching down Yonge Street. Huge puppets, theme floats, banners, drums, trumpets, red cheeks, husky voices, laughs, hoots...a big carnival poured out onto the street. They were all there, provincial opposition politicians, municipal mayors, public celebrities, artists, journalists, rock groups, and citizens. It didn't feel like a student sit-in, an ethnic carnival, or a gay pride day. But the streets belonged, for an afternoon to angry grannies, mothers, professionals, teenagers, intellectuals; just plain anyone. C4LD took over the streets, staging fun demonstrations like the "Democracy Parade," the "Rebellion of 97." It was fun, but it was also very much embedded in the middle-class action space as it used a great symbol of Canadian liberalism: William Lyon MacKenzie (1795-1861). MacKenzie directed a newspaper, the Colonial

Advocate, he was several times elected in the "House of Assembly" and fought for democracy against aristocratic control. In 1834, he became first mayor of the newly created City of Toronto and continued to advocate democracy. In December 1837, he marched on Yonge Street and attempted an armed insurrection, which was quickly defeated by the government troops, but nonetheless made history. MacKenzie served as the "unofficial, honorary historical patron of Citizens for Local Democracy," symbol of the middle class against the aristocracy.[73]

A few months later, Queen's Park was taken over by another carnival. On April 21, 1997, the day Bill 103 was scheduled to be voted, Citizens for Local Democracy organized a rally in front of the Legislature.

> It was a beautiful spring day. Perfect for the "outside" troops to perform their miracles on drums, whistles, megaphones, saxophones, and sundry other instruments of the people—all in an effort to penetrate the great thick walls of the Pink Palace with a cacophony of democratic sentiment.[74]

This protest is interesting in its symbolism. While some C4LD members were sitting inside the Legislature in the public gallery, inside the realm of formal politics, others were making sure that outside noise was being heard by elected representatives, illustrating the importance of the spaces of civil society.

October 1997 came with angry teachers on the streets across the province. C4LD was very active in supporting their struggles against Bill 160, the legislation that centralizes decisions concerning education in the Cabinet of the Premier without possibilities of review by the courts, the bill that introduced drastic cuts to the education system, reserves for government the right to hire unqualified teachers, and terminates existing collective agreements between school boards and teachers' organizations. C4LD supported struggles against such sweeping reforms, including the province-wide teachers' general strike. For C4LD, Bill 160, like Bill 104 (the Fewer School Board Act) before it, seriously harms democracy. "This legislation smacks of what is expected in a totalitarian state where the rule of law is denigrated," it is written in Newsletter #20, "One fears for the worst when the government tries to limit access to the courts. It is ironic that the government is seeking the help of the courts (through an injunction) to stop protests against legislation which tries to limit access by the public to the courts."[75]

Taking over the streets, C4LD toyed with the idea of creating a slogan for the movement. Some members were openly against the idea;

others found the exercise fun and possibly useful. The point of mentioning this activity here is that it serves to outline the most important values in the movement. A slogan captures the vision people have of their movement. It is an exercise of self-definition. Themes that came out played with the Tories' 1995 electoral slogan: Common Sense Revolution. Harris' reforms do not make sense, most suggestions said, because it does not include due democratic process. "Mike's really common but he doesn't make sense!" Many other suggestions emphasized the role of people in democratic societies. "My Ontario includes people," "Democracy doesn't lock people out!" Another theme was identification to, and "ownership" of, the province by the people, not by the government. "Take Back Our Province." Some propositions played with the idea of freedom. "Free Ontario." Others conveyed the fear of revolution, which brings chaos, and proposed instead the common "decency" of democracy. Decency is a word that has strong moral undertone and is closely related to other phrases such as community or family values. "The revolution makes me nervous—I'd rather just have common sense." "In community I can find common sense—in revolution I find chaos." "Common Decency!"

In sum, the role of a slogan is to create a sense of identity with the entity it represents. In this case, C4LD perhaps saw this slogan as a tool for the 1999 provincial elections, or simply as a means to engrave its action into public memory. Later on, the *Toronto Star* launched a campaign to find a motto for the new Megacity:

> Verily, a city cannot hold up its head without an epigram that defines it to the rest of the world. Paris is the city of lights. Rome is the eternal city. Los Angeles is the city of angels. New Orleans is the city that care forgot, when it is not being the Big Easy. And I—you, me, we—love New York.[76]

In the end, the new Megacity adopted the motto "Diversity is our Strength," recalling the literal meaning of Toronto as the "meeting place." As we will discuss in the next chapter, the new City embarked in an important marketing/visioning strategy to create an image for the city. A slogan for Citizens for Local Democracy is a means to create a space for action, a space where people rally around similar values, values that are captured in a catchy phrase. Producing space in the city means much more than toying with catchy phrases. Space is about 1) physical location and distance, actual places and ways to get there; 2) symbols associated with physical spaces, such as the importance of Queen's Park as a symbol of democracy for instance; and 3) space is also about banal places of everyday life, from the grocery store, to the house, to the emotional meaning of falling leaves in autumn, to the image of Toronto in memory, and so on.[77] How are these spaces emotionally charged? Who is excluded? What can people learn from experiencing these sites? How can these sites be appropriated, produced, used, inhabited, memorized? How can they provide a sense of orientation, of location, of identity?

In the case of the Megacity saga, the sites of mobilization cut across multiple scales: the province of Ontario (through e-mail links and provincial-wide municipal restructuring policies, provincial elections), the whole metropolitan region, local cities, ward organizations, downtown churches where the Monday night meetings took place, the public hearing room, the public gallery of the provincial Legislature, the front yard at Queen's Park, downtown streets, Toronto City Hall, the subway where newsletters were distributed, electric poles where flyers were posted, press rooms, alternative newspapers, cybernetic networks, closed-down hospitals, high schools, university campuses, homeless camp-outs, living rooms, and so on. In other words, mobilization occurred in homes, in public spaces, in communities, in the anonymous spaces of the street...C4LD was sometimes aware of the importance of place for mobilization. In its document giving ideas about organizing, it is mentioned that the chosen place of meeting should be pleasant to be in, "it should feel like community space, in a place that is seen as open to the public. City Hall might be a good place to start, given the idea that citizens should have access to this place. Churches are also accommodating."[78] Beyond the physical issue of the place of meeting and its importance for mobilization, C4LD knew the importance of people's identification to a place, the sense of "ownership," the sense of community. Downtown Toronto has a different feeling than the suburbs, and downtown residents felt strongly about this, fearing that putting these different lifestyles under the same name would dissolve them. As the song by Joanne Cohen goes:

> Living in the proposed megacity, You will find it very pretty
> Only two things to beware: No representation, and no 'there' there
> Megacity, megacity, They'll eliminate fiscal waste,
> And local colour, And all sense of place.[79]

*The Middle-Class Action Space: Differing Protest Cultures*

Members of C4LD fought many battles, against hospital closures, against the government's education reform, against the new property tax policy, against library or police reforms, and the list goes on. A common thread of argument runs through all these fights: democracy. The Harris government, the movement argued, has slashed democracy in all of the new legislation rushed through Queen's Park. A member on the forum e-mail list called for the organization of a "Democracy Congress," where all activists in Ontario would develop a united stand on democracy against Mike Harris and his government. Democracy is the mantra of progressive urban middle-class activism. It is the rallying value that cuts across ideologies.

Nevertheless, differing cultures of activism clashed. The kind of action undertaken was divided along spatial and class lines. On the one hand, well established, usually non-politicized communities were demanding more time to the government because such "communities like to think of themselves as leading rational, ordered lives and feel they are in command of their environments and able to influence decision-makers."[80] Many participants in Citizens for Local Democracy felt uncomfortable with the label of activist. As one of them put it:

> I don't do things like powerfax MPPs or chant. I prefer to keep myself a bit more dignified than that and find more effective means of dealing with these problems, such as convincing people through good arguments. Just because you see a few strange ideas floating around here such as people sticking their nose into politicians' faces and going on spontaneous marches doesn't mean everyone is doing it. When for example Ruth throws an idea into the e-mail about some action on Wellesley, I don't jump off my chair and go down there. I like to think things through first. (Sorry, Ruth.)"[81]

On the other hand, other participants had extensive political experience and were pushing for more radical actions. Some of them were also involved in other organizations such as the Metro Network for Social Justice and the Ontario Coalition against Poverty, and were more concerned with outreach and alternative lifestyle issues. Regardless of this noticeable tension, "you could close your eyes and swear you were at a 1960s student demonstration. Then you open them and see all those Rosedale [a wealthy neighbourhood] matrons and guys in suits just convulsed in anger."[82] The tension followed class, background, and interest lines, but it also transpired within the leadership at different times. John Sewell himself often balanced from democratic lobbying to radical actions such as chases, shouting, and chanting. And this is probably a great strength of the movement. It was fascinating to observe people becoming politically active both in the formal channels of participation and on the streets. When thousands of teachers took to the street in anger, not to ask for better salaries but to defend the quality of the education system; when usually quiet professionals dressed in yellow to attend the public gallery of the legislature, it became clear that C4LD participated in a very intense moment of insurgency in Toronto.

At some point, the movement was emotionally charged with this tension. Some people felt C4LD was becoming too moderate. As a participant on the forum e-mail list wrote: "Of course if we are not a resistance group, then what are we? A collaborator group?"[83] Other people resisted the idea of establishing a well-defined organization with membership lists to determine who has right to vote on organizational matters. "C4LD is a citizen's group, not a government. It doesn't tax me. Hold my pension money, or control health care, and I don't consider myself governed by it in any ways," wrote another participant.[84] C4LD was a movement that served for mobilization and consciousness-raising purposes. It did not become such a formalized organization providing individuals with a sense of who they are and to whom they should be loyal. C4LD did not impose rules of conduct or mandatory actions, people came in and out without having to legitimize their presence or absence. Participants strongly reacted to other adherents' willingness to push a more collective agenda in the movement. These debates were sometimes quite aggressive and emotional.

> I conceived the phrase Local Democracy to mean the right of citizens to have an effective local government, not a huge, remote, undemocratic, and inefficient one. Democracy is not about everyone agreeing on a point of view but rather is a system for managing a diversity of views and interests without bloodshed or (common sense?) revolutions.[85]

Socialism, unionism, and anarchism, spurred much flaming interchanges in a movement crossing over ideologies. To resistance in defining C4LD boundaries and establishing a membership list, others responded that a memberless group promotes libertarian principles that encourage people to simply leave if they do not agree with the group's values and strategies. "I think libertarian is the word," wrote Gary Morton, "C4LD is some sort of libertarian group that says it isn't a group but just a bunch of individuals who individually agree to aid the group in certain actions."[86] This is the "voice" against "exit" argument.[87] If an individual is not satisfied with an organization, she or he is confronted with the decision of either leaving, voicing her/his concerns, or staying out of loyalty. To conceive of a social movement this way implied, for some participants to C4LD, privileging an individualistic and self-interested vision over one of solidarity and collective action. The decision to continue as a movement rather than institutionalizing itself into a hierarchical organization draws upon a certain middle-class tendency to privilege individual over collective political involvement, precisely the reason why the concept of middle class had such a negative connotation in studies of collective action. However, C4LD's decision to remain a "movement" rather than a formalized organization should not be judged according to this simplified individual/collective dichotomy. As mentioned above, Tarrow explains there is much confusion between three aspects of movement organization.[88] While C4LD participants understood "organization" as a form of institutionalization into a formal and hierarchical body, a second meaning could be the "organization of collective action at the point of contact with opponents." The movement was actually very successful at this level of organization in supporting assemblies of active citizens and social networks. The third meaning of movement organization, the "connective structures," links the different parts of the movement "sector" and permitting the coalition of different formal organizations. C4LD initiated some of this with its outreach strategies and its value statement. It seems that participants who remained active in C4LD until now tend to be comfortable with the labels of activists, and most of them have long-time experience in socio-political activism in Toronto.

During the peak months of the Megacity saga and despite internal tensions on ideologies and strategies, most people in the movement despised the media and the government's depiction of active citizens as "angry radicals," instead of "ordinary people:"

> The people, according to Mike Harris and his government, is a mob who needs to be controlled by strong-arm authority. I remember an extremely offensive and truly propagandistic drawing done in the Sun [Toronto's tabloid newspaper]...showing the protesters as being an enraged beast that was reflected in the visor of an OPP [Ontario Provincial Police] riot squad member (who was of course presented as being an heroic figure). This theme has been played out again where anyone, and everyone, who has stood up to the

> bullying of Harris has been dismissed. This has included politicians, professionals, working people, the poor—just plain anyone.[89]

There were also concerns in the movement with the trend of not only labelling active citizens "socialist bums,"[90] but also with intimidation of protesters. In its December 1997 newsletter, C4LD asked the question:

> Is the Harris government well down the slippery road to tyranny? Or is that a wild overstatement drawn from a few debatable incidents? Should we fear that the steps the government has taken are preludes to much more repressive actions? Or is it business as usual?[91]

C4LD avoided alarmist reactions, but nevertheless asked the question and provided "the best information available so you, the reader, can decide for yourself how serious the situation in Ontario is, and then act as you think most appropriate." Again, this very rational, tamed, and reasonable approach is reassuring and credible for many participants. The newsletter outlined three "worrisome trends":

- The government's legislation restraining public debate in the Legislature, public consultation, access to information, etc.;
- Examples of vocal and persistent critics being threatened of being banned from Queen's Park;
- Examples of personal intimidation of demonstrators

### *Beware of the Gentle Angry People*

What comes out of this tale of resistance is that most strategies were aimed at preserving municipal institutions for the sake of democracy. Citizens for Local Democracy played a crucial role in mobilizing the urban middle class to challenge the Tory government who had targeted middle class people, public sector employees, health care or education professionals since its first election in 1995. The main analytical point I wish to raise here is the importance of middle class politics and of municipal institutions in the processes of restructuring occurring around the world today. The middle class can react very fiercely to the disappearance of its venue for influencing the state. It was very revealing to observe how citizens attempted to use one level of government to influence another one. As an emotional citizen said to the hearing committee on Bill 103: "Just because we are a city—not a country—doesn't make it any less a curtailment of our historically hard-won rights."[92] The Toronto experience has shown that many attacks on different fronts may not prompt co-ordinated resistance until the very city in which these people live is under attack. As its first goal, C4LD resisted Harris' restructuring that destroyed these crucial tools for progressive middle-class activism in Toronto. It resisted it, not in the name of middle-class comfort, but in the name of progressive and democratic politics, the kind of politics in which the middle class plays a crucial role. And I leave the final words to Keil's observation:

> The mix of these bourgeois traditions of running a city and their rejuvenation as a potential social movement has presented a number of interesting challenges for the immediate future of progressive urban politics in Toronto.[93]

## NOTES

1. Rosie DiManno, "Give our city a slogan," *Toronto Star* (December 21, 1997), A1.
2. Elaine Carey, "Minorities set to be majority," *Toronto Star* (June 7, 1998).
3. Ekos Research Associates conducted interviews between August 25 to August 29, 1997. Out of a sample of 1,200 residents, 500 were from Metro Toronto. GTA-wide results have a margin of error of 2.8 percent 19 in 20 times, whereas Metro results have a big margin of error of 4.4 percent and for outer-GTA the margin is 3.7 percent. See John Spears, "Voters set clear goals for super city," *Toronto Star* (September 15, 1997), A1; John Spears, "Your vision for region: Caring, safe, affordable," *Toronto Star* (September 15, 1997), B1.
4. Sidney Tarrow, *Power in Movement: Social Movements and Contentious Politics*, Second Edition (Cambridge: Cambridge University Press, 1998).
5. Ibid., 123
6. Ibid., 124
7. Posted on the C4LD list server (January 30, 1997).
8. www.c4ld.org
9. Ibid.
10. Janice Etter, *The Death of a Thousand Cuts* (community.web.net/citizens, April 1, 1997).
11. Ijeoma Ross, "Neighbours rally to fight amalgamation in Metro Toronto," *Globe and Mail* (February 1, 1997), A6.
12. Jon Caulfield, *City Form and Everyday Life: Toronto's Gentrification and Critical Social Practice* (Toronto: University of Toronto Press, 1994), 67-74.
13. In order to avoid confusion, the term liberal is used here to refer to political liberalism and more specifically liberal democracy. When referring to the political party, Liberal is capitalized. The use of the term "liberal" in the sense of progressive, common in the United States, is avoided. Moreover, it is important not to confuse political liberalism (a democratic process based on representation, pluralism, and basic individual rights) with neoliberalism (a series of economic policies).
14. Engin Isin, "Governing Toronto Without Government: Liberalism and Neoliberalism," *Studies in Political Economy* 56 (1998), 169-191.
15. Klaus Eder, *The New Politics of Class: Social Movements and Cultural Dynamics in Advanced Societies* (London: Sage, 1993).

16. Pierre Bourdieu, *La Distinction : Critique sociale du jugement* (Paris : Minuit, 1979). See also texts on the urban role of the middle class: Warren Magnusson, "Bourgeois Theories of Local Government," *Political Studies* XXXIV (1986), 1-18; Mike Davis, *City of Quartz: Excavating the Future of Los Angeles* (New York: Verso, 1990); Jon Caulfield, *City Form and Everyday Life*; Wallace Clement and John Myles, *Relations of Ruling: Class and Gender in Postindustrial Societies* (Montreal and Kingston: McGill-Queen's University Press, 1994); Tim Butler and Mike Savage, eds., *Social Change and the Middle Classes* (London: UCL Press, 1995); David Ley, *The New Middle Class and the Remaking of the Central City* (New York: Oxford University Press, 1996); Erik Olin Wright, *Class Counts: Comparative Studies in Class Analysis* (Cambridge: Cambridge University Press, 1997); Engin Isin, "Citizenship, Class and the Global City," *Citizenship Studies* 3, no. 2 (1999); Robert Beauregard, "The Politics of Urbanism: Mike Davis and the Neo-Conservatives," *Capitalism, Nature, Socialism* (May 1999).
17. Eder, *The New Politics of Class*, 166.
18. Ibid., 175.
19. Lorinc, "Making of the Megacity"
20. Ibid.
21. Kipfer, "Urban Politics in the 1990s"
22. I insist on the word symbolic. In fact, despite the persistence of this dichotomy in the popular imagery, the reality is that poverty, diversity, and crime are increasing in many suburbs in the Greater Toronto Area.
23. Isin, "Governing Toronto," 184.
24. The PC won every single seat in these regions in the 1995 provincial elections, whereas they won only 16 out of the 30 seats in Metropolitan Toronto. In the 1999 provincial elections, the PC won again every single seat in the 905 region, and 7 out of 22 seats in the new amalgamated city. Please note that there was a reduction of electoral districts effective for the 1999 elections.
25. Citizens for Local Democracy, *What's Going On Here?* Newsletter 1 (December 1996).
26. Gerry Caplan, *Address to the Monday night meeting* (February 17, 1997).
27. Elaine Prescod, Coalition of Visible Minority Women, *Deputation to the hearing committee on Bill 103* (February 20, 1997).
28. Lyba Spring, *Deputation to the hearing committee on Bill 103* (February 12, 1997).
29. Lester Brown, posted on the C4LD list server (January 15, 1998).
30. Task Force on Community Access and Equity, *Consultation Guide*.
31. Eric Jackson, posted on the C4LD list server (February 17, 1998). I suppose that by "multiculturalist racism," Jackson meant discrimination on the part of the Government based on the fact that Toronto is a very diverse society.
32. This document was adopted by Citizens for Local Democracy on March 21, 1997. Please refer to Appendix C for the full text. All emphasis is mine.
33. David Held, *Democracy and the Global Order: From the Modern State to Cosmopolitan Governance* (Stanford: Stanford University Press, 1995).
34. Michael Mann, "The Autonomous Power of the State" *European Journal of Sociology* 25 (1984), 185-213.
35. As a journalist wrote: "The government wants to avoid the appearance of property tax hikes caused by the new city, but it also doesn't want to be perceived to be anti-democratic by denying elected councilors their tax-and-spend powers." See William Walker, "Harris calls big megacity meeting," *Toronto Star* (March 20, 1997).
36. Engin Isin, *Cities Without Citizens* (Montreal: Black Rose Books, 1992).

37. Please see Martha A. Ackelsberg, "Communities, Resistance, and Women's Activism: Some Implications for a Democratic Polity," in *Women and the Politics of Empowerment*. eds. Ann Bookman and Sandra Morgen (Philadelphia: Temple University Press, 1988).
38. Adopted on September 15, 1997. Please refer to Appendix A for the full text. Emphasis mine.
39. Adopted on March 9, 1998. Please refer to Appendix B for the full text.
40. Jane Jacobs, quoted in Christopher Hume, "The city that Jane helped build," *Toronto Star* (October 12, 1997), F5.
41. John Sewell, *Address to the Monday night meeting* (posted on the C4LD list server, April 28, 1997).
42. Nelly Auster Young, *Deputation to the hearing committee on Bill 103* (February 12, 1997).
43. Globe and Mail Editorial, "What's good for Toronto is good for Ontario," *Globe and Mail* (January 21, 1997).
44. Roger Greenwald, *Deputation to the hearing committee on Bill 103* (February 12, 1997), emphasis is original.
45. Ann Phillips, "Dealing with Difference: A Politics of Ideas, or a Politics of Presence?" in *Democracy and Difference: Contesting the Boundaries of the Political*, ed. Seyla Benhabib (Princeton: Princeton University Press, 1996).
46. William Walker, "Queen's Park on 're' alert: MPPs ready for megacity trouble," *Toronto Star* (March 31, 1997).
47. See A. B. Stodart, "Letter to the Editor," *Now Magazine* (March 6-12, 1997), 10. Also, in chapter 6, I discuss an interesting exchange on the e-mail forum list about local voting rights (see Nigel Blumenthal, posted on the C4LD list server, March 23, 1998).
48. Spring, *Deputation.*
49. Arthur Lofsky, *Deputation to the hearing committee on Bill 103* (February 3, 1997).
50. Wally Brooker, *Deputation to the hearing committee on Bill 103* (February 17, 1997).
51. John Sewell, *Deputation to the hearing committee on Bill 103* (February 13, 1997).
52. Eder, *The New Politics of Class*, 149-151.
53. Jocelyn Stratton, *Deputation to the hearing committee on Bill 103* (February 5, 1997).
54. Kristen Fahrig, *Deputation to the hearing committee on Bill 103* (February 10, 1997); David Farrant, *Deputation to the hearing committee on Bill 103* (February 12, 1997).
55. Greenwald, *Deputation.*
56. Bob Olsen, *Deputation to the hearing committee on Bill 103* (February 5, 1997).
57. Joe Mihvec, *Deputation to the hearing committee on Bill 103* (February 25, 1997).
58. Don Young, *Deputation to the hearing committee on Bill 103* (February 12, 1997).
59. Young, *Deputation.*
60. Ruth Cohen, *Deputation to the hearing committee on Bill 103* (February 3, 1997).
61. Citizens for Local Democracy, *Harris clamps down: Should anyone be worried?* Newsletter 21 (December 1997).
62. These were Parkdale-High Park, York South-Weston, York West, York Centre.
63. E-mail exchange with Joey Schwartz (February 16, 2000).

64. Citizens for Local Democracy, *Local democracy is an issue across Canada*, Newsletter 11 (May 1997).

65. www.c4ld.org

66. Edward S. Herman and Noam Chomsky, *Manufacturing Consent: The Political Economy of the Mass Media* (New York: Pantheon Books, 1988).

67. Posted on the C4LD list server (November 20, 1997).

68. *Toronto Star* Editorial, *Toronto Star* (February 15, 1997).

69. John Sewell, *Address to the Monday night meeting* (March 10, 1997).

70. Gary Morton, posted on the C4LD list server (March 23, 1998).

71. Globe and Mail Editorial, "Four steps to Toronto," *Globe and Mail* (April 23, 1997); John Sewell, "The fight was for democracy," *Globe and Mail*, Letters to the Editor (April 26, 1997).

72. Eric Peterson, "William Lyon MacKenzie Lives!" Address to the Monday night meeting (January 20, 1997), recorded on *no mega-cd [no – megacity]*.

73. www.c4ld.org

74. S. D. Gibson, posted on the C4LD list server (April 22, 1997).

75. Citizens for Local Democracy, *First they took our city government, then our hospitals, now our schools, next*… Newsletter 20 (November 1997).

76. DiManno, "Give our city a slogan," A4

77. Henri Lefebvre, *The Production of Space* (Oxford: Blackwell, 1991).

78. www.c4ld.org

79. Joanne Cohen, *Megacity Drive!* To the tune of "Pollution" by humourist Tom Lehrer.

80. Colin Vaughan, "Ratepayers' groups gear up for megacity," *Globe and Mail* (February 3, 1997), A3.

81. Will Rutherdale, posted on the C4LD list server (May 30, 1997).

82. Reported in the *Globe and Mail* (February 21, 1997), A10.

83. Ruth Cohen, posted on the C4LD list server (July 18, 1997).

84. Tara Dier, posted on the C4LD list server (June 14, 1997).

85. Eric Jackson, posted on the C4LD list server (November 22, 1997).

86. Gary Morton, posted on the C4LD list server (November 9, 1997).

87. See Albert Hirschman, *Exit, Voice, and Loyalty: Responses to Decline in Firms, Organizations, and States* (Cambridge: Cambridge University Press, 1970); Stefano Bartolini, *Exit Options, Boundary Building, Political Restructuring*, EUI Working Paper SPS No. 98/1 (Florence: European University Institute, 1998).

88. Tarrow, *Power in Movement*, 123-124.

89. Joseph Cooper, posted on the C4LD list server (March 18, 1998).

90. Reported by Gary Morton on the C4LD list server (February 18, 1998).

91. Citizens for Local Democracy, *Harris clams down*.

92. Stratton, *Deputation*.

93. Roger Keil, "Toronto in the 1990s: Dissociated Governance?" *Studies in Political Economy* 56 (1998), 163.

## CHAPTER 3

# WITHIN THE BELLY OF A GLOBAL MONSTER: DISCOURSES ON GLOBALIZATION AND THE STATE

In "The Promises of Monsters: A Regenerative Politics for Inappropriate/d Others," Donna Haraway explores the possibilities opened up by advanced technologies and globalization. "How to move and what to fear in the topography of an impossible but all-too-real present?" she asks. What to fear about globalization, the buzzword on the lips of local politicians, journalists, financial advisers, but also of you and I, residents of big cities, of global cities? What to do with this fearful but also promising reality? Some have even given up on the possibility of doing anything; some chose to take advantage of the promises offered by globalization; and others have decided to fight the "monster" against all odds.[1] What to do within the belly of a global monster?

The populist discourse on globalization sustains the illusion that nothing else can be done but to abide to the necessities of a globalized world. It is this discourse the Tory government adopted to legitimate municipal restructuring in Toronto. The Common Sense Revolution, the platform on which the government was elected in 1995, meant the common sense of reducing the deficit and creating a business-friendly environment in order to become one of the great players of globalization. One of the concrete effects of this discourse has been the redefinition of local boundaries in Toronto, partly with the aim of reducing the power of the urban progressive middle class, which had control over municipal institutions. As Al Leach said, "We simply don't need every layer of government that we have now, and the cumbersome bureaucracies supporting them. And we certainly don't need as many politicians as we have now."[2]

It is important to understand this "impossible but all-too-real present." When the Conservative government says it wants to put Toronto on the map of global cities, what does it mean? When the same government uses this excuse to change democratic procedures, what does it entail? When state institutions adopt the "fight the deficit arithmetic," how much power is left in the hands of citizens? There is a general confusion between ideological discourses on globalization and empirical facts about economic, political, cultural, and social globalization. In this chapter, I will focus mostly on ideological discourses in order to understand the popular government rhetoric, before turning to the transformation of Toronto into a global city and exploring the avenues open for democratic citizen actions.

### *Discourses on Globalization*

These days, governments tend to explain social change mostly in economic terms. They argue the state no longer has the power to counter global economic decisions made by transnational corporations, banks, or global economic organizations. The state has limited autonomy in this age of global competition. It may indeed be less powerful because it is more open to external influences, but these influences are not only economical. Important political, social, cultural, and demographic forces flow through nation-states as well. Economism, defined as the prioritization of economic forces over others in influencing social change, nurtures the illusion that globalization is an inevitable economic force legitimising neoliberal policies.

More than half-century ago, Karl Polanyi argued that the economy cannot simply be a distinct sphere isolated from the rest of socio-cultural activities. The myth of the auto-regulated market does not correspond to socio-economic reality. Therefore, Polanyi concluded, this economistic ideology is to be rejected. The economy and other social spheres are closely related in their concrete functionings. Against economistic research, Polanyi used anthropological, sociological, and historical methods to demonstrate the "embeddedness" of the economy into society.[3] With the dominance of neoliberal ideas today, Polanyi's warnings are still very contemporary. Much of the current discussion on globalization assumes that what the global economy gains, the political sphere of the nation-state loses. This is a zero-sum assumption that falls directly into the trap of economism.

At the local level, economistic explanations focus on elements of intensified competition for investments between cities. Local economic development policies "are best developed away from the distractions of democracy, if necessary, in independent authorities," critically observes Swanstrom.[4] However, economic development and influxes of money in cities do not depend solely on what the Conservative government of Ontario labels a "business-friendly climate." For Harris and Leach, a "business-friendly climate" entails a slim bureaucracy, low taxes, much less political power in the hands of elected councillors and much more power in the hands of independent, non-elected advisory boards with which developers and investors deal directly, away from the "chaos" of democracy. Real-estate developers push for easier urban planning guidelines and less public consultation on new development projects. If it does not happen, they might bring their development money somewhere else. But local elites insist on keeping this money on their territory, because development creates the infrastructure necessary to attract more investment. Economism ultimately results in pushing politics away and privatizing decision-making processes.

This ideology rests on the reduction of citizens to consumers /spectators. It is assumed that as consumers we approve development projects such as sport stadiums or entertainment complexes, therefore municipal administrators do not see the usefulness of asking the political citizenry what it thinks. Keil points out that the Megacity saga has exacerbated the "dissociation" between the discourse on democratic rights and processes on the one hand, and urban growth and spatial development on the other hand. While the progressive urban middle class was busy fighting for a fair democratic process, major urban development projects such as the airport extension, or the new sports complex Air Canada Centre, have been approved without much outcry from the same group of people who had fought fiercely against the Spadina Expressway in the 1970s.[5]

Despite these real pressures for depoliticizing economic development in order to adapt to global competition, many have argued before that corporate capital cannot flee as easily from one city to another. Corporations depend on the physical infrastructure, land, support networks, and the concentration of facilities specific to the locality. They cannot relocate that easily.[6] Places differ from one another in their labour pool, their culture, their networks, and their synergy. They compete with one another for capital investments exploiting certain comparative advantages. Local elites embark in this competition by promoting and marketing their city to developers, investors, and consumers. Zukin as well as Urry argue that cultural services, tourism, and gentrification are becoming central strategies of place construction in the global economy. Indeed, firms' locational and investment decisions are influenced not only by specific local assets, knowledges, skills, informational infrastructures, but also by the availability of "world-class" entertainment services to "world-class" professionals. As Zukin puts it, there is a general strategy of mythologizing the city in order to sell it. This cultural strategy exploits the uniqueness of fixed capital (such as monuments, art collections, shopping streets), gentrifies it, and uses it as a scenario of economic development.[7] Keil explains that:

> Although statistically it appears as if global capital is moving through cities like an invader from outer space, local space entrepreneurs (who can themselves head offices of the subsidiaries of transnational firms) provide the necessary means to facilitate the spatial and social integration of these investments locally. They do this by using the local political and planning process as a mediating instrument.[8]

*Reprinted with permission from Tom Dolighan*

Place marketing and gentrification do not come without resistance. Harvey notes that "the historical geography of place construction is full of examples of struggles fought for socially just reinvestment (to meet community needs), for the development of 'community' expressive of values other than those of money and exchange…The upper classes have been just as active (and of course more effective) as the lower classes in this resistance."[9] Toronto's reformists of the 1970s are a good example of such resistance to pro-development policies. People invest places of their labour, loyalties, and culture. The means by which these investments are made will differ, but Harvey's point is well taken that global economic forces do not erase local agency. Transnational flows are actively re-appropriated in local places and tend to become specific to these places. Cities differ in their experiences with global economic forces.[10] While cities may respond differently to global pressures, many embark in place construction strategies. But the mere variation in responses to globalization "indicate that these choices are essentially political, not determined by larger economic forces."[11]

If economism is a first characteristic of the popular discourse on globalization which tends to benefit real-estate developers and corporate investors, the recent period of economic austerity also led governments to abide to the panic surrounding the "fiscal crisis." Austerity has not always been the "normal" and "reasonable" way of governing society. But with the raging tide of the discourse of economistic (read neoliberal) globalization, austerity seemed to be the "only" strategy to remain in the game. When governments cut social services dramatically, when electoral campaigns are won on the promise of fighting the deficit, when core social values such as education and health are considered too expensive, one wonders why such discourse did not encounter more resistance. Thom Workman explains that the rhetoric on the "fiscal crisis" played on the use of common sense and culturally specific expressions.[12] People certainly understood what the government meant when it qualified the economy as "sick," when it associated a "healthy society" with deficit-zero institutions. These metaphors are very strong and created a sort of public state of panic. Sickness is not something a society wants. Most people do not think about the effects of using these expressions. Is a society really "sick" because of a difficult public financial situation? What if other assessment criteria such as social solidarity, cultural vitality, or democratic politics were to be used? The idea behind the discourse of "fiscal crisis" dictated that letting "social greed" continue its course would be catastrophic.

Upon a close examination of the vocabulary used in the public realm, Workman found that most words have masculine and military connotations. To "fight" the deficit, Mike Harris was elected in 1995 on the promise of "tough change." An "army" of "debt-fighters" took over the legislature. They took "firm steps" to regain "mastery" over public services. This was the "reasonable" way to go; "special interest groups" had to be "muted." All this was said with "gravity" instead of "frivolity." "Strength" won over "weakness," and so on. When the need for change in the structure of social services is conveyed in such an aggressive way, who would opt for "weakness," "frivolity," or "special interest groups?" Only a few movements have explicitly challenged this rhetoric. One can think of the Quebec's "Bread and Roses" march in the summer of 1996, or the resistance to the Toronto Olympic bid organized under the banner of "Bread not Circuses," revived in 1998. Both movements fought for a greater consideration of social issues such as poverty and the condition of women, and they both chose less aggressive words to convey their message.

While it is interesting to note the rhetorical tropes used to legitimate neoliberal policies, it is also important to highlight the moralistic twist to this aspect of the discourse on globalization. People were told they were individually responsible for the public deficit. Because the discourse of "fiscal crisis" was integrated into daily life, into the underlying worldviews of society, people accepted immense cutbacks in the public system. The deficit became a popular household preoccupation and was no longer the sole interest of financial experts.

Despite huge cutbacks and the panic surrounding the "fiscal crisis," studies have demonstrated that government spending as a percentage of gross domestic product continued to increase.[13] What had changed was not the absolute amount of money dedicated to public services, but rather the way governments organized social management. An ideological shift occurred from liberal democracy to neoliberalism (or "advanced liberalism" to use Nikolas Rose's term). This meant a profound transformation of values in the government with repercussions throughout society. Isin explains that the shift towards neoliberal governance implied a new basis for decision-making.[14] Rather than a reliance on scientific knowledge, governments now base their decisions on criteria of performance and marketable "formulas." Legitimacy relies on calculation and monitoring by private agencies staffed by accountants, managerial engineers, and marketing experts. Social prestige is gradually fading for lawyers, academics, doctors, psychologists, and social workers.

Given that benefactors from public services are now defined as "clients," "customer," and "taxpayers" rather than the "ill," "patients" or the "poor," occupations specializing in calculation have taken over occupations specialising in human services (Table 4).

*Forms of Rule: Liberal versus "Advanced Liberal"*

| | **Liberal** | **"Advanced Liberal"** |
|---|---|---|
| Source of authority | Expertise based on truth-claims; knowledge as a foundation of authority | Emphasis on performance and efficacy; knowledge as foundation of marketability |
| Mode of legitimacy | Verify, validity, reliability | Enumeration, calculation, monitoring, evaluation |
| Subjects of government | Ill, patient, poor | Client, customer, taxpayer |
| Object of government | Risk reduction is collective responsibility | Risk reduction is individual responsibility |
| Technologies of government | State is governed via public institutional arrangements (e.g., municipality); steering, guiding, disciplining | State enabled by "quasi-private" or "private" institutional arrangements; self-control, self-modulation |
| Characteristic occupations | Law, academe, medicine and social guidance professions; social trustee professions | Accountancy, managerial, engineering, advertising; promotional professionals based on marketable expertise |

**Table 5:** Changes in Social Management
*Source: Engin F. Isin. 1998 "Governing Toronto Without Government: Liberalism and Neoliberalism" in Studies in Political Economy, Vol.56:176*

The ultimate goal behind the neoliberal discourse on globalization is to reduce the size of the bureaucracy, not the power of the state. Political power partly resides in the state's capacity to convince people through the use of rhetorical tropes such as the ones highlighted above. Convincing citizens of the urgency to implement neoliberal policies in order to remain afloat in a globalized world is a strategy of "authoritarian populism."[15] Authoritarian populism means appealing to popular fears and values in order to legitimize drastic restructuring policies. It is no coincidence that most right-wing platforms use the term "revolution" to point to the necessity to act rapidly in responding to economic globalization. "The idea of revolution suggests something overwhelming, all-encompassing and new. Much of the rhetoric surrounding the current right-wing transformation of Canada," argues Paul Leduc Browne, "implies that the Right is innovative and creative, while the Centre is stagnant and the Left is nostalgic for the past."[16]

This playful analysis of the popular rhetoric of globalization serves as the background against which proponents and opponents of amalgamation in Toronto developed their arguments. Clarke and Gaile rightfully note that "the interpretation of globalization and restructuring processes is a political process of problem definition; as such, the causes identified by policy makers drive the solution chosen."[17] I will not attempt to provide a definition of globalization here.[18] Instead, it will be more useful to examine the articulation of global economic forces with state political power in order to better understand how the economistic, neoliberal, and populist discourse on globalization could explain municipal restructuring in Toronto.

### *The End of State?*

"Around the globe, the state is in the spotlight," this is the first sentence of the World Bank's World Development Report 1997.[19] From international agencies' official discourse on the state, to governments' right-wing agenda to reduce the state's involvement in social welfare, to popular cynicism about electoral politics, to local "drop-out" attitudes, what is left for the state? What kind of state? Many observers are quite pessimistic about the role of the state in this age of globalization. In the face of the increasing pace and scope of global economic developments, some have declared the "end of geography," "the end of territories," "the end of cities," and the "end of the nation-state."[20] While the relationship between economic and political forces has been significantly transformed since the 1970s, there is certainly much power left in the hands of nation-states, albeit different kinds of nation-states.

Much of the literature on the "withering away of the nation-state" focuses on the new regulatory powers of supranational institutions and of private entities such as credit-rating agencies. Thus it is often assumed that changes in the regulatory framework lead to a decreasing importance of the nation-state.[21] On the other hand, because globalization is often times understood as a form neoliberalism, it is also argued that it takes democratic power away from the nation-state.[22] While increasing transnational flows, the development of a transnational regulatory regime, and neoliberal state policies such as privatization and deregulation seem to point towards a decreasing margin of manoeuver for the nation-state, I wish to argue here that this correlation is based on a particular definition of the state. Indeed, the state is usually defined as a hierarchical bureaucratic entity exercising control over a bounded territory by monopolizing the means of legitimate violence. The modern ideal of a closed national sovereign territory rose out of the ruins of other systems of spatial organization such as city-states, empires, feudalism, and the administrative territorial organization of the Catholic Church.[23] A triggering element in this development was the 17th century Westphalia Treaties concluded after the Thirty Years War. The treaties determined that national territories were to become the jurisdictional space providing the foundation for sovereign political authority and the exclusive monopoly over order, security, protection, and redistribution. No other modes of spatio-political organization could then be tolerated. With transnational flows ignoring territorial boundaries, with privatized and decentralized governing agencies, and with a weakening grip on the social world, the nation-state does indeed seem in a difficult position.

Nevertheless, the state is not necessarily losing its power. Rather, it is changing its organizational structure. To fully understand these transformations, a more flexible definition of the nation-state is needed. The basis of this new definition is that the current shift in the geography of governance does not entail the end of the state. In fact, the state is re-scaling, that is it devolves more power to the supranational level, on the one hand, and to the provincial and local levels, on the other hand.[24] For example, the North American Free Trade Agreement (NAFTA) has created a transnational legal regime that regulates trade and pressures national governments to enforce their labour and environmental laws. This transnational regime modifies certain rules, but it does not necessarily weaken national states. Each country still designs its own laws.

NAFTA creates a supranational entity that pressures them to enforce their own laws. It does not impose what kind of health and safety regulations Canada ought to adopt, for instance. But it does give citizens, unions, businesses, and the U.S. and Mexican governments the opportunity to force the Canadian government to properly enforce its own laws. This example illustrates the fact that, despite the introduction of external pressures, re-scaling is not the same thing as weakening.

Modifications in state institutional structures are also occurring by devolving power to lower levels of government. Decentralization is the new mantra. In a climate of fiscal panic, central governments offloaded many responsibilities to provinces, which in turn passed the buck to municipalities. This was the case not only in Ontario, but all over Canada and in many other countries in the world. The Canadian case is particular because Quebec's particular pressures for greater provincial autonomy have been a founding element of the federal system. The Canadian constitution clearly identifies which level of government has jurisdiction over which sectors. Despite this longer history of decentralization, Canada is nevertheless going through a profound restructuring of its state organizational structure, like many other countries.

What does this re-scaling process entail? The World Bank affirms that "the state has grown everywhere." According to its 1997 report, total government expenditure has increased by 40 percent since the beginning of the century, with a major increase of 25 percent since the 1980s.[25] The question remains however: What kind of state? These figures probably include provincial and local government expenditures, although it is not specified. The fact that many of these lower levels of government have increased their responsibilities is not mentioned. States are not weaker, they have modified their organizational structure, both in terms of sharing responsibilities between different jurisdictions and in terms of their approach to governance. How did this happen in Toronto?

### *Toronto, the Global City*

> The ideological and political context for Toronto's restructuring thus lies in local fiscal policy and the rhetoric of global competitiveness—which the Progressive Conservatives quickly adapted to their own agenda.[26]

In 1986, John Friedmann ranked Toronto as a "secondary" global city within core countries of the global economy. Toronto, was thus comparable to Miami, Houston, or San Francisco in terms of its participation in the global economy.[27] Ten years later, Graham Todd held that "the relative weight of financial sector activity in the Canadian economy places the country well apart from advanced industrialized nations such as France or Germany, and closer to those national economies where global cities such as New York, Tokyo, and London, mediate massive volumes of international financial transactions."[28] In fact, Toronto stands apart as a "secondary" global city, behind leaders such as New York, London, Tokyo, because of its high concentration of financial services relative to the Canadian economy.[29] Todd explains that the process of "going global" in Toronto began in the 1980s, but was building on Toronto's success in outranking Montreal as the Canadian financial centre in the 1960s. Toronto's Redevelopment Advisory Commission, a business coalition of the 1960s, was very successful in attracting headquarters and major financial institutions to Toronto, in response to leaving industrial plants threatening the regional economic balance.[30] As Canada's undisputed financial and commercial services centre, Toronto hosted in 1991, 42 of the 56 Canadian foreign bank head offices, half of Canada's top 50 foreign-owned companies, the executive functions of Canada's top 5 banks, the headquarters of 6 out of the 10 largest life insurance headquarters.[31] Throughout the 1990s, Toronto gained more headquarters. There is no doubt, Toronto has become a global city, a process that began in the 1980s with this sectoral transformation of the regional economy from an industrial base to a financial base. Such transformation did not occur on its own; specific planning and political incentives have consciously been crafted to put Toronto on the map of global cities.

Filion distinguishes two recent periods of planning initiatives in Toronto.[32] The years between 1959-62 were the years of boosterism and economic growth, where the city was built through accelerated infrastructure development, urban renewal, and urban sprawl. From 1969 onwards, a reform movement swept the City of Toronto Council, committed to social equity, public participation and environmentalism. Reform councillors never formed a formal political party, instead they constituted a loose alliance voting together on a number of issues. This progressive regime in the central city was not replicated in the suburbs of the metropolitan area, where power remained decisively in the hands of pro-development politicians. Filion explains the political specificity of the central city regime by two socio-economic factors. The old city of Toronto had a higher proportion of renters (62.6 percent against 42 percent in the greater metropolitan region). This could explain the concern for issues not directly related to property values. The second socio-economic characteristic is the concentration of middle-class professionals in the central city.[33] The more radical wing of the reform movement ultimately lost to the more socially minded conservative wing, which re-initiated a compromise with business interests in the 1980s.[34]

Filion's second distinctive period in planning practices in Toronto spans from 1989 to 1992, characterized by tensions between a new wave of urban reform centred around issues of racism, feminism, and environmentalism on the one hand, and a boosterist world-class city vision on the other hand.[35] The slower economic recovery from the severe recession of 1989-90 in the central city, coupled with the imposed amalgamated structure brought the boosterist, suburban, world-class vision to the forefront. Kipfer and Keil argue that this signals a third period in Toronto's planning history, moulding the city according to criteria of competitiveness and neoliberal policies.[36]

The 1996 GTA Task Force Report is a good example of a political project that underpins the processes of transforming Toronto ino a global city.[37] The report clearly situates the Greater Toronto Area within the global economy and states that "the GTA's challenge is to reinvent itself into a city-region that is economically and socially sustainable in today's global context."[38] The GTA Report insists on the necessity to restructure governance in the GTA because "in an era of fiscal constraint and intense global competition, the costs associated with this level of inefficiency are no longer tolerable."[39] Indeed, at the fiscal level, the old City of Toronto was in a peculiar situation, which was infuriating large corporations. With the high concentration of headquarters in the central business district, the City could rely on an important influx of business property taxes, and thus permitting to maintain low residential taxes. When the Harris government used provincial legislation to ease the fiscal burden of large capital, it clearly marked the willingness to turn towards the needs of powerful actors in the global economy. Furthermore, other provincial Tory initiatives such as changes in the Planning Act, the Municipal Act, and the Environmental Assessment Act, have weakened local capacity to control development. In the end, the project of restructuring the governance and fiscal structure of Toronto is more than a response to concerns about efficiencies of the public sector, it is clearly a response to global competitiveness.[40]

In addition to economic sectoral transformations and political responses through structural changes in governance, the face of Toronto slowly came to resemble other global cities. A set of gentrifying projects, entertainment complexes, conference centres, luxury condominiums, and harbourfront developments, ensured the construction of the spatial infrastructure of the global city.[41] Global cities, as Sassen explains, play a particular role in the process of economic globalization, they are the production sites, the organizing nodes of global flows. Economic globalization requires a concrete physical infrastructure to work: ranging from telematics circuits hidden under the ground, to airports, to satellite connections, to high-scale restaurants and hotels, to entertainment stadiums or theatres, to training universities, to star architect's buildings. Sassen points that the economy of global cities is highly polarized between high-end and low-end jobs. She explains:

> A focus on the *work* behind command functions, on *production* in the finance and service complex, and on the market*places* has the effect of incorporating the material facilities underlying globalization and the whole infrastructure of jobs and workers typically not seen as belonging to the corporate sector of the economy: secretaries and cleaners, the truckers who deliver the software, the variety of technicians and repair workers, and all the jobs having to do with the maintenance, painting, and renovation of the buildings where it is all housed.[42]

Toronto has come a long way to become a global city. But its history has long been filled with boosterism. In the postwar years, war industries had to be converted into branch plant manufacturing. The period was marked by a high influx of immigration and major infrastructure development. From the 1960s until the mid-1980s, the city saw a dramatic growth in the auto industry and a steady migration of headquarters from Montreal to Toronto. With the advent of free trade after 1988, there was a decline of branch manufacturing, which was gradually replaced by telecommunications and computer industries and a film industry cluster. The GTA Report indicates that "we are poised to begin a new era, which is marked by global competitiveness."[43] It is striking that the history of governance restructuring in Toronto is connected with these economic "eras." For instance, the metropolitan structure was created in 1953 by Fred Gardiner's boosterist initiative. His words fifty years ago could now potentially be mistaken with the Harris government's arguments for amalgamation:

> A municipality is no different from an industrial undertaking. Both must provide adequate plant and equipment to carry on their business. If a municipality does not have adequate plant and equipment, which are the lifeblood of a city, industry and commerce will go elsewhere. Industry needs water, sewers, roads, public transit and residential accommodation for its work force. We

> are now equipped so that in due time in accordance with well-defined plans we can provide all of these.[44]

In 1953, with the new and unique metropolitan structure, Gardiner felt "equipped" to plan the infrastructure development necessary to support industrial growth. Now with the Megacity, boosterists have the power to build the "world-class" infrastructure sustaining economic globalization. Changing the governance structure has long been seen as a means to stabilize and consolidate new economic "eras."[45] As Isabel Bassett, Tory Representative of St.Andrew/St.Patrick wrote in response to a citizen's letter:

> I support Bill 103 because I believe in the long-term benefits of unification. The global trend is toward strong, habitable city-states, with strong regional governments such as Rotterdam, Frankfurt and New York. Metro Toronto, with a population of 2.3 million, must be in that league in order to compete for investment, business and jobs in the global marketplace.[46]

Marketing the Greater Toronto Area has become very important. The Greater Toronto Marketing Alliance has been commended in the Transition Team Report as an excellent illustration of public/private partnership to "let everyone know about [our] achievements and attractions."[47] At the scale of the new amalgamated city, praising of the size and importance of the city became a central rhetorical strategy. It is constantly highlighted that with 2.3 million of population, the new City is the fifth largest in North America, after Mexico City (16 million), New York (7.4 million), Los Angeles (3.6 million), and Chicago (2.7 million). Of course, these figures represent the population of municipalities, certainly not the urban region. In the case of Los Angeles, with a fragmented municipal structure, 3.6 million may not seem big, but in reality, the urbanized region has over 14.5 million people (8.8 million in the county of Los Angeles, and about 5 million in the four other counties of the region).[48] But beyond size, amalgamation is used to highlight the difference between Toronto, a good Canadian city, from fragmented and "decaying" American cities. The Transition Team report spelled out a "Vision for Toronto in the Next Decade":

> We are a City of vision and pride. We are considered a globally significant City not only for our economic dynamism, but also because we pay as much attention to quality of life—social, cultural and environmental vitality—as we do to economic growth.

> We recognize that the measure of our social strength lies in how well we share and care for those who are most vulnerable. We may not have eliminated poverty or homelessness or violence or prejudice, but we are committed to continuing the battle. There is no move here for the well-to-do to retreat behind gated neighbourhoods.[49]

There is a broad-based consensus in Toronto on the necessity for institutional changes in governance. The general goal is to develop infrastructure and human capital, to enhance and maintain the quality of life (which is seen as Toronto's competitive advantage), and to attain government efficiency and effectiveness.[50] While the Tory government, the GTA Task Force, local mayors, and even Citizens for Local Democracy converged on these issues, they varied in their prioritization of them. In the end, however, Toronto's quality of life remained central. Why then, did the Tory amalgamation legislation spur so much resistance?

### *Urban Politics*

The means by which Toronto's quality of life is to be enhanced and maintained differed immensely between Citizens for Local Democracy and the Tory government. The conflict could be boiled down to opposing views on the role of local governments and whom they serve. Referring to the liberal democratic ideals of Alexis de Tocqueville and John Stuart Mill, C4LD saw local governments as the training ground for democracy. Local governments' democratic role was thought to be much more direct and fundamental; it is the level at which the democratic ideal is to be fulfilled. In contrast to this, the Harris government sees local government as an administrative arm of the state, mostly preoccupied with property owners and with the provision of services to property. The Harris government's view of municipal politics stands in direct continuation to more than seventy years of developments that undermined the operating independence of local governments. Tindal and Tindal explain that in the 1930s, the Depression resulted in an increased provincial surveillance over municipal financial activities. During the 1940s, the war effort led to the loss of municipal involvement in fields such as income tax and sales tax, and thus confined municipalities to a dependence upon property taxes as their main source of revenues. With increasing urbanization and demands for services, the 1950s brought further provincial and federal involvement in municipal affairs.[51] In the end,

> ...municipal governments in Canada never really had an opportunity to develop as an extension of the community, as a political

> mechanism which allows local citizens to decide what services they want and need (and are willing to pay for with their taxes).[52]

In fact, municipalities are constitutionally accountable to the province, not to citizens. The 1867 British North America Act enshrines the concept of municipalities as "creatures" of provincial governments. The courts have traditionally interpreted very narrowly the powers of municipalities. The "Dillon's Rule," in reference to a treatise on municipalities published in 1872 by an Iowa Chief Justice named John F. Dillon, establishes that local administration is unwise and dangerous. Dillon stated that it was necessary "to protect citizens from the excesses of the municipal corporations to which they belong."[53] Canadian courts have often referred to the Dillon's Rule to justify restrictive rulings on municipal powers. Legally, therefore, municipalities have long been prevented from playing an important role as a training ground for democracy. In some American States, however, the Dillon Rule eventually fell into desuetude. The Home Rule principle gave municipalities power to determine their own charters. In Canada, Tindal and Tindal plead that:

> Rather than regarding municipalities as analogous to private corporations, as corporate bodies which must be tightly controlled to protect citizens from their excesses, it is suggested that the courts should be more appreciative of municipalities as a level of government with a mandate from the electorate and with a legitimate political role to fulfil.[54]

In his book on the history of municipal incorporation, Engin F. Isin explains that from the twelfth to the fifteenth century in England, cities were autonomous from any central authority and rose out of sworn associations of citizens declaring themselves a city. Around the fifteenth century, these autonomous cities were gradually subjected to the State governed by an appointed elite that derived its authority directly from the central state. The central state needed their support for governing. By forcing them to choose a representative to sit on the King's parliament in England, the city slowly became and entity in itself (a unitary fictitious person), rather than a collective association of citizens. In the early nineteenth century, the city became a municipal corporation that was authorized by the central state and governed by a council chosen by city dwellers. Municipalities became part of the state apparatus and became tools for governing and maintaining order. They became a "governmental franchise of the State."[55] "Corporation" means the city becomes a legal, abstract entity rather than an embodied association of citizens. It means that the city would continue to exist even if all the citizens would die, an entity capable of holding property separate from the property of its members, capable of suing and being sued, and of issuing regulations and by-laws. By focusing on municipalities, the state could emphasize the hierarchical nature of the municipality within the state's administrative structure. The state was thus conceived as a layered system of distinct jurisdictions. The municipal corporation became responsible for a number of issues difficult to govern from a remote centre of power, such as schooling, public health, and infrastructures. In the case of British imperial Canada, the colonial government was also eager to use cities as state tools to maintain order in the colony, in order to prevent another American Revolution. Settling towns had the purpose of populating the territory, foster loyalty by using the municipality as an arm of the state and by compacting people in order to induce "appropriate" habits instead of letting people conglomerate irregularly and without discipline.

At the turn of the twentieth century, a first reform movement further confirmed this administrative role of municipalities. Reformists called for the depoliticization of municipal governments in order to attain more efficient administration and remove corruption. The second reformist wave of the 1960s and 1970s did not change the situation much. The main preoccupation then was the improvement of service delivery to respond to community needs, more than a political reform of the role of municipal governments. Not only do municipal administrations not have a constitutional standing as a level of government, their structure is not conducive to politics either.

Nevertheless, building upon a gradual politicization of the municipal role, the Toronto Megacity saga transformed such a depoliticized interpretation of municipal politics. For a few months, municipal politics became a central focus of political activity in the city. It became a vector through which a battle raged to define the political direction of the global city. With their polarized economic structure, global cities are intense sites of contestation.[56] But interestingly in the case of Toronto, a political battle was waged less on economic and urban development issues, and more specifically on issues of governance structure and democratic principles.[57] The case of Toronto is rich in illustrations of the importance of municipal politics in this world where the urban reality has no doubt become central to politics. We live in an urban world, a world in which everything is urbanized, whether one lives in the city or not. The most rural village is urban because it is intimately connected with the city. When the farmer turns on his television set at the end of the day, when he buys canned soup, when he congratulates himself for avoiding the evils of the big city, when he thinks about selling his crop, when he militates in favour of environmentally-friendly lifestyles, he is living in an urban world. And the urban world challenges the organization of the state centred on the national level. The city becomes a key site of construction for the "post-national," re-scaled state.[58]

In the current context of globalization, it becomes clear that urban politics often disrupts the regular processes of democratic elections and bureaucratic administration. The city generates different legal regimes and tolerates certain forms of illegality that explode the rigid boundaries of the national state. "This unstable mix of the legal and the illegal, and of various forms of each," argue Holston and Appadurai, "turns the city into a honeycomb of jurisdictions."[59] The city is the place where global forces are concretely experienced, the place where economic changes are felt, the place where cultures meet, the place where social ills are endured, the place where the media produces its entertainment, the place where innovation emerge, the place where people live, work, and resist. Urban politics has already indicated its potential for progressive Left politics.[60] Places like Berkeley, Santa Monica, London in the times of the Greater London Council, or Toronto in the reform years of the 1970s have been the site of radical urban politics using the powers vested to municipal institutions to act on issues such as nuclear proliferation, the Vietnam war, capitalism, civil rights, women's rights, or sustainable development. They also acted on issues less "radical" but certainly as passionate, issues like housing, transportation, or development control.

Municipalities are particularly well situated to play an important political role, despite restrictions on their jurisdictional powers. Municipalities are situated at the juncture of the city and social movements, to paraphrase Warren Magnusson.[61] The city is the place where social movements arise and meet. The municipality is designed to fix and control the elusive slippery boundaries of the city, and insert it within the reach of the state apparatus. At the same time, by virtue of its connection with the realm of daily life, it is particularly susceptible to the critiques arising from social movements. The municipality is thus an intense site for political action. Nevertheless, mobilization around the organization of the municipal governance system *per se* is rare. This makes the Toronto Megacity saga quite interesting. The amazing mobilization against amalgamation illustrates the importance of municipal politics in this age of globalization. Toronto witnessed tensions between urban and suburban interests, and between the progressive middle class and the economic and political elites. While urban and progressive middle class interests were closely allied with downtown municipal institutions, suburban and corporate business interests tended to ally more with the provincial government. These spatial and class tensions had repercussions on state re-scaling strategies. Indeed, restructuring of governance in Toronto took the form of a struggle between the provincial and the municipal levels of governance and their spatial and class interests.

Citizens for Local Democracy fought for the recognition of municipal governments as legitimate democratic institutions. In a context of state re-scaling strategies, it is clear that the municipality itself does not ask for overriding loyalty. It does not ask its inhabitants to die for it, but it still serves to foster a certain sense of coherence, of living-together, using the same streets, subways, reading the same newspapers, listening to the same radio stations, living under the same smoggy sky. "The municipality signifies the claims of a territorial community that does not pretend to be sufficient unto itself," Magnusson indicates, "it exists within a state, within a global economy, and within an ensemble of social relations that it can affect locally but cannot by itself transform."[62] The municipal structure is situated within the web of the state, but it does not necessarily entail a hierarchical positioning of different scales of government. Magnusson deplores the spatial hierarchy people have in mind when thinking about politics, assuming that important issues are dealt with at the top (at the level of nation-states) while municipalities are left with trivialities.[63] Within the context of state re-scaling strategies, this hierarchical understanding of the state cannot stand. Brenner argues instead that cities are *co-ordinates* embedded within the state matrix and within the multiple regulatory networks through which the state is configured on differential spatial scales.[64] As an ensemble of institutionalized compromises between scales, the state has become more, rather than less important within the belly of a global monster. As Keil puts it:

> Globalization makes states, but the local state is neither a closed system in the sense of a governmental-administrative institution nor simply a derivative of the nation-state. Rather, the local state has perforations at its interface with the dynamized, global city civil society. In these perforations are openings for resistance and alternatives to hegemonic globalization."[65]

"The wider world is never simply outside: it is always potentially and most constructively the subject of local politics," writes Magnusson.[66] A good way to fully grasp the importance of urban politics in this globalized world, is to abandon the idea that the nation-state can still pretend to secure its unified and sovereign territory. Magnusson names this, the illusion of "enclosure," which pervades every aspect of the political imaginary. It is assumed that without clearly demarcating where the political community begins and ends—its boundaries—governance is impossible. Within these boundaries, the state centres politics upon itself, "it creates its own vortex, which pulls the media, the movements, the parties, the pressure groups, and the political scientists toward it."[67] There is the belief that something must hold the system together, that governance needs fixture. Ultimately, such assumptions result in purging politics out of everyday life and centring conflicts around the state system. In the end, this is a means to "contain" democracy, so to render politics "safe for the state, the market, and the other forms of government to which we are subject."[68] To impose such political containers cannot be the role of the state anymore, for politics escapes definite boundaries. This is not to say, however, that we should not have any institutions and that society can govern itself by intuition. To fix boundaries, write rules down, organize violence, redistribute wealth, are crucial elements of a system of governance. Municipalities here again demonstrate their privileged situation. Being at once part of the state and part of civil society and daily life, its rules, fixings, constitutions, boundaries, are more prone to evolve as society evolves.

In other words, municipalities play a central in the reconfiguration of the state. Such a decentred view of the state also entails understanding what Jessop calls the "governance of complexity," by which he means the articulation of formal politics and civil society, and a shift from govern*ment* to gover*nance*.[69] Because the "supralocal economic environment" and the "extra-economic local environment" are more complex than local actors can possibly understand, and because they will always involve more complex causalities than it is possible to control, we need to develop means to govern complexity.[70] A first step is thus to *analytically* distinguish between the sphere of local economic development, the extra-economic local environment, and other scales (the supralocal) in the political environment. In reality, these environments are hardly distinguishable. Jessop notes that any solution to the problem of governing complexity "depends as much on the spatial imaginary and the links between state and civil society…as on formal territorial demarcations and the reallocation of formal legal and political powers."[71]

Complexity is scary, and it is also pragmatically very difficult to manage. But once we turn this analysis upside down and focus on multiplying the points of access to power instead of gearing towards seizing it by creating little pockets of enclosed sovereignty, we understand what re-scaling really is. It should not be about offloading responsibilities without giving municipalities the tools to deal with them, or even breaking away from the existing state in imagining that sovereignty will solve all the problems. State re-scaling, in fact, means governing complexity. It means understanding the state as a terrain of social relations in which different nodes radiate from different agencies, different access points, different people. This is very unsettling because it implies refusing to see the state as a container, with clear boundaries of inside/outside, fixed, and secure.

It would be dangerous to envision a municipality independent from the other components of the state, be it the provincial, the federal, or any other state agencies. The city cannot have definite boundaries like those arbitrarily traced for the purposes of administration and institutionalized politics. The city can hardly be captured in a sealed container as a city-state. This is simply reproducing the illusion of nation-state sovereignty at a smaller scale. As Magnusson says, "the locality is preserved as an imaginary place where the like can be with the like—and forget about the rest of the world."[72] A little like gated communities, he continues, "localities are no doubt a comfort to those who can afford the localities they want. For everyone else, they may appear as another dimension of imprisonment." When Mel Lastman declared that Toronto should be a province in November 1999, he unleashed ideas of autonomy and enclosure in the metropolitan region. The idea was that it would give Toronto some political leverage at the federal level, bypassing the obstacles of the municipal status as a "creature" of the province. "Look for MPs to start springing money for Harbourfront cultural endeavours, for housing programs, maybe even for Toronto's universities. They won't want the city-state debate to engulf Ottawa the way the Quebec separatist debate has," wrote Sewell.[73] Jane Jacobs has also supported the idea for a while. In her deputation to the hearing committee on Bill 103 she said:

> There are ways out of relationships if and when they become intolerable and destructive. One possible escape could be to create a new province, South Ontario. In that event, South Ontario and North Ontario could each set its own preferred tax and other provincial policies. North Ontario of course would still depend heavily on subsidies from South Ontario's economy, but only indirectly through Ottawa, much as if North Ontario were an Atlantic province. However, it would be much, much more sensible

> to avoid an intolerable future leading to deterioration and disruption, by intelligently and courageously facing realities in the fine province of Ontario we do have.[74]

Vaughan raised two important difficulties with the proposal of transforming Toronto's status from that of a municipality "creature of the province" to that of a city-state. The first one is the necessity to give the city-state power to levy income taxes in order to avoid the dependence on property taxes. But most importantly here, Vaughan pinpoints to the disadvantage of fixed boundaries entailed in a constitutional status for Toronto. As the city would expand, economically and socially, it would be very difficult to redraw its boundaries if it necessitated a constitutional change, just like in the case of provinces.[75] Reproducing enclosure at a smaller scale can be problematic. However, bypassing the provincial level to establish a direct relationship between the metropolis and the Federal government is a consistent proposal of state re-scaling, albeit difficult to imagine in the current political climate.

The state is not disappearing, it is the illusion of national sovereignty that falls apart in the face of the current process of re-scaling. The state has changed enormously, but it is still very powerful. Globalization makes new kinds of states, to use Keil's phrase.[76] The state is decentred in a web of agencies, administrative scales, and political jurisdictions, from the local to the global. In this intertwined web, the municipality plays a key role. In this urban world, municipal institutions provide important leverage to the urban progressive middle class who can mobilize constituencies on issues dear to mainstream Canadian society: education, universal health care, access and equity, human rights, etc. Even though these issues are not controlled by municipalities—they are rather under the jurisdiction of higher levels of government—they are issues impacting the quality of everyday life in the city. In this sense, municipal institutions are key sites for political action as they are situated within the web of the state and within the confines of everyday life. It is this very interweaving that gives the city administration its vitality. Discussion about the size of government and the mechanics of administrative boundaries, while important, remains but a small part of the pragmatics of governing. What is governing after all? It is co-ordinating the "living together," the "rubbing of shoulders" in the city. It is finding fair and effective ways to redistribute resources. It is forming an identifiable place, a sense of place, a sense of solidarity. Governance pushes the traditional functions of the state (providing public goods such as defence, law, property rights, basic education, social insurance) to include co-ordinating mechanisms operating in civil society.

## NOTES

1. Donna Haraway, "The Promises of Monsters: A Regenerative Politics for Inappropriate/d Others" in *Cultural Studies,* eds. L. Grossberg, C. Nelson, and P. Treichler (London and New York: Routledge, 1992).
2. Leach, *Statement to the Legislature.*
3. Karl Polanyi, *La Grande Transformation: Aux origines politiques et économiques de notre temps.* Trans. by Catherine Malamoud (Paris: Éditions Gallimard, [1944] 1988).
4. Todd Swanstrom, "Beyond Economism: Urban Political Economy and the Postmodern Challenge," *Journal of Urban Affairs* 15, no. 1 (1993),61.
5. Keil, "Dissociated Governance."
6. J. R. Logan and H. L. Molotch, *Urban Fortunes: the political economy of place* (Berkeley: University of California Press, 1987); Saskia Sassen, *Cities in a World Economy* (Thousand Oaks: Pine Forge Press, 1994); Manuel Castells, "The Spaces of Flows," in *The Rise of the Network Society* (Cambridge: Blackwell, 1996), 376-428; Kevin Cox, ed. *Spaces of globalization: Reasserting the Power of the Local* (New York: Guilford Press, 1997); Susan E. Clarke and Gary L. Gaile, *The Work of Cities* (Minneapolis: University of Minnesota Press, 1998).
7. Sharon Zukin, *Landscapes of Power: From Detroit to Disney World* (Berkeley and Los Angeles: University of California Press, 1991); Sharon Zukin, *The Cultures of Cities* (Cambridge: Blackwell, 1995); John Urry, *Consuming Places* (London and New York: Routledge, 1995).
8. Roger Keil, *Los Angeles: Globalization, Urbanization and Social Struggles* (Chichester: John Wiley & Sons, 1998), 146.
9. Harvey, *Justice,* 298.
10. Andrew Kirby, *Power/Resistance local politics and the chaotic state* (Bloomington and Indianapolis: Indiana University Press, 1993).
11. Clarke and Gaile, *The Work of Cities,* 2.
12. Thom Workman, *Banking on Deception The Discourse of Fiscal Crisis* (Halifax: Fernwood Publishing, 1996).
13. Michael Hardt and Antonio Negri, "Postmodern Law and the Withering of Civil Society" in *Labor of Dionysos: A critique of the state-form* (Minneapolis: University of Minnesota Press, 1994).
14. Isin, "Governing Toronto."
15. The expression was coined by Stuart Hall et al. *Policing the Crisis: Mugging, the State and Law and Order* (London: Verso, 1978); Stuart Hall, *The Hard Road to Renewal: Tatcherism and the Crisis of the Left* (London: Verso, 1988); See also Colin Leys, "Neo-Conservatism and the Organic Crisis in Britain," *Studies in Political Economy* 4 (1980), 41-63.
16. Paul Leduc Browne, "Déjà Vu: Tatcherism in Ontario" in *Open for Business Closed to People,* eds. D. Ralph, A. Régimbald, and N. St-Amand (Halifax: Fernwood Publishing, 1997), 37.
17. Clarke and Gaile, *The Work of Cities,* 2.
18. The reader may refer to Amin and Thrift's general definition of the global economy as including the following aspects: 1) the increasing centrality of the financial structure; 2) the importance of the knowledge structure; 3) the transnationalization of technology, coupled with an enormous increase in the rapidity of redundancy of given technologies; 4) the rise of global oligopolies; 5) the rise of transnational economic diplomacy and the globalization of state power; 6) the rise of global cultural flows; and 7) the rise of new global geographies. See A. Amin and N. Thrift, eds., *Globalization, Institutions, and Regional Development in Europe* (Oxford: Oxford University Press, 1994), 2-5.

19. World Bank, *The State in a Changing World: World Development Report 1997* (Oxford: Oxford University Press, 1997).

20. Richard O'Brien, *Global Financial Integration: The End of Geography* (London: Pinter Publishers, 1992); Bertrand Badie, *La fin des territoires: Essai sur le désordre international et sur l'utilité sociale du respect* (Paris: Fayard, 1995); Alain Touraine, "Das Ende der Städte?" *Die Zeit* 23, no. 31 (1996), cited in Roger Keil, "Globalization makes states," 629; Kenichi Ohmae, *The End of the Nation State* (New York: Free Press, 1995).

21. Mann lists four lines of arguments used to support the thesis of a "weakening state": 1) global capitalism is undermining the nation-state; 2) social and environmental problems of a global nature grow beyond the reach of a singular state; 3) identity-based movements compete with national and class identities; and 4) the end of the cold war ends the military necessity for sovereign super-powers. Quoted in Keil, "Globalization makes states," 622.

22. Leo Panitch, "Globalization and the State," in *Socialist Register 1994*, eds. R. Miliband and L. Panitch (London: Merlin Press, 1994), 60-93.

23. Badie, *La fin des territoires*; Robert David Sack, *Human Territoriality: Its theory and history* (Cambridge: Cambridge University Press, 1986).

24. Neil Brenner, "Global cities, glocal states: Global city formation and state territorial restructuring in contemporary Europe," *Review of International Political Economy* 5, no. 1 (1998), 1-37; Bob Jessop, "Capitalism and its Future: Remarks on Regulation, Government and Governance," *Review of International Political Economy* 4, no. 3 (1997), 561-581; Bob Jessop, "A Neo-Gramscian Approach to the Regulation of Urban Regimes: Accumulation Strategies, Hegemonic Projects, and Governance" in *Reconstructing Urban Regime theory: Regulating Urban Politics in a Global Economy*, ed. Mickey Lauria (Thousand Oaks: Sage, 1997).

25. World Bank, *The State*, 2.

26. Todd, "Megacity."

27. John Friedmann, "The World City Hypothesis," *Development and Change* 17, no. 1 (1986), 68-84.

28. Graham Todd, "'Going global' in the semi-periphery: world cities as political projects. The case of Toronto" in *World Cities in a World-System*, eds. P. Knox and P. Taylor (Cambridge: Cambridge University Press, 1995), 198.

29. Sassen, *Cities in a World Economy*; Todd, "'Going global'."

30. It could be argued that this success was also partly influenced by the election of the Parti Québécois on a nationalist platform, the result of which was a migration of headquarters from Montreal to Toronto after 1976.

31. Todd, "'Going global'."

32. Pierre Filion, "Rupture or Continuity? Modern and Postmodern Planning in Toronto," *International Journal of Urban and Regional Research* 23, no. 3 (1999), 421-445.

33. Ibid., 432.

34. Kipfer and Keil, "Still Planning to be Different?"

35. Filion, "Rupture or continuity?" 433

36. Kipfer and Keil, "Still Planning to be Different?"

37. Todd, "Megacity."

38. Greater Toronto Area Task Force, *Report*, 34.

39. Ibid., 37

40. Todd, "Megacity."

41. Ibid.; Keil, "Dissociated Governance."

42. Sassen, *Cities in a World Economy*, 123, emphasis is original. There is often a racial divide between low-end and high-end jobs. Global cities are also attracting points for international migration. Toronto is not the exception; it is an important destination point for international migrants, particularly from the Caribbean, South East Asia, Latin America, and China. In 1996, 40 percent of the GTA was foreign-born. See Kipfer and Keil, "Still Planning to be Different?"
43. Greater Toronto Area Task Force, *Report*, 46.
44. Frederick G. Gardiner, quoted in Timothy J. Colton, *Big Daddy: Frederick G. Gardiner and the Building of Metropolitan Toronto* (Toronto: University of Toronto Press, 1980), 94.
45. Todd, "Megacity."
46. Isabel Bassett, Letter posted on the C4LD list server (March 18, 1997).
47. Transition Team, *New City New Opportunities*, 91.
48. Keil, *Los Angeles*, xix.
49. Transition Team, *New City New Opportunities*, 36.
50. Greater Toronto Area Task Force, *Report*, 59.
51. C. Richard Tindal and Susan Nobes Tindal, *Local Government in Canada*, Fourth Edition (Toronto: McGraw-Hill Ryerson Limited, 1995), 198.
52. Ibid., 5.
53. Ibid., 193.
54. Ibid., 194.
55. Isin, *Cities Without Citizens*, 18.
56. Keil, "Globalization makes states"; Sassen, *Cities in a World Economy*.
57. Keil, "Dissociated Governance."
58. Yasemin Soysal, *Limits of Citizenship: Migrants and Postnational Membership in Europe* (London and Chicago: University of Chicago Press, 1994); Brenner, "Global cities."
59. James Holston and Arjun Appadurai, "Cities and Citizenship," *Public Culture* 8, no. 2 (1996), 199.
60. Keil, *Los Angeles*; Magnusson, *The Search for Political Space*.
61. Magnusson, *The Search for Political Space*, 73.
62. Ibid., 106.
63. Ibid., 11.
64. Brenner, "Global cities," 17.
65. Keil, "Globalization makes states," 617.
66. Magnusson, *The Search for Political Space*, 63.
67. Ibid., 10.
68. Ibid.
69. Jessop, "A Neo-Gramscian Approach," 58.
70. Ibid., 60.
71. Ibid., 65.
72. Magnusson, *The Search for Political Space*, 62.
73. Sewell, "Welcome to the Year."
74. Jacobs, *Deputation*.
75. Colin Vaughan, "Toronto can learn much from German city-states," *Toronto Star* (November 8, 1999).
76. Keil, "Globalization makes states."

CHAPTER 4

# THE LIVING SPONGE OF THE CITY: THE POLITICS OF EVERYDAY LIFE

The city is like a sponge, absorbing various flows of ideas, capital, labour, religions, lifestyles, peoples, colours, neon tubes, trees, speed. The city is a living sponge clogged with the legacy of the past, the intensity of the present and dreams of the future. City life penetrates your skin, breathes in and out of all social realities, be it economic transactions, knowledge formation, creation, innovation, political deliberation, reproduction, cultural deployment, identification. It is more than a point on a map. The city, in fact, is a place that moves, teaming with activity that perpetually reshape the landscape. Italo Calvino tells the story of Kublai Khan, an Emperor who thought of all his conquered cities as pieces on a chessboard. However, his emissary Marco Polo always reported on his visits to the new corners of the empire with an abundance of details, giving depth to the black and white squares of the Emperor's chessboard. As a result, the story says, Khan realized that a city is more than a flat square piece of wood, a simple location on a map; it is a dynamic place of interaction. It is an urban living sponge.[1]

Moving from the global arena to the very local spaces of everyday life, this chapter first discusses how urbanity was defined by Citizens for Local Democracy and the tensions created with suburbanity. This progressive middle-class conception of urbanity can be traced back to the reformist regime of the 1970s. Through its struggle for preserving and enhancing this regime, Citizens for Local Democracy asserted the importance of the politics of everyday life in the face of the provincial government's rationale for globalization. C4LD was in fact able to redefine the issue of globalization as urban, or perhaps was it mostly as a local issue?

*Urbanity and the Politics of Everyday Life*

Why has it become so hip to mock suburban life and to glorify downtown cappuccino lifestyle? Urbanity has come to be seen as a "solution" to suburban alienation, to urban sprawl, to segregation, to economic development, and to boredom. The concept of urbanity is also confused with other notions such as cosmopolitanism, centrality, or civility. One can think of Jane Jacobs' appreciation of the subtle ballet of street life; of the New Urbanist School calls for gentrification and the creation of town-community life in cities; or middle class resettlement in downtown areas. One can also think of Richard Sennett's work on the loss of public life and civility. Or again, Iris Marion Young's call for city life and differences as opposed to exclusive communities.[2] The "normative ideal" of city life, she holds, is a form of social relations defined as the being-together of strangers. It is based on the principles of social differentiation without exclusion, that is the ability to live with difference. The ideal city life also relies on a variety of multifunctional streets, parks, and neighbourhoods. Young adds a third principle, city life needs to be acknowledged as an erotic form of human life. It is erotic in the sense of attraction to the other, of the willingness to live with different people. Finally, city life is based on publicity, that is on access for everyone.

An urban world is a cosmopolitan world. Cities are cosmopolitan, a bursting of demographic, cultural, ethnic, class, and sexual diversity. But an urban world is also a public and civic world. The word city says it: *city, civic, civilisation, citizen*. An urban world is a world in which, ideally, citizens participate in public life, negotiate the rules of the game and the codes of interaction in society. Urbanity does indeed encompass the negotiation of this civic code of behaviour, but reducing it to this would be a mistake. Civic codes of behaviour tend to represent middle-class values and norms, and can be exclusive for those who do not have the cultural, historical, economic, and educational background to really understand and participate in this joyful civic play.

Kevin Robins critically describes this culture of cities understood as a consensual belief in public spaces, bringing a sense of territorial identity, and encouraging regeneration and gentrification in order to create a city of consumers. Urbanity in the strict sense of centrality and civility, is a means to "safely [consign] to the historical dustbin" all "the "dysfunctions" of the "modernist city." "Disenchantment is buried in the past, while the future can be unproblematically given over to the project of re-enchantment."[3] It is thus very important to avoid reducing urbanity to centrality, civility, or cosmopolitanism, because it could easily become an exclusive and parochial device.

Nevertheless, this definition of urbanity has numerous merits as a possible solution to alienation, depoliticization, and oppression. One should not reject the idea of urbanity based on civility, centrality and cosmopolitanism, as discussed by Sennett, Jacobs and Young, to name just a few. The urban, however, is much more than this. Henri Lefebvre depicts a textured notion of the urban. For him, urbanity means a set of specific practices different from rural practices. The world is not merely rural or industrialized anymore, it is mostly urbanized (a change in perspective formalized with the United Nations World Conference on cities, Habitat II). In Richard Sennett's words, the urban is "a mode of cognition which originates in the Capital City and then spreads out through the whole society, so that regardless of geography, people come to see with the eyes of those who come from a special place."[4] Urbanity is not only a lifestyle located in cities, but a worldview diffused throughout society, in the Annex of Toronto, the financial districts of global cities, but also in Kapuskasing, Temagami, or Brampton.

The city evolves through a variety of scales, actions, biographies, and schedules. How can we understand this complexity? Geographer Jacques Lévy suggests to consider different scales and speeds of time.[6] For instance, to get to really know the urban space, what could be better than to follow one person around, to focus on "individual time"? The local space, the house, the neighbours, work on the "time of the everyday," of daily routines. The regional scale is part of someone's imaginary in so far as the region becomes the "context" of one's life, a point of identity closer than that of national or transnational space.

The everyday—where the urban is lived, experienced, created—overlaps with other speeds and spaces in the city. Fundamentally, the everyday is a very rich site of resistance to the overwhelming power of globalization because of its raw simplicity and concrete-ness. The everyday is where you and I live most of our life. It is where we can feel at home, where we have control over our schedule and the spaces we use, build, appropriate. Because we are soaked into it, we tend to dismiss these spaces and times as trivial, ordinary, unimportant. But I wish to argue that the everyday is in large part defining the city, it is its life and its dynamism. The everyday is an important point for political mobilization, from mothers organising a co-operative kitchen, to marches planned on the corner of a kitchen table, to discussions about the impacts of government policies, to solidarity for the neighbour who lost his job, to the education of our children, to the consumption of international products, to the fascination with Disney cartoons or the church choir. The everyday is real for all of us, it is concrete, we can touch and feel it, it is material. Urbanity in this sense is very much about materiality. It entails going "beneath the surface" of the readily observable world to understand what is really going on behind the glossy picture of the global city.

It is in the sites of everyday life that people "produce space" to use Henri Lefebvre's expression.[7] People shape their surroundings according to their needs, desires, and visions. They appropriate spaces that were used differently by different peoples, sometimes peacefully, and sometimes violently. People create different spaces through their daily trajectories around the city. They represent these spaces according to the perception they have of them, and according to the image they want to project. People describe their houses, their street, their neighbourhood, and their city. Artists, writers, tourists or marketing agencies represent spaces in the city perhaps differently than people living there would. Squatters appropriating a shelter, a gang taking over a street, planners designing the city, you and I landscaping our front yard, or sending a postcard of our city to friends, these are but only a few examples of what it means to produce space. Space is not a fixed, dead, container in which life unfolds. Space is not only the territories drawn on world maps, or the surface of the earth. It is something that we create in our daily social interactions, putting to life the built form that humans shaped over the course of history. Space is also something we create in our mind, something that we perceive and then represent in writing, in arts, in tourist promotion, in architectural and urban design or planning...Spaces are constructed by the stories told about them, they are constructed in our memories. The values, images, and rules that shape one space provide a sense of orientation and identification. In certain spaces, people feel more secure because they know where they are and who they are.

The construction, production, and appropriation of places are at once a physical, imaginary, and lived process.[8] Place-building can be a means of resistance. When gays mark a neighbourhood with rainbow flags, or when people take over a public park and organize demonstrations, place-building is a physical resistance tool. When immigrant groups advocate for better services, or when women challenge the paternalistic domestic division of labour, people are building spaces for minorities in the imagination of the mainstream society, they are working on carving a space in the social mentality.

From these examples, it is clear that spaces cannot be captured by rigid divisions of the world in isolated scales, from the local, to the provincial, the national, to the global. Jessop's concept of "governing complexity" requires envisioning the state as a network of different institutions, public or private, at different scales and levels. It challenges the bureaucratic notion of strictly defined hierarchical levels of organization. Similarly, spaces are produced at all scales, from the home to the globe. Jacques Lévy suggested different speeds of time useful to grasp the spaces of the city, from the individual time of someone living the city, to the time of the everyday, to the historical context.

Some spaces are public and others are private. The boundaries between them is constrained by the rights to property, whether one thinks of the small scale in terms of the right to own land, or the larger scale, as the right to secure a national territory. In this sense, spaces are regulated by the legal and political system, and everyday life evolves in and through these legal rules, be they territorial sovereignty or private property. Ownership, legally defined, is a means to pragmatically manage spaces, to control entries and exits, activities and violence. We all live with these legal boundaries projected on spaces in our daily lives. Some of us respect them, some of us trespass them, some of us challenge them, and some of us create new boundaries and new spaces. When people put together a co-operative, for instance, or when a group of artists turn a loft into an art gallery at night, they are creating new spaces, with new boundaries determining who is in the group and who is not. Resistance groups often produce space in this way, by establishing boundaries in which adherents feel secure to act, talk, and live an alternative life. Ownership of a space, be it *de jure* or *de facto*, legally or extra-legally, does not only provide a sense of security by defining the inside and the outside, but also can provide a feeling of accountability and identity. Territorial identity is the best example of this. People feel this corner of the earth is theirs, because they feel something for it. Territorial identity fosters a sense of collective ownership of space.

Ownership, nevertheless, can be a powerful means of repression. If territorial boundaries, in our political system, give the national state monopoly over legitimate violence, it also gives it tremendous power in defining who is in (the citizens) and who is out (the strangers, the aliens). In the same way, gated communities clearly define who has the right of passage and who does not. When everyday life is enmeshed in so many boundaries, it can create a sense of alienation. The image of a suburban housewife trapped in her house on her private lawn is often given as an example of this darker side of ownership.

The establishment of boundaries, or control over the existing one, is a good way to understand urban politics. Politics takes place somewhere, in the city, in the sites of everyday life, in our homes, on the streets, in the parks, in our minds. Boundaries, rules, tacit conventions, emotions, laws, walls, maps, all these elements shape political struggles:

> A politically significant *locality* at present is both a zone of intervention within a global process and a moment of meaning within a larger movement. It is a spot/moment at which people come together—as at Tiananmen Square or Sproule Hall—for action that may resonate far beyond. In the affairs of a global city like Brisbane [or Toronto], these significant sites/ times appear and reappear as people recompose their political location. The spots/ moments/locales at which people can act effectively are constantly changing.[9]

## *Megacity Toronto: A "Class Struggle in Space"*

Kipfer coined this very effective expression to describe the Megacity saga.[10] It could indeed be interpreted as a struggle about who will get to shape the city to its vision. On the one side, the Harris government framed its amalgamation package in terms of enabling Toronto to compete on the global marketplace and this implied being able to exhibit the golden badge of "Toronto, global city." Becoming "global" gave the city a passport to the world of wealth, prestige and entertainment. This rosy picture of the world city, this fascination for *grandeur*, is reflected in the term "Megacity" to describe the new Toronto. On the other side, opposing the government's "boosterist" view, Citizens for Local Democracy criticized specifically the name of the new city on the grounds that the "Megacity" is too remote from people. Furthermore, identity, history, and memory were too important to allow the re-appropriation of the name Toronto as the name of the new Megacity. John Sewell said: "Usually, when new cities are forged, they are named after the person who did it. Hence, Ho Chi Min City, or Stalingrad. This one should be called Harris City, or Leachtown. They shouldn't be allowed to steal our name."[11] But more importantly, the privileging of the global city image was resisted by C4LD on old reformist grounds. John Sewell, after all, was the mayor of Toronto from 1978-80, years of the progressive reformist movement. Resistance against prioritizing financial districts, highway development, and office spaces over small-scale urban life in central neighbourhoods, is based, to a certain extent, on homeowners' concern with property values and the quality of life.

The city is an intense site of contestation, not only between the poor and marginalized on the one hand and the very rich on the other. But the city is also a site used by urban middle class people as a tool to regain control over daily life. Downtown old neighbourhoods have slowly been re-appropriated by the middle class. In the name of downtown's dense pattern of interaction in which their children are exposed to a "particular texture of daily experience" in a place that "has a history and has ghosts,"[12] the urban progressive middle class has learned to use municipal institutions to secure this lifeworld. The Megacity saga was in fact the clash between these two visions of the city: the global city versus the hipness of urbanity constructed by a particular segment of the middle class.

Within Citizens for Local Democracy, urbanity was mostly understood in terms of centrality and civility. C4LD's rhetoric was imbued with fear of losing Toronto's exceptional quality of life by North American standards. It fought the government's boosterist discourse about the global city by giving examples of American inner-city problems, illustrating the loss of civility. Many feared Toronto would become as derelict as Harlem, the Bronx, the core of Chicago or Detroit:

> When I was at school in Albuquerque, New Mexico (way back when) the town was a veritable jewel in the sun—a main street with all kinds of fascinating stores, neighbourhoods with cozy adobe houses, Old Town with its smell of pinon wafting over colonial buildings. When I visited again 15 years later, I was shocked to find the downtown completely gone—looking like a bombed out area, all boarded up, literally overrun with rats.
>
> That has been the American experience repeated over and over again, the one we have avoided here in Toronto. Those of us who have participated in making our town livable will not allow that to happen here. We've been through too much to get to where we are, the place known the world over as the most livable city in the world, to see it demolished through the current ideology of privatization.
>
> Yes, it's true there are experiments going all over the U.S. in privatizing welfare, privatizing Schools, privatizing Hospitals, but that's not us, not here, not now, not ever. We will be a beacon here

> in Toronto. We will stand fast and continue on the route to sane policies for a sane society. We are educated people here, the product of our school system and our municipal and provincial institutions. We are quite capable of determining our own future within the kind of enlightened, intelligent representation we have had up to now.[13]

This kind of perspective on Toronto illustrates the progressive urban middle-class regime that evolved over the years through the work of people like those active in C4LD. It was a regime prioritizing universal health care and quality education, public services and redistribution. Proud of this regime, C4LD's rhetoric was very focused on centrality. Many arguments against amalgamation were framed in opposition to suburban life. John Sewell himself in many public speeches built his argument against amalgamation in terms of older city progressive and specific needs versus suburban conservatism.[14] Many deputations presented to the hearing committee emphasized differences in lifestyle between central urbanity and suburban sprawl. As an example, in C4LD's first newsletter, we can read:

> Metro is made up of two different kinds of cities. The older compact city with its active street life and jumble of shops, apartments, houses and businesses defines Toronto, East York and York—and contrasts sharply with the newer suburban style of low density, single use areas, and reliance on automobile travel, found in Scarborough, North York and Etobicoke.[15]

To dichotomize centrality/suburbanity in such a clear-cutting manner precludes the possibility of viewing the region as a whole, in all its diversity. After all, urbanity is a way to understand and live in the world that is diffused throughout society.

This kind of "class struggle in space" was particularly acute in Toronto, but it is occurring in many other global cities. As Beauregard bluntly notes:

> Liberals, progressives and neo-conservatives struggled over who would represent the city…Hardly the defenders of the city we would expect, neo-conservatives now do more than advocate for real estate investment and tax subsidies. They also claim to be the champions of the city's urbanity…This has left liberals and progressives with an urbanity that privileges groups that are disappearing and morally problematic while marginalizing groups that are politically powerful and ascendant. The liberal-progressive view no longer

> resonates...Although the euphoria surrounding the cities in the 1990s might well be short-lived, it is defining a new politics of urbanism whose momentum belongs to neo-conservatives. All others are critics or spectators.[16]

The old City of Toronto's progressive urban regime developed since the 1970s was characterized by a number of progressive policies and a very open tradition of public participation. For instance, more than 130 boards of management, city agencies, and advisory committees benefited directly from members of the public.[17] Moreover, countless public meetings, task forces, special committees, working groups, roundtables, community groups, city programs, constantly sought citizen input. According to a report by the old City of Toronto, the City has done three important things: 1) provided opportunities to contribute to the decision making process; 2) provided resources like meeting space, staff time, translators, and in many cases a budget; 3) made citizen input central to its decision making process and created a culture where a community-driven approach is valued.[18] Specifically progressive grant programs included: AIDS Prevention Program, Breaking the Cycle of Violence Grants, Daycare Grants, Drug Abuse Prevention Program, Homeless Initiative Fund, Major Recreation Grants, School Food Program, Toronto Art Council Grants, Youth at Risk Grants, and Occupancy Cost Grants (i.e., the use of City property by non-profit corporations at below market charges). The same report notes that while Toronto has only 27% of Megacity's total population, it has 44% of single, low-income households, 80% of people with HIV/AIDS, and 90% of hostel beds for people at risk.[19]

A quick look at voting patterns in downtown Toronto over the past years, clearly demonstrates its progressive bent. Three downtown provincial electoral districts have been decisively New Democrat since 1987, while four others have been oscillating between the Liberal Party and the New Democratic Party (Table 5). It is the potential loss of that progressive haven that many downtown residents feared. As Sewell put it:

> There's a dangerous and frightening edge to provincial politicians saying that people and their opinions don't matter. That approach encourages an attitude of not caring about other people. The first people to suffer from this attitude are those already at the margins, those who don't have much a voice in society...Yet an uncaring kind of society is what the provincial politicians are signaling when they reject people's opinions. It is this moral spillover of Bill 103 that really frightens me.[20]

| Provincial Electoral Districts | Provincial Parties | 1999 | 1995 | 1990 | 1987 | Average |
|---|---|---|---|---|---|---|
| Beaches-East York | PC | 29.8 | 38.4 | 17.0 | 19.5 | 26.2 |
| | LIB | 21.8 | 24.6 | 26.7 | 39.2 | 28.1 |
| | **NDP** | **45.9** | **34.0** | **50.4** | **38.3** | **42.5** |
| Broadview-Greenwood | PC | 24.7 | 29.5 | 10.3 | 15.7 | 20.1 |
| | LIB | 24.7 | 24.7 | 27.4 | 43.3 | 30.0 |
| | **NDP** | **46.9** | **42.8** | **54.8** | **38.8** | **45.8** |
| Davenport | PC | 15.8 | 17.0 | 4.9 | 5.7 | 10.9 |
| | **LIB** | **49.7** | **39.1** | **39.4** | **55.8** | **46.0** |
| | NDP | 31.8 | 39.5 | 49.1 | 35.6 | 39.0 |
| Parkdale-High Park | PC | 30.2 | 34.4 | 15.3 | 22.2 | 25.5 |
| | **LIB** | **54.9** | **30.6** | **33.8** | **44.9** | **41.1** |
| | NDP | 11.8 | 32.5 | 45.1 | 29.8 | 29.6 |
| St. Paul's | PC | 40.4 | 40.1 | 27.6 | 30.3 | 34.6 |
| | **LIB** | **50.6** | **34.1** | **34.9** | **46.6** | **41.6** |
| | NDP | 7.1 | 23.1 | 31.4 | 21.0 | 20.7 |
| Toronto-Rosedale | PC | 29.9 | 33.9 | 20.9 | 25.2 | 27.6 |
| | **LIB** | **38.9** | **31.0** | **35.5** | **48.3** | **38.4** |
| | NDP | 8.8 | 32.3 | 37.1 | 23.4 | 25.4 |
| | Ind(Sewell) | 19.3 | -- | -- | -- | -- |
| Trintiy-Spadina | PC | 20.5 | 19.1 | 9.2 | 10.5 | 14.8 |
| | LIB | 27.5 | 31.8 | 35.1 | 45.5 | 35.0 |
| | **NDP** | **47.9** | **45.2** | **49.4** | **40.1** | **45.7** |

**Table 6:** Downtown Toronto Provincial Electoral Results 1987-1999
*Source: www.electiosontario.on.ca, www.c4ld.org*

This tension between higher levels of government and citizen control over municipal institutions has been operating since the beginning of British colonial city-formation in Canada. As Engin F. Isin puts it, "the essence of this tension was how to build cities without citizens, for it was thought that without building cities it was impossible to establish a civilization, whereas at the same time it was recognized that cities must be subordinated to the centralized authority."[21]

Citizens for Local Democracy was able to reassert the importance of the politics of everyday life in Toronto. They insisted on political mobilization to carve a space in civil society, as well as on the use of municipal institutions to further progressive goals and enhance the quality of life. The movement was able to get the authorities to pay attention to what the city means to its inhabitants.

### *Mobilization and Political Action*

The Megacity saga, through the leadership of C4LD, has awakened a considerable segment of the population usually politically inactive. "The huge upsurge of civic awareness in Toronto—the passion of ordinary people are bringing to the defence of their city—is monumental." This is how John Barber, one of the few columnists supporting the fight against amalgamation, described political motivation for Toronto.[22] There was a strong sense of living through a historic struggle, and that provoked a public discussion on civic space in Toronto. The day following the referendums organized by the former local municipalities; journalists were quite enthusiastic about Toronto's political awakening:

> If there was anything worth celebrating yesterday morning, it was the citizenry, awake—if only for the moment—to the truth that they, not the politicians or planners or architects or urban activists, are Toronto's true creators each day, and always.[23]

> Imagine politics without politicians. The Megacity fight hasn't been politician-free, but the politicians have been chasing the people, trying either to catch up with merger opposition or to trip up citizens' efforts to scuttle the plan.[24]

Political mobilization is an attempt to affect history. When the political scene explodes in vitality, in vibrant moments where performative citizenship is clearly enacted, the sparkling flame is most often the perceived necessity to react to broader forces. The Megacity saga indicates that people were furiously reacting against the loss of control over their daily lives. Social movements, for the most part, also operate in reaction to an enemy, be it capitalism, patriarchy, pollution, or racism for example. Political mobilization also comes out of quests for emancipation and human flourishing. In other instances, mobilization springs out of the desire to build alternative worlds. Mobilization thus happens within a social context, either in reaction to an abrupt disruption of everyday life and politics, like in the case of the Megacity saga, or as a means to emancipate from the heavy burden of oppression. As Kipfer mentions, any form of collective action relies on organization, resource-mobilization and identity formation.[25] It relies on people putting their time and energies to encourage other people to join the collective efforts to emancipate or resist. It appeals to people's memory of previous excitement in marching shoulder to shoulder on the street, of group solidarity, of rewarding efforts.[26] Collective action also explodes when the glass is too full, when people can't take it anymore. This can happen in an organized, orderly fashion, as it was the case during the Days of Action in Toronto, or as a spontaneous moment of insurgency, like we saw during the Los Angeles riots of 1992. One way or the other, collective action is spurred by hopes of something better, ideas of a possible better world, and lots of frustration. Action is a way to set something new in the world without knowing the long-term consequences. Nobody really knows what will happen next, but energies, excitement, and frustration are boiling; something needs to be done!

Different theories seek to understand why and how people get together to collectively act, resist or emancipate. Basically, a first set of explanations focuses on the individual motivations behind collective action and the means to gather resources. A second set of explanations emphasizes the visionary aspect driving collective action, where people decide to act in order to change the course of history. A third set of explanations explores the psychological elements at play to push people to act collectively, particularly in the context of a crowd. At a smaller scale, other explanations focus on communication and interaction between individuals.[27]

Three elements seem relevant here: 1) the kind of collective action emerging depends on the context; 2) individuals have moral motivations to act to transform things or to resist in the loss of control over their lifeworld; but these individual motivations are shaped by people's relations with one another, thus the problem becomes one of co-ordination of actions rather than the mere aggregation of individual actions; and 3) the very fact of people acting together changes the context in which collective action emerged, whether the actions taken were successful or not, because it creates a new space for action.[28] When people get together to resist oppression or a sudden transformation of their lifeworld, something happens, whether their tactics and strategies are successful or not. As activist Toronto Sandra Van writes:

> The strength of advocacy work, or any other civic participation activity rests with the process. It is here that we can easily identify and achieve meaningful milestones. Through participation, we know that there is a strong possibility that community residents will develop skills, increase their capacity to mobilize and bond as a community. Often times, important skills are developed through the experience and in our case, many learned how to navigate and participate within the bureaucracy maze.[29]

Collective action also depends on the political, social, and cultural system as well as on the conjuncture. The "political opportunity structure" in place[30] will influence the kind of mobilization that is most likely to arise. In the case of the Megacity saga, the instability brought by the Harris amalgamation act and the relative stability and institutionalization of the urban progressive middle class in the former municipal structure, have largely determined who would be part of political action. Citizens for Local Democracy is a movement situated in the action space of the progressive urban middle class, even if not all its adherent are part of the middle class. Many of them were active in creating the urban progressive regime in Toronto and reacted to its disappearance.

Middle-class activism pops up momentarily and then tends to fade away. Most middle-class people are not usually willing to give up their houses, their jobs, their living standards, to create a commune or live in a local barter community. They will support social and environmental causes, promote social justice and human rights, provide a critical education to their children, but most of them do not like to be labelled activists, or associated with the stereotype of a "young hippy-ish radical person wearing sandals or eating bird seeds." Middle-class people will most of the time integrate activism in their daily lives, slightly modifying it when they feel efforts can change things, like recycling, volunteering in different social organizations, use the public transit instead of having two cars, avoid buying clothes made in sweatshops, buy a coffee for a homeless person, buy organic vegetables, vote on the Left, and invest in institutions they feel they can shape to their progressive goals. They rise up occasionally against outrageous events, but mostly against imposed changes in their daily lives, disturbing their human, social, and moral principles. The Megacity saga was one of these moments of intense political mobilization that rose out of latent energies in the city. Middle-class activism is an insurgent form of political action, a moment of explosion in the life of the city, an explosion of rage against reactive transformations or sometimes against the lack of it. Insurgent moments emerge out of the sites of daily life because these are sites where life can easily condense and explode intermittently. Outside these explosive insurgent moments, the politics of everyday life is also a creative site. The city is created by its inhabitants on a daily basis, created by the inhabitants' use, production, and appropriation of space. In this sense, the city is an evolving project.

The politics of everyday life, for Citizens for Local Democracy, tended to privilege the use and preservation of municipal institutions over these incremental acts in daily life. This meant focusing on the "right *of* the city" rather than the "right *to* the city."[31] C4LD is very concerned by the weakening of municipalities as an important progressive political tool. In fact, Donzelot would argue that this shift from a focus on the *quality* of the city in the face of industrial development to the city's *political capacity* to create mutual obligation in society (*faire société*), constitute the new urban question today.[32]

Overall, Citizens for Local Democracy offered a good response to the discourse of globalization. It effectively redefined the field of social conflict as *urban* and this process fostered a sense of collective identity among the urban progressive middle class in Toronto. Middle-class urbanism is not a revolutionary movement. Nevertheless, it is a form of political activism that is very powerful.

### *The Politics of Everyday Life in Regional Perspective*

With its energies focused on the spaces of daily life in the city, Citizens for Local Democracy struggled for a local notion of urbanity. In opposition, the provincial government explicitly located Bill 103 within the discourse of neoliberal globalization. In contrast with previous attempts to restructure governance in the Greater Toronto Area, amalgamation for the Harris government was not meant to solve problems of urban sprawl and environmental degradation. It was rather a neoliberal means to re-scale the state in order to respond to globalization. As Isin and Wolfson note:

> The GTA Task Force was about a problem—regional governance—that the Tories were not interested in addressing. The Harris government was not interested in bringing about a

> new style of governance to the entire region. If anything, it was interested in *reducing* governmental regulation in the GTA which it believed was hampering economic growth.[33]

For the neoconservative government, amalgamation would solve many economic problems in Toronto by reducing costs, eliminating duplication and red tape, and depoliticizing the planning process through the reduction of the number of local politicians (from 106 before amalgamation to 57, and 44 for the 2000 elections). Harris hired a consulting firm to evaluate these savings.[34] Amalgamation was also the only way for poorer municipalities within the metropolitan region to absorb the extra financial burden of downloading imposed by the provincial government. Indeed, Harris promised in his 1995 electoral campaign to eliminate Metro Toronto. However, the government quickly realized that eliminating the upper-tier governance structure would entail ending tax pooling and thus poorer municipalities would not be able to receive extra financial responsibilities. Furthermore, eliminating Metro Toronto would entail important difficulties in dividing already-integrated services such as policing, fire, or welfare back into six municipalities. The Harris government was convinced that the global economy requires big and strong cities. It was important for Toronto to project the image of a large global city to the rest of the world.

The government's decision to amalgamate only Metro Toronto and its rejection of the GTA Task Force proposals for regional governance, puzzled most observers. Harris chose the wrong scale for restructuring. Neoliberalism would dictate smaller competitive units rather than bigger bureaucracies.[35] But a competitive advantage in the global economy seems to point more towards broader regional co-ordination in order to include exurbs and edge cities where growth occurs. Keating argued that:

> The proposed megacity is too small to meet the needs of truly metropolitan planning, and far bigger than needed to realize economies of scale. Indeed, it may be the size at which dis-economies set in. It is at best an irrelevance, and at worst a diversion of community energies from the real tasks of creating a viable city for the next century.[36]

The GTA Task Force proposal of a Greater Toronto regional government coupled with measures to strengthen local municipalities seemed to respond to prevalent necessities of the global economy. The Report established four principles for restructuring governance: co-ordination, fairness, efficiency, and accountability and responsiveness.[37] With language such as "the structure should respect the importance of the urban core," or "the structure should be as understandable as possible to promote public access, participation, and accountability," or again "it should respect and accommodate diversity and be responsive to the needs and preferences of local communities," the GTA Task Force proposal generally gained the support of the progressive urban middle class.[38] But politically, Harris could not support such a proposal. He faced strong opposition to the elimination of two-tier governments in the exurbs (the 905 area), where he won almost all the seats in the 1995 and all of them in the 1999 provincial elections. Moreover, Isin and Wolfson point out that the proposed Greater Toronto Council would have represented almost half the population of the province, and its Chairman would have been as powerful as the premier of Ontario.[39]

Regardless, Harris had to act. The momentum created by the GTA Task Force and increasing pressures from Metro Toronto pushed the government that prides itself for "getting things done" to find another solution.[40] The decision to amalgamate the six local municipalities and Metro Toronto was a means to act, while sparing the 905 area where the government had a strong political support. Bill 103 was also a way to keep the electoral promise of eliminating Metro Toronto. Politically, amalgamating Metro Toronto was a way to dilute the voice of progressive councillors in downtown Toronto. But as Isin and Wolfson remind us, this was not simply a personal vendetta against progressive politicians in the old City of Toronto. Instead, the Harris government firmly located its actions within the discourse of neoliberal globalization:

> When amalgamation is viewed from the perspective of regulation theory, one sees that the role of government has changed in recent years. Add to that the effects of globalization on Toronto's economy and it becomes clear that the Harris government's support of capital took the form of reducing the extent of the workers' social contract. In order to do that municipal social service programs, especially those provided by the former City of Toronto, had to be curtailed.[41]

Citizens for Local Democracy did not put as much emphasis on the effects of globalization on Toronto, nor on the centrality of this element in the Harris government's decision-making rationale. Despite the movement's great success in asserting the politics of everyday life, to focus on the local and on its disappearing governance structure was a strategically weak response to the provincial government's manipulation of new urban dynamics such as demographic changes and labour market restructuring. The Harris government directly addressed issues of economic growth in order to respond to fears about unemployment and fiscal constraints. Characteristic of populism, and albeit in a neoliberal fashion, the government still addressed tensions and fears caused by economic restructuring and demographic changes. C4LD chose to address these issues by blaming globalization and corporate capital for social problems. The solution proposed was to reassert the importance of everyday life, social movements, and municipal institutions. I would concur with this argument. However, a complementary regional vision is also necessary, for municipalities are not perceived as strong enough to engage in the powerful game of the global economy.

There is an abundant literature on the importance of regions. Economic geographers have demonstrated the importance of regional clusters such as Silicon Valley and the Third Italy.[42] But in terms of regional political structures, the literature abounds with studies on the importance of regional co-ordination for success in the global economy. There is, according to Scott, a "new global mosaic of regional economies." The forces reshaping the economic geography of the world propel political responses that are usually lagging behind economic changes. But once regions acquire a "collective consciousness of themselves, not just as grateful recipients of individual business investments, but also as guarantors of overall local competitive advantage and economic performance," then they become more aggressively politicized.[43] This politicization is further stimulated by the development, most notably in Europe, of jurisdictional powers to the meso-level of regions. Regions now represent identifiable if limited communities of interest, identity, and organization. The GTA Task Force Report sought exactly this: "The new structure should encompass the interests of the entire city-region and foster a common regional identity and purpose."[44] The Task Force understood quite well the importance of a political structure to secure Toronto's competitive advantage.

Despite its ubiquity in academic discourse, regionalization is an issue that is still very loosely defined.[46] Conceptually, Keating proposes to differentiate between the region as a territorial space (i.e., as an intermediary level between the state and municipalities); the region as a functional space for planning, state intervention, and co-ordination; and the region as a political space where legitimate decisions are made through public debate.[49] He argues that regions are formed by a top-down process instigated by the state, on the one hand, and a bottom-up process mobilized directly on the ground, on the other hand. Toronto was long known for its regional perspective. Already in 1943, the City of Toronto voted to apply to the province for the annexation of the built-up areas outside the city in order to resolve problems arising out of the population boom and urban expansion. An upper-tier regional governance structure was finally created in 1953, the Municipality of Metropolitan Toronto. But with the goal of fostering economic growth, and well-known for facilitating suburban expansion, Metro Toronto spurred much anger in the City of Toronto.[47] In 1967, the thirteen lower-tier municipalities were consolidated into six. The City of Toronto lost its majority in Metro Toronto with only twelve votes out of thirty-three. Meanwhile, in 1966, the provincial government embarked in regional planning and designated the Toronto Centred Region (TCR). It covered 14,000 $km^2$ and was three times the size of the current Greater Toronto Area (GTA), which was formalized in the 1980s. The four regional municipalities surrounding Metro Toronto (York, Durham, Peel, Halton) were created in the 1970s.

Bottom-up mobilization has also developed over the years and peaked during the GTA Task Force consultations. However, the decision to amalgamate only the core area of the GTA and the overwhelming resistance to it, polarized the debate around issues of localism versus regionalism, and urban versus suburban interests. It prompted a "class struggle in space" which dominated the debate and pushed to the background regionalist mobilization.

While this chapter was devoted to exploring the politics of everyday life in urban settings, it is also crucial not to lose sight of the bridges between local everyday politics and regional mobilization. The case of Toronto illustrates more a split between urbanity and suburbanity that has shadowed the grassroots regional agenda. Kipfer and Wirsig convincingly argue that perhaps strategically important social spaces are not only located in downtown neighbourhoods but in the postwar suburbs of Etobicoke, North York, or Scarborough. The postwar suburbs have been politically neglected by downtown-centred progressive forces in Toronto from the beginning of the reform years.[48] The politics of everyday life is often contrasted with institutional politics and forces such as globalization. However, Citizens for Local Democracy was quite successful in transgressing this dichotomy through both insurgent political actions and a deep understanding of institutional politics, particularly at the municipal level. Unfortunately, the movement was unable to break out of the local to address regional issues. Such a shift in scale does not preclude working in the sites of everyday life, it simply means placing them in a broader spatial, political, social, and economic perspective.

## NOTES

1. Italo Calvino, *Les villes invisibles* (Paris: Éditions du Seuil, 1972).
2. Jane Jacobs, *The Death and Life of Great American Cities* (New York: Vintage Books, 1961); Richard Sennett, *The Fall of Public Man* (New York, London: W.W. Norton & Company, 1974); Iris Marion Young, *Justice and the Politics of Difference* (Princeton: Princeton University Press, 1990).
3. Kevin Robins, "Prisoners of the City: Whatever Could a Postmodern City Be?" in *Space and Place Theories of Identity and Location*, eds. E. Carter, J. Donald, and J. Squires (London: Lawrence & Wishart, 1993), 312.
4. Sennett, *The Fall of Public Man*, 239.
5. Henri Lefebvre, *Writings on Cities*, translated and edited by Eleonore Kofman and Elizabeth Lebas (Oxford: Blackwell, 1996).
6. Jacques Lévy, "Urbanité: à inventer," *Annales de la recherche urbaine* 64 (1994), 11-16.
7. Lefebvre, *The Production of Space*.
8. Ibid.
9. Magnusson, *The Search for Political Space*.
10. Kipfer, "Urban Politics in the 1990s."
11. John Sewell, *Address to the Monday night meeting* (February 3, 1997).
12. Caulfield, *City Form and Everyday Life*.
13. Cohen, *Deputation*.
14. Among other speeches, see John Sewell, "Democracy in Toronto," prepared for the International Symposium on *The Rights to the City: Citizenship, Democracy, and Cities in a Global Age* (York University, June 26-28, 1998).
15. Citizens for Local Democracy, *What's Going On Here?*
16. Beauregard, "The Politics of Urbanism."
17. City of Toronto, *Community Consultation*, 28-29.
18. Ibid., 15.
19. Ibid., 10.
20. John Sewell, *Address to the Monday night meeting* (April 14, 1997).
21. Isin, *Cities Without Citizens*, 88.
22. Barber, "Sending a message."
23. John Bentley Mays, "Monitoring Toronto's pulse," *Globe and Mail* (March 5, 1997). It is interesting to note that the journalist differentiates between citizens and urban activists.
24. Michael Hollett, "Oh What A Night," *Now Magazine* (March 6-12, 1997), 17.
25. Stefan Kipfer, "Global-city politics in the 1990s: Facing the dilemmas of oppositional politics in Toronto," prepared for the Annual Meeting of the Research Committee 21 of the *International Sociological Association* (Berlin, July 21-23, 1997).
26. Tarrow, *Power in Movement*.
27. See John D. McCarthy and Mayer N. Zald, "Resource Mobilization and Social Movements: A Partial Theory," *American Journal of Sociology* 82, no. 6 (1977), 1212-1241; Alain Touraine, "An Introduction to the Study of Social Movements," *Social Research* 52, no. 4 (1985), 749-787; Herbert Blumer, *Symbolic Interactionism* (Englewood Cliffs: Prentice Hall, 1969).
28. Eder, *The New Politics of Class*.

29. Sandra Van, "Getting to the Root of the Matter?" *Cityscope*, Newsletter of the Community Social Planning Council of Toronto (Winter 1999-2000), 19.
30. See D. McAdam, J. D. McCarthy and M. N. Zald, eds., *Comparative Perspectives on Social Movements* (Cambridge: Cambridge University Press, 1996).
31. Engin Isin, "Rights to the City," prepared for the International Symposium on *The Rights to the City: Citizenship, Democracy, and Cities in a Global Age* (York University, June 26-28, 1998).
32. Donzelot, "La nouvelle question urbaine."
33. Isin and Wolfson, *The Making of the Toronto Megacity*, 69, emphasis is original.
34. KPMG, *Fresh Start: An Estimate of Potential Savings And Costs From The Creation of a Single-Tier Local Government for Toronto, Executive Summary* (www.kpmg.ca/centre/vl/cg_gta.htm, January 27, 1997).
35. The Tiebout model states that fragmentation of the governance structure is preferable for individuals because they can chose where to live depending on the "basket of services" offered to them in return for the level of taxes they are willing to pay. Fragmentation, in this public choice model, is essential to maintain competition between municipalities and give individuals the possibility to "vote with their feet." See Charles Tiebout, "A Pure Theory of Local Expenditures," *Journal of Political Economy* 64 (1956), 416-424.
36. Michael Keating, "Megacity: not big enough, not small enough," *Globe and Mail* (February 4, 1997).
37. Greater Toronto Area Task Force, *Report*, 161-162.
38. Ibid.
39. Isin and Wolson, *The Making of the Toronto Megacity*.
40. Ibid.
41. Ibid., 76-77.
42. See for example, Michael Storper, *The Regional World: Territorial Development in a Global Economy* (New York, London: Guilford Press, 1997).
43. Allen Scott, *Regions and the World Economy: The Coming Shape of Global Production, Competition, and Political Order* (Oxford: Oxford University Press, 1998), 149.
44. Greater Toronto Area Task Force, *Report*, 161.
45. See for example, David Rusk, *Cities Without Suburbs*, Second Edition (Washington, DC: The Woodrow Wilson Center Press, 1995); Neal R. Peirce, with Curtis W. Johnson and John Stuart Hall, *Citistates: How Urban America Can Prosper in a Competitive World* (Washington, DC: Seven Locks Press, 1993); L. J. Sharpe, ed., *The Government of World Cities: The Future of the Metro Model* (New York: John Wiley and Sons, 1995); Christian Lefèvre, "Metropolitan Government and Governance in Western Countries: A Critical Review," *International Journal of Urban and Regional Research* 22, no. 1 (1998), 9-25.
46. Michael Keating, "Les régions constituent-elles un niveau de gouvernement en Europe?" in *Les paradoxes des régions en Europe*, eds. P. Le Galès and C. Lequesne (Paris: Éditions La Découverte, 1997), 26-29.
47. Warren Magnusson, "Toronto," in *City Politics in Canada*, eds. Warren Magnusson and Andrew Sancton (Toronto: University of Toronto Press, 1983), 110.
48. Stefan Kipfer and Karen Wirsig, "Politics and Possibilities: Re-Living the Suburban Paradox in the New Toronto," *Inura Bulletin* 17 (Fall 1999).

CHAPTER 5

# FROM CONSTITUTIONALISM TO THE RIGHTS TO THE CITY

Citizens for Local Democracy created an intense moment of political mobilization in Toronto. These were very exciting times. The new city of Toronto was incorporated, a new Megacouncil was elected, and the city is now going through the transition. C4LD did not succeed in stopping amalgamation. Nevertheless, it played a crucial role in shaping the political discourse in Toronto, in Ontario, but also in academia. The movement provides a rich illustration of current struggles over the redefinition of democracy, citizenship, and governance in the city. It is an interesting case study because with the raging tide of identity politics, social movements tend to underestimate the regulative presence of the state.[1] C4LD focused most of its energies on local governance. To choose the city as a starting point for the redefinition of democracy, citizenship, and governance, entails thinking through the tension between being a resident of the city and being a legal citizen of a country. C4LD inscribed "new" unexpected issues on the public agenda and opened up a window of opportunity for a redefinition of citizenship and democracy in this age of globalization. It pushed away concerns about efficiency and fiscal neatness and swept Toronto and Ontario with concerns about fairness, quality of life, and participation.

It is no surprise that in these times of political and economic restructuring, and in these times of massive socio-demographic transformations, many cultural claims emerge to challenge a system of governance based on sovereign nation-states. Membership in society can no longer be contained in the legal notion of citizenship. Citizens for Local Democracy and other activists around the world re-appropriate more than ever the concept of citizenship enlarging its meaning to fit with the values of human rights, local rights, the rights to the city. In the wake of these important trends, a "citizenship debate" has developed in academia. From theories of multiculturalism, cosmopolitanism, radical democracy, to deliberative democracy and the revival of civil society, citizenship has become a new rallying point for the Left, which is increasingly facing a Right gaining in influence and seemingly better equipped to respond to the changing political and economic climate. This chapter offers a theoretical look at the changing discourse on democracy and citizenship. In the next chapter, this theoretical discourse will be tied back to the political reality of Toronto and the impact of Citizens for Local Democracy.

For all their nuances, theories of democracy and citizenship meet on their grounding in constitutional/legal systems of rights. Regardless of how open to diversity these democratic theories claim to be, they all remain closely attached to a conception of citizenship clearly defined in legal/constitutional and national terms. Citizenship is seen as a privileged status that provides rights to its holder as well as membership on a national territory. But it is one thing to have rights well defined in legal terms, it is another story to *enact* these rights, and to eradicate discrimination and inequalities.

I wish to argue that a reliance on political liberalism is not sufficient anymore. Liberal definitions of citizenship have not been able to truly incorporate differences of identities, lifestyles, and cultures. Liberalism states that everyone is equal, but inequality still persists in reality. Consequently, many people have become politically active specifically to defend different identities. They have been asserting the right to their differences on the public place, thus exploding the ordered and formal conception of democracy. The terrain of politics, in other words, has been broadened to include personal attributes and lifestyles as possible political claims in the public sphere. Hence gender politics, ethnic politics, gay and lesbian politics, all have brought their personal issues on the public agenda. Politics draws on everyday life. And identity is the new buzzword on the political scene.

The politics of identity is a response to liberalism, which places the individual as the primary social unit, as the core of social, economic, and political life. In terms of identity, liberal politics has been reduced to the struggles surrounding the legal definition of the individual. Who is the ideal Canadian citizen? Understanding citizenship simply as a legal status, consequently, alienates many people who do not fit in the norms of ideal Canadian-ness. It has failed to foster a sense of belonging and civic and political participation. A citizen writing a letter to the Now Magazine that analyzes the lack of participation of Black people in the struggle against the Megacity, illustrates this lack of substance in legal citizenship:

> The absence of African Canadians, their reluctance to select themselves as citizens of a broader polity is not the fault of a particular organization. Rather, it speaks to a deep and troubling alienation of the black community from the civic life of this city...Issues that affect them as "African" are addressed, those that affect them as "Canadian" are not. This may be the most unfortunate consequence of our multicultural policies.[2]

Legal citizenship frameworks may be considered more and more obsolete if we consider the set of rights and privileges formerly restricted to citizens, which are now accorded residents without the citizenship status. This extension of citizenship social and civic rights to residents challenges the idea that citizenship brings about a series of privileges by virtue of membership and loyalty to a society. Furthermore, some countries, like Denmark, give the right to vote in local elections to non-citizens after three years of residence. Moreover, the current wave of neoliberalism has prompted a redefinition of the means to foster social justice and solidarity. Two major forces influence these discussions. On the one hand, the discourse of human rights pushes towards an expansion of people entitled to social rights, be they citizens or not. On the other hand, the neoliberal discourse pushes for a contraction of available social rights for everyone, be they citizens or not. One way or the other, there seems to be a strong trend towards less rigidity in the definition of the boundaries of citizenship.

The anxiety caused by changing civic norms and rules of the game, by multicultural negotiations of everyday interactions, and by the dissolution of national identification, has often been translated into urban violence, civic apathy, and exclusion. Toronto illustrates all these shortcomings of the liberal democratic governance structure. It is the stage of diverse expressions of identity and differences that challenge the legal definition of Canadian citizenship. It is a host for many new members politically active and for "formal" citizens politically apathetic. It participates in intense discussions on social services and entitlement to them. It is even victim of urban violence and the fragmentation of identity allegiances. It is in the city that we see the incompleteness of modern constitutionalism when it comes to envisioning "performative" citizenship practices. The right to inhabit the city, to be there, to be politically active regardless of one's legal status, and the right to claim rights, are written nowhere in constitutional definitions of citizenship. This chapter discusses ways of bringing the "citizenship debate" down in the city.

### *Critiques of Modern Constitutionalism*

In an excellent book entitled *Strange Multiplicity*, philosopher James Tully affronts the difficult question of the role of constitutionalism in an age of diversity. "Can a modern constitution recognize and accommodate cultural diversity?" he asks.[3] Tully begins with the assumption that cultural diversity is more than just a factual reality; it is a legitimate "constitutional problem" of our time. His central argument is that by approaching constitutionalism from the perspectives of those who have been erased from the 19th century "universal" declarations of human rights (Aboriginal peoples, cultural minorities, women, and so on), one can uncover the constitutions' current limitations and open new paths for "mutual recognition" and "cultural accommodation." Unlike postmodern political and legal theorists, Tully does not advocate for the "deconstruction" or even abandonment of constitutions as "meta-narratives." Instead, for him "the question is whether a constitution can give recognition to the legitimate demands of the members of diverse cultures in a manner that renders everyone their due, so that all would freely consent to this form of constitutional association."[4]

While Tully's treatment of constitutionalism in an age of diversity provides very interesting venues for addressing the question of constitutional and political legitimacy at the dawn of the 21st century, I argue here that it is not sufficient. Before turning to this argument, let me first recall the principal aspects of modern constitutionalism and their different interpretations. To begin with, modern constitutionalism developed around two basic principles: 1) the equality of independent nation-states; and 2) the equality of individual citizens. And, as Tully reminds us, it also developed in opposition to imperialism.[5] He identifies seven features of modern constitutionalism: 1) it is based on the principle of popular sovereignty; 2) it contrasts with "ancient" constitutions; 3) it assumes regularity and organization; 4) it is based on a theory of progress and modernization; 5) it follows the republican model; 6) it assumes that each state possesses an individual identity as a nation; and 7) this "foundational moment" is a precondition to democracy rather than being part of it.[6]

The modern constitution, in sum, imposes a framework for maintaining order in a "constructed" polity (the nation-state). Henceforth, it assumes a bounded society; the state is seen as a container for the flourishing of the people.[7] In this age of globalization and transnationalism the premise of a well-defined sovereign state over which constitutional principles have exclusive authority is a contestable statement. Importantly as well is the assumption that modern constitutionalism sharply divides the public from the private spheres. The feminist critique challenges this sharp distinction.[8]

The underlying purpose of this reflection is to question the assumption present in the "citizenship debate" that it is theoretically possible to resolve the problems of exclusion, inequalities and political apathy without engaging with the relationship between constitutionalism and concrete urban political practices. There is, in other words, a gap between the abstract/theoretical peoplehood of the constitution and the actual reality of living together, the "we-ness in present time." This is what Lee calls the "performative paradox."[9] Put differently, the performative paradox is in fact a tension between civic and political actions and the imposed constitutional democratic order. Reality is far from being abstract enough to fit in the normative democratic models of modern constitutionalism. It is important to articulate the constellation of procedures, theories, conditions, and resources through which democracy is enacted, understood, organized, and represented.

Tully's work on constitutionalism in an age of diversity provides an interesting attempt to go beyond the dichotomy between the legal constitution (*de jure*) and political practices (*de facto*). By uncovering the many "hidden constitutions" that developed along with modern constitutionalism, he emphasises the importance of the *application* of constitutional law; i.e., the common law and the jurisprudence.[10] These many interpretations of the constitution intersect with both *de jure* and *de facto* practices. This "common constitutionalism," as he calls it, is based on three conventions: mutual recognition of the groups, continuity of interpretations, and consent. In his words: "Constitutional 'conventions' in this common-law sense are norms that come into being and come to be accepted as authoritative in the course of constitutional practice, including criticism and contestation of that practice."[11] In legal practice, however, a law is supposed to be interpreted according to the "author's intent." Nevertheless, the law is usually read to the benefit of the client. It is the text as read, not as written, that becomes law. Legal texts are indeed read in a context very different from that of their creation. Hence, they should be viewed as interactive and adaptable to the constantly changing social base. Tully's response to the performative paradox of modern constitutions is to propose a constant constitutional dialogue, bringing dynamism to the legal text.[12]

A second critique of modern constitutionalism is not pursued by Tully, but it was central to Citizens for Local Democracy. Modern constitutionalism conceives the state as a monolithic entity solidly anchored in nationally bounded societies. In doing so, it focuses on the national state at the expense of other levels of governance, be it the transnational, the regional, or the local. Moreover, the monolithic and clearly identified state implies a rigid distinction with what is non-state, that is civil society and the private sphere. "The state is not a monolith. It is, rather, to be viewed as a complicated political, legal, and administrative jigsaw puzzle that contains a vast number of pieces," writes Andrew Kirby, "Most important is the recognition that the state apparatus is not a bureaucracy confined to office buildings in a capital city."[13] The state apparatus, therefore, cannot simply be imagined as a pyramid in which the Federal government has power over provinces and provinces over municipalities. Instead, the state is a complex field of tension between different levels of government, between state institutions and civil society, between state institutions and global pressures. Henceforth, municipalities are located in the national state apparatus itself; they do not simply constitute a lower level of government. Municipal governments are vectors through which the national state penetrates into society, into everyday life, and vice-versa. This conceptualization of the state apparatus is helpful to capture democracy, as it is practised, not only as it is defined in constitutions.

Tully's argument serves Citizens for Local Democracy's struggle very well. It was particularly striking during the Citizens' Legal Challenge. The case was built on the argument that Bill 103 was violating the *convention* of reasonable autonomy for local governments in Canada. The argument was built on traditions and practice to counter the actual wording of the constitution stating that municipalities are "creatures" of the provinces. In other words, C4LD relied on what Tully calls "common constitutionalism." The movement further adhered to the second critique of modern constitutionalism concerning the view of the nation-state as a unified and centralized sovereign unit. Seeking more power for municipal institutions displaces the authority of other levels of government.

If modern constitutionalism is lacking the means to address the current conjuncture, what else should help define what it means to be a citizen within the belly of a global monster? That is not to say that we ought to reject all of its principles and procedures. Human rights, governance by the people, universal suffrage, free periodic elections, freedom of speech, assembly, association, freedom from arbitrary arrest, public independent media, non-partisan legal system, are certainly fundamental attributes of a valuable redefinition of citizenship. What is needed is a critical assessment of the enactment of the principles of liberal democracies already institutionalized. How are they performed in reality? How is liberal citizenship practised *de facto*?

### *Democratic Theories*

In 1963, T.H. Marshall proposed to extend citizenship not only to political and civil rights but also to social rights.[14] As Turner notes, "at the heart of Marshall's account of citizenship lies the contradiction between the formal political equality of the franchise and the persistence of extensive social and economic inequality, ultimately rooted in the character of the capitalist marketplace and the existence of private property."[15] Marshall's trilogy of rights has been criticized, and the "citizenship debate" still struggles with means to link the basic infrastructure of democratic citizenship inscribed in constitutions and citizenship politics and practices. Most new citizenship conceptualizations attempt to link the passive view of citizenship-as-a-status with the construction of active citizenship in political participation. It is Habermas who noted that "the institutions of constitutional freedom are only worth as much as a population makes of them."[16]

Attempts to overcome this performative paradox have led to a dual concern in the "citizenship debate": 1) attempts to respond to the "ills" of democracy in "the age of diversity" through a focus on citizenship identity; and 2) attempts to link rights and responsibilities through a focus on civic virtues and political participation.[17] The first concern is related to a willingness to justify liberal norms institutionalized in the nation-state and the international regime, whereas the second concern deals more directly with the question of the distribution of the privilege to participate in democratic governance for the sake of social unity and the stability of the regime.[18]

### *Liberal Multiculturalism*

Multiculturalism and multiethnicity are factual realities in many contemporary societies. In this "age of diversity," multicultural perspectives on citizenship are genuine attempts to understand, manage, and respond to this factual diversity. What has by now become "buzzwords" in the citizenship debate are in fact theoretical and practical endeavours to respond to the factual socio-cultural diversity by developing the idea of a functional multicultural democratic polity; by "stipulating the procedural and substantive principles ordering a multicultural society."[19] The argument stresses that by recognizing differences and by installing mechanisms to ensure the effective participation of different groups, liberalism could overcome the performative paradox.

Indeed, multicultural perspectives are political commitments that range from conservative, to liberal and radical on the political spectrum. According to Goldberg, conservative multiculturalism promulgates "assimilation," i.e., "the extension of established values and protections over the formerly excluded group."[20] Liberal multiculturalism, for its part, promotes "integration," i.e., tolerance and recognition of differences without breaking established boundaries between groups. Will Kymlicka illustrates this view quite famously in Canada.[21] He distinguishes between nations and ethnic groups. The former are groups that share a common history, that are institutionally complete, occupy a homeland, and share a distinct language. Quebec would be an example. In the latter, difference is manifested mostly in the private realm and should not affect institutional integration in public life. An example of ethnic groups would be the Chinese-Canadian community. From these two types of differences stem three distinct types of rights. The first ones are self-government rights that would apply to nations or peoples. The second are polyethnic rights, which grant minorities the possibility to express their cultural pride. The third type of rights are special representation rights which serve to remedy the "unrepresentativeness" of the political process by reserving a certain number of seats in the Legislature to persons with particular features (race, gender, class, regional origin, etc.). To the argument that group recognition will harm social unity, Kymlicka responds that these rights are in fact demands for inclusion (with the exception of self-government rights) based on ideas of social justice. A shared conception of justice does not necessarily lead to a sense of solidarity. What is needed is a collective will to live together that can only be stimulated by a recognition of differences and a commitment to build mechanisms to provide more access to disadvantaged groups.

Iris Marion Young is an essential figure for both liberal and radical multicultural perspectives. She is cited as an authority by many in the citizenship debate. And as exemplified below, she is sometimes cited by authors with different positions. In fact, depending on their position, authors will emphasize one of the following two related aspects of her work on the "politics of difference":

1. Inspired by feminism, Young develops the idea of an "heterogeneous public," which rests on the principle that no persons or actions should be forced into privacy, therefore no subjects should be a priori excluded from public discussion. Given that the primary meaning of "public" is openness and accessibility, a democratic public sphere cannot imply the homogeneous adoption of a universal standpoint in contemporary diverse societies.[22] This aspect is central for perspectives on radical democracy discussed below.

2. To guarantee the openness and accessibility of all to the public sphere, a democratic polity should provide specific mechanisms for oppressed groups to enter the decision-making process. Institutional mechanisms such as support for group self-organization, group analysis in policy making, and group veto power regarding specific policies that affect a group directly should be developed.[23] Differentiated group representation is not the same as proportional representation; it is closer to the formation of group caucuses, or requirements of group representation in leadership positions. Young warns that these special mechanisms should be designed solely for social, not ideological or interest groups. She defines a social group as "a collective of people who have affinity with one another because of a set of practices or way of life; they differentiate themselves from or are differentiated by at least one other group according to these cultural forms...Shared political and moral beliefs, even when they are deeply and passionately held, however, do not themselves constitute a social group."[24] It is this aspect of her work that clearly situates Young within liberal multiculturalism.

### *Radical Democracy*

The fact that radical and liberal theorists both refer to Young as an authority is not a paradoxical conceptual slippage. Radical theorists of citizenship and democracy acknowledge their faith in basic liberal democratic principles of equality and liberty.[25] Liberalism has valuable principles to offer, it is argued, but they need to be radicalized. In their 1985 book on hegemony and democracy, Chantal Mouffe and Ernesto Laclau began to develop what has by now been known as radical democracy.[26] Their starting point is a poststructuralist critique of essentialism. More specifically in later work, Mouffe takes issue with Rawls.[27] She posits that neutral and rational "objectivity," the basis of

Rawls' and others' liberal theory of justice, is always invested with power, thus it is always political. What is decided to be "objective" always includes in itself what was excluded when making the original choice (the "constitutive outside"). It follows from this that power is not something floating outside people and enacted in interactions and relationships, but rather something inherent to each person's identity by the very fact of having made a choice between one identity and another. At the social scale, this confluence between what is labelled "objective" and its inherent power is what Mouffe and Laclau have termed "hegemony," simply because it is disguised as "objective," thus not contestable. This anti-essentialist point of view reminds us that for democracy to exist, no one should be able to claim control over the foundation of society. Democracy is not a perfectible dream of harmony, because perfect harmony will always silence the constitutive outside. Liberal rationality and neutrality hide the unrecognized excluded option.

Mouffe criticizes Rawls' liberalism for essentializing norms and identities by camouflaging them as rationality. In his work, Rawls establishes "reasonable" grounds of co-existence of differences by seeking a moral consensus on "fundamental principles." In this sense, those who do not accept liberal principles are "unreasonable." But the elaboration of these liberal principles is "the expression of an eminently *political* decision, not a moral requirement," answers Mouffe.[28] Democracy is not a fixed system that maintains order. It is, according to Mouffe, a regime in which participants accept a "grammar of conduct."[29] And there will be as many interpretations of this grammar of conduct as there are interpreters, and this is not necessarily harmful for democratic governance for it is based on a common will to live together without demanding overriding loyalty to hegemonic moral values. She writes, "Why is there not any space left in his [Rawls] well-ordered society for contested interpretations of the shared liberal democratic principles?"[30] Rawls eliminates the element of undecidability in his liberal democratic utopia. Mouffe contests the idea that there could be a rational definite solution to pluralism and justice. Democracy is an unending process that cannot eliminate conflict and antagonism.

On these grounds, Mouffe also criticizes Young's solution of group-differentiated citizenship. Already-constituted groups and interests cannot provide a new hegemonic radical common ground of equality without creating new identities and interests. Groups need to cross-fertilize, to modify one another. Goldberg expands on this idea by replacing the liberal multicultural principle of integration with that of "incorporation," which "involves the dual transformations that take place in the dominant values and in those of the insurgent group as the latter insists on more complete incorporations into the body politics and the former grudgingly gives way."[31] With its emphasis on dialogue, hybridity and heterogeneity, Goldberg's principle of incorporation highlights conflicting interactions between evolving *fluid* groups.

What Goldberg calls "multicultural heterogeneity" based on incorporation is in fact akin to Tully's insistence on "interculturalism." He states that "cultural diversity is a tangled labyrinth of intertwining cultural differences *and* similarities, not a panopticon of fixed, independent and incommensurable worldviews in which we are either prisoners or cosmopolitan spectators in the central tower."[32] Similar to Goldberg, Tully criticizes liberal multiculturalism for reifying cultural groups in an effort to extend citizenship rights without modifying existing majority norms and values. More than the constitutional right to speak and act politically within prevailing institutions, what is needed, he contends, is a continual intercultural constitutional dialogue that transforms the institutional framework.

Overall, we could organize the radical and liberal multicultural perspectives according to the two concerns presented at the onset of this literature review.[33] In responding to diversity, liberal multicultural perspectives are animated by the will to legitimate liberal norms and values. Kymlicka's, and to a lesser degree, Young's work illustrate this first concern very well. However, their work has been criticized and developed by others such as Mouffe and Goldberg, who seek to create a new radical democracy based on social unity in diversity. Radical democracy calls for the development of a new radical hegemonic common ground for democratic governance. This means conceptualizing citizenship as an articulating principle "to which we constantly refer" when acting politically, "but that can never be reached."[34] In this view, Kymlicka and Young's call for group-differentiated citizenship cannot offer the "solution" to calls for recognition of differences because it lacks a radically new common ground. Radical democracy begins with the acceptance of individual rather than group differences. The emphasis is placed on the right to individually interpret the "grammar of conduct" more than on political participation. In sum, radical democracy does not necessarily aim at resolving the "performative paradox." Instead, radical democrats insist on the necessity to create a democratic framework that can adapt to continual contestation of the very political norms upon which it rests.

### *Deliberative Democracy and Civil Society*

Let us now turn from attempts to reconceptualize liberalism to address the question of diversity, towards a body of literature inspired by Habermas and explicitly concerned with the question of civic virtues and social unity through political participation. Perspectives on "deliberative democracy" are the clearest endeavour to address the performative paradox of modern constitutionalism identified at the beginning of this chapter, that is the dichotomy between legal principles and political practices. Habermas posits that "democratic will-formation draws its legitimating force not from a previous convergence of settled ethical convictions but both from the communicative presuppositions that allow the better arguments to come into play in various forms of deliberation and from the procedures that secure fair bargaining processes."[35] The legitimacy, stability, and unity of the political system, in the deliberative model, would emerge out of collective interchanges rather than out of some moral notion of the common good. The public sphere, in this view, is the site where democracy is enacted, and out of which ethical principles emerge *politically*.

The stability of the political system thus requires a certain institutionalization of deliberation in the public sphere by providing the necessary conditions for participation, association, and expression. The only benchmarks prior to deliberations, out of which ethical and moral principles collectively evolve, are clear and fair rules of procedure to manage the functioning of the public sphere. These procedures are based on the premise of mutual equal respect for all. Benhabib adds that all citizens have the right "to initiate reflexive arguments about the very rules of the discourse procedure."[36] Therefore, even basic human rights could be challenged, but paradoxically this would entail the suspension of democracy. In this sense, the strongest safeguards for democratic procedures are the moral principle of egalitarian reciprocity and the collective will to live under a democratic system.

Habermas writes that deliberative democracy implies a "decentred society" where the public sphere is defined much more broadly than according to the political centrality of the state. The public sphere, in fact, is composed of a plurality of associations. According to Habermas, the self-organizing principle of democracy can only be satisfied through the use of practical rationality. Deliberations are based on the cross-cultural use of rationality in argumentation. Practical rationality guides the process of give-and-take in a common loyalty to the best argument.

One of the basic critiques of the deliberative model of democracy is its inadequate response to the problem of exclusion and its difficulties to foster meaningful participation. Young criticizes the exclusionary bias entrenched in the deliberative model of democracy through the imposition of a culturally loaded and dominant communicative framework. The deliberative model adopts a Western, modern, and scientific conception of what debates ought to be. Deliberations are based on competition, combativeness, and assertiveness. Such a conception privileges those who are competitive and know the rules of the game. Moreover, dispassionate and disembodied speech is privileged. These are culture and gender specific rules.[37]

### *Cosmopolitanism and Human Rights*

Radical democracy means giving up on the dream of a "place called home," to use Honig's expression, a place where one can retreat from the conflicts of the public sphere.[38] The home and the private sphere are politicized. Similarly, at another scale, this entails for cosmopolitanism, rejecting the idea that the national constitution is a "vouchsafe" for the "privilege of withdrawal" from the chaos of global political and economic life. Therefore, the boundary between the national state and the global arena is blurred and in constant state of flux. Contrary to the liberal distinction between these spheres, for cosmopolitanism, such fuzziness does not lead to a lack of democracy as long as the regime respects individual autonomy. The individual right to autonomy of choice is different from the definition of an exclusive sphere like the home or the nation-state. In this sense, argues Appiah, cosmopolitanism is perfectly compatible with liberal individualism. He writes, "the cosmopolitan ideal—take your roots with you—is one in which people are free to elect the local forms of human life within which they will live."[39] Hence, cosmopolitanism is located within the individual as a normative set of values and choices. But just like in radical democracy, citizens need to adhere to a common "grammar of conduct" to "share the political culture of the state. And sharing that political culture does not require them to be centred on it, and certainly does not require them to be centred on a culture wider than the political. What *is* essential is only—though this is, in fact, a great deal—that all of us share respect for the political culture of liberalism and the constitutional order it entails."[40]

Cosmopolitanism is not about a privileged detachment from the local, but rather a reality of re-attachments, multiple memberships, and belonging at a distance. But as Robbins warns, "cosmopolitanisms" are more than "a gallery of virtuous, eligible identities," they point instead to a domain of contested politics. In other words, cosmopolitanism is not about an idealized global community or global consciousness. There are different types of cosmopolitanisms that compete politically. They are not simply a single normative ideal, "but habits of thought and feeling that have already shaped and been shaped by particular collectivities, that are socially and geographically situated, hence both limited and empowered."[41]

"Habits of thought and feeling" are difficult to detect empirically. Nevertheless, there is a growing literature on diasporas, networks, "postnationalism," etc. that attempts to empirically and theoretically come to grips with the effects of transnational flows, migration, and globalization.[42] Cosmopolitanism is a theoretical normative attempt to redefine liberal citizenship in this context. But perhaps the more empirically developed and the less abstract aspect of cosmopolitanism is the growing international human rights regime.

Human rights, beginning with the United Nations Universal Declaration of Human Rights in 1948, are inspired by liberal rights originating in the French and American revolutions. They are not dependent on nationality or citizenship but on the notion of "peoplehood." Sassen holds that parallel to a developing international legal economic regime, the international human rights regime is also growing in strength and influence. She gives the examples of many conventions such as the International Convention adopted by the General Assembly of the UN (December 18, 1990) on the protection of the rights of all migrant workers and members of their families (Resolution 45/158), the Convention on the Political Rights of Women (1981), the opening of the Protocol to the Covenant on Civil and Political Rights (1976) enabling private parties to file complaints to the UN Human Rights committee, the International Convention on the Elimination of All Forms of Racial Discrimination (1965), etc. She writes:

> The growing accountability of the state to international human rights codes and institutions, together with the fact that individuals and nonstate actors can make claims on states based on those codes, signals a development that goes beyond the expansion of human rights within the framework of nation-states. It contributes to a redefinition of the bases of the legitimacy of states under the rule of law and the notion of nationality.[43]

David Jacobson advances a slightly different conclusion. The active role of nation-states in the expansion of the international human rights regime, to him, signals instead a strategic response to growing transnational challenges:

> Human rights codes are taking on such salience not because of any intrinsic normative concerns about human rights in the states involved. The rather marginal movements that devote themselves to human rights have not been a major factor either. International human rights have come to the fore as a result of the piecemeal and incremental strategies of states to confront growing transnational challenges.[44]

In other words, Jacobson argues that nation-states are not conceding authority to supranational institutions, but redefine their role from exclusiveness to inclusiveness. In fact, national legal institutions are still central to the enforcement of human rights. Jacobson converges with Sassen in stating that this very process redefines the notion of nationality. Rights are more and more granted, in his view, to "persons" according to the principle of residency, rather than to "citizens" according to the principle of nationality. This way, the state *includes* many more people in its legal web. Soysal confirms this statement with empirical data from different European countries.[45] There is a general trend toward a decline in naturalization rates.[46] Permanent residents and in some cases undocumented immigrants are "incorporated" in the host society.[47] She found that for access to social services, what is important is a physical presence and a legal status in the country. For economic rights, it is a legal status and the passage of time (with civil employment as a major exception). Even in terms of political rights, some countries grant local voting rights. Civil rights are most of the time guaranteed by constitutions. In Canada, for instance, the only rights exclusive to citizens are the right to mobility, the right to vote, and the right to be elected to the Legislative Assembly.[48] Citizenship as a legal status loses ground according to this perspective, which leads Soysal to propose a "postnational model of membership." Membership into a society should permit dual citizenship status and multiple status in terms of rights, distinguishing between nationality, identity and rights.[49]

Cosmopolitanism and human rights are still faithful to liberalism, but interestingly grounded in multiple regimes and allegiances. These perspectives are too often wrongfully accused of naively believing in the emergence of a "global community" or a "global super-state." In fact, their main motive is simply to challenge the modern constitutional assumptions about the absolute sovereignty of the nation-state.

Questions of diversity, globalization, migration and transnationalism have been central to the renewed interest in citizenship in academia. But, the perspectives reviewed in this section were in most parts silent about the concrete realities created by these phenomenon experienced in urban settings. Statements about the hollowing-out of the state, the loss of control over borders, and the emergence of a transnational legal regime, remain abstract without linking them to their materialization in most of the world's major cities.

*Urban Critiques*

> Although one of the essential projects of nation-building has been to dismantle the historic primacy of urban citizenship and to replace it with the national, cities remain the strategic arena for the development of citizenship. They are not the only arenas. And not all cities are strategic. But with their concentrations of the nonlocal, the strange, the mixed, and the public, cities engaged most palpably the tumult of citizenship. Their crowds catalyze processes which decisively expand and erode the rules, meanings, and practices of citizenship. Their streets conflate identities of territory and contract with those of race, religion, class, culture, and gender to produce the reactive ingredients of both progressive and reactionary political movements.[50]

Democratic theory necessitates a certain dose of normative or utopian plans, but it is often difficult to predict the feasibility of these normative frameworks. It is thus crucial to bring to the debate a crucial and usually ignored element: the urban lived experiences. The project of rethinking citizenship and democracy needs to explore "a realm of the possible that is rooted in the heterogeneity of lived experience, which is to say, in the ethnographic present and not in utopian futures."[51] Because current socio-political and economic trends are condensed within cities, they are particularly rich sites to explore the "ethnographic present." And because the typical of everyday life is obvious, assumed, and hard to detect, "it is often by their deformations and counters that we learn about them."[52] In an effort to resolve the performative paradox, Holston proposes to hunt for "situations which engage, in practice, the problematic nature of belonging to society."[53] He calls these situations the "spaces of insurgent citizenship," which include "the realm of the homeless, networks of migration, neighbourhoods of Queer Nation, autoconstructed peripheries, ganglands, fortified condominiums, employee-owned factories, squatter settlements, suburban migrant labour camps, sweat shops, and the zones of the so-called new racism,"[54] and we could add homeless campouts, the Democracy Parade, or a public gallery filled with people dressed in yellow...The academic citizenship debate, in other words, lacks this concern for the lived citizenship experiences condensed in diversified cities.

### *The Fluidity of Membership*

To define who is a member of a polity and the rights and obligations attached to this membership is the primary function of citizenship. Cosmopolitan writers have opened the door to a more fluid conception of membership by challenging the absolute sovereignty of nation-states on the definition of membership. Nevertheless, most of these writers usually do not address the "ethnographic present" condensed in cities. Perhaps we can begin here with the work of Hannah Arendt.

In the midst of her discussion of totalitarianism in the mid-20th century, Hannah Arendt initiated a reflection on the "right to have rights."[55] Considering the increasing number of "stateless people," Arendt wrote on the right to belong to a state, to a political community. More than "human rights," for Arendt, the right to have rights is a right to incorporation into a polity, a right to participate in the creation of a political and judicial situations.[56] Thus, more than mere individual rights, the right to have rights consists of the possibility for the individual to *act*. The right to have rights is a concept that breaks the static view of the modern constitution as a simple framework providing the necessary conditions for democracy and injects dynamism by emphasising the necessity to constantly enact the constitution in political practices.

Arendt depicts stateless people as active subjects in constant search of liberty, liberty attainable only through the incorporation into a political community. Their "presence-event" (always non-predictable), to use Caloz-Tschopp's term, disrupts the legal, philosophical and political categories of modern constitutionalism and forces the integration of movements and displacements into the concept of citizenship. Rights become attached to individuals according to "personal criteria" more than territory. Arendt, it is important to remember, writes during World War II, thinking about a transnational Jewish citizenship, independent of territory.[57] In light of more recent discussions of rights and democracy, such "personal criteria" might be taxed of essentialism as discussed above.[58] I suggest instead to take Arendt's concept of the "right to have rights" on the terrain of its implications for citizenship practices in urban settings. Rather than emphasizing the "personal criteria" of rights attached to individuals in their displacements and movements, what if we emphasized the integration of movement within modern constitutional definitions of citizenship? In this sense, the right to have rights would mean the recognition of residency, the right to "be here and there," the right of presence. This would mean respecting the "principle of welcoming." As Smaïn Laacher explains, hospitality, in contrast to welcoming, implies that the visitor ought to respect the internal affairs of the host. The guest acts as a spectator. While the "principle of hospitality" is a universal human right, welcoming remains under national jurisdiction. To welcome means to permit the incorporation of the stranger at home; it means recognizing the "permanency" of the stay and the right to act politically. Of course this means accepting the presence of the "stranger" and redefining politics, everyday life, and identity according to the relations between the indigenous and the new members of the polity.[59]

The right of presence is in fact the right to socially, culturally, economically, and politically *inhabit*. The right to have rights and the right to inhabit are also present in Henri Lefebvre's work on the "right to the city." The right to the city is a right of access to daily necessities such as housing, sanitation, health services, education, childcare, etc. It is also a right to claim rights regardless of one's legal status. Rights, here, are not only something citizens possess. Rights to the city are more about living in the city than about becoming a legal citizen of a country. "These rights," writes Holston, "generally address the social dramas of the new collective and personal spaces of the city, especially its impoverished residential neighbourhoods."[60] These new demands often result in new legislation, enshrining the "unprecedented participation of new kinds of citizens in making law and even in administrating urban reform and local government."[61]

Henceforth, membership could be defined according to residency criteria. Legally, "residency" means the factual physical presence of a person. However, it becomes clearer that "residency" means much more than the legal "permanent resident" status. It means, "inhabiting the city," "being-in-the-city." Such a broad category includes taxpayers, homeless people, immigrants (legal or not), and other people who have been living there long enough to call it home (this excludes tourists, but not students or temporary workers). Transient migrants are more difficult to categorize as residents if they are just passing by, but sometimes their "passing by" lasts many years, or sometimes they are forced back to this transient point by deportation, as in the case of the U.S.-Mexico border-crossing for instance.

To be a "resident" implies demonstrating some kind of loyalty to the polity, be it a very minimal indication of the intention to stay there for a reasonable period of time (as in the case of residency status in American states), or a more demanding statement of loyalty (as in the case of countries such as Sweden, Ireland, Denmark, Norway, or the Netherlands where voting rights are granted to non-citizens in local elections).[61] The time required to obtain such a status may vary in different settings, but the important factor is to demonstrate the willingness to become a member of the polity. As Iris Marion Young indicates, "membership in a social group is a function not of satisfying some objective criteria, but of a subjective affirmation of affinity with that group, the affirmation of that affinity by other members of the group, and the attribution of membership in that group by persons identifying with other groups."[62]

*Performative Citizenship*

The will to become a member of a polity, it should be clear by now, does not necessarily entail restrictions on mobility. Fluid membership, therefore, is about multiple status (legal and extra-legal), dual citizenship, residency in more than a single site, complex and multiple allegiances. Nevertheless, willingness to become a member remains an important element of membership, for it is a basic requirement of active political citizenship. Beyond liberal citizenship as a passive status, active citizenship is a set of performative rights and moral obligations that are negotiated through conventions by residents of a specific place. If membership is fluid, and if constitutional rules are in flux, then performative citizenship has to rely on obligations and not only rights in order to sustain the sense of solidarity and cohesion necessary for governance and redistribution. Performative citizenship is also a device to foster a sense of belonging to a place, to develop a stake in the polity. Citizenship thus becomes an expression of society rather than of the state, "an aspect of social relatedness" rather than "an inherent and natural property of individuals."[63] Performative citizenship is a new response to the performative paradox of modern constitutionalism. "Performed" rights that need to constantly be claimed and materialized expand the framework of liberal rights. These rights include rights to the city such as housing, for example, and the right to have rights and to be politically active. Affirming the importance of these rights and of creating space for claiming and materializing them is an important step. However, the difficulties of meeting, delivering, and monitoring them remains. As Rocco puts it: "the difficulty with this emphasis and interpretation, however, is that it does not address the connection between these enabling conditions and practices and the dimension of institutionalisation."[64] Henceforth, the opening of institutional and constitutional structures is another building element necessary for bringing the new citizenship debate down in the city.

### *Intercultural Constitutional Dialogue*

Performative citizenship, particularly in urban settings, challenges the organization of the nationally centred state. As it stands within the Canadian legal framework, municipalities are not vested with rights and obligations as legal corporations, like citizens who are individually vested with rights and obligations derived from the national state. Thus, inhabitants of a city are not vested with any rights as "citizens" of the city, but rather as citizens of the national state regardless of their dwelling place. However, the urban reality often disrupts the regular processes of democratic elections and bureaucratic administration. The city generates different legal regimes and tolerates certain forms of illegality that explode the rigid boundaries around nation-states and between different levels of government.[65] It follows that the fluidity of membership and performative citizenship have to rely on a flexible constitutional framework. Radical democrats insist on the necessity to leave open a space for the critique of the democratic rules and norms. Tully proposes more concretely to persistently stimulate an intercultural constitutional dialogue in order to sustain a healthy and inclusive democracy. But this is not easy to implement, because the idea of a well-bounded sovereign territory as a basic condition for democracy is so entrenched. Jessop addresses these difficulties by elaborating on what he calls the "governance of complexity," which means, placing boundaries of institutional jurisdictions not into administrative units, but rather to politicize them and thus to collectively determine the boundaries of moral obligation.[66] Who is eligible to rights, who is part of the trust network? These obligations should guide public administration and policy-makers, much more than administrative or jurisdictional borders. Such an arrangement does not mean the abolishment of all forms of social discipline and control, for sanctions and rules are necessary to avoid terrorism, dictatorship, and extreme violence. It means however, not locating the power to provide this security in well-bounded societies, for this is not the reality.

### *Towards a Lived Definition of Citizenship*

In concluding this chapter, I wish to engage a discussion on a very legitimate fear about the definition of citizenship proposed here. If citizenship is that inclusive, it might become totalizing and thus subject to dictatorial manipulations, because it is not clearly defined. In other words, why is such radical openness a desirable goal?

Many people would feel uncomfortable to radically opening citizenship to include all those living "here" in the city. This would imply dramatically open our borders to immigrants. In a society where people constantly attempt to define who they are collectively, cultural openness can be very scary. Cultural radical openness presents for many people a challenge to one's culture and self-identity, a challenge to the way things are and the way things work in one's homeland. Indeed, when the cultural majority shifts with demographic changes, people feel threatened. They talk about assimilation of these other groups into the essence of Canadian-ness. Clear boundaries define a society and provide to its constituents a sense of security and identity. It also provides the necessary institutions to organize society, for without a clear notion of where the polity begins and ends, it is difficult to govern it. Redistribution is difficult to imagine without a clear notion of who is in the group of citizens, who gives through income taxes and who receives through welfare benefits. A territorially well-defined society can assert who is in and who is out. This way, it provides basic security to its constituents who recognize their surrounding world and know the conventions to function in it. People in this polity developed the necessary skills to act in it, thus they have the necessary autonomy to live without constantly asking themselves what to do next and how to react when they don't know what is coming next. This basic security system, to use Anthony Giddens' expression, is enacted by practical gestures, habits, and routines that are there in the society as benchmarks and enable people to function.[67] In the face of changing demographic realities and shifting identity patterns, people feel a sense of despair and fear. The problem thus becomes one of co-ordination and co-existence rather than one of assimilation and integration. Because at the level of public discourse and legal frameworks, Canada will not adopt overtly racist policies, many people do not consciously believe that some people are inferior than others. But racism still exists. Why is that? Because people fear the loss of their own security system, and feel that their everyday life is changing, basic conventions are evolving.

This is a very difficult question. Why would openness, not only at the level of discourse but also at the level of political practice and thus changing the basic security system, be seen as a desired goal? The moral response would be to eradicate oppression and cultural imperialism. Although these fears are understandable, they do not necessarily represent what would really happen if we opened our borders and were receptive to important changes in our everyday lives. Even though interaction with people on a daily basis changes when the society changes demographically, it takes a long time to completely transform a society and modify all its conventions. The legacy of institutional arrangements, of the built environment of the city, of social rhythms and of the history of the society (history from all perspectives, not only from the mainstream), do not fade easily when there is a shift in the cultural background of the new majority of people. A place has ghosts, memories, ways of working, physical layouts, geographical characteristics that constantly speak to the newcomers about the people living there before them. The slow modification of social conventions is a process that takes place in the conversation between the newcomers and the people who were there before. It is not a process where there is a complete take-over of the place by another group.[68] Groups may appropriate places and shape them according to their cultural values, like in the cases of Chinatowns for instance, but these Chinatowns are not taking over the society and transforming it into a Chinese society. People modify their own cultural background when in contact with the host society. It is rather a process of hybridization. The problem is that oftentime the last society is not receptive to change its own cultural values in this process of hybridization. Can people really claim rights over a territory because they were there for longer than the newcomers? I don't think so. What people can claim is the right to negotiate with newcomers what the new rules of the game will be. And this means rethinking membership, institutions, constitutions, and political agency. The academic leftist discourse tends to avoid facing these fears, leaving open space for the populist Right to exploit them. But reality often surpasses academic and ideological discourses. Within the belly of a global monster, the vitality urban politics illustrates that many people are in fact living the culture, in all its diversity and openness.

## NOTES

1. Henri Lustiger-Thaler, "New Social Movement Discourse: The Unsolved Democracy" in *Organizing Dissent: Contemporary Social Movements in Theory and Practice*, ed. W.K. Carroll (Toronto: Garamond Press, 1992).
2. A. B. Stodart, "Letter to the Editor," *Now Magazine* (March 6-12, 1997), 10.
3. James Tully, *Strange Multiplicity: Constitutionalism in an age of diversity* (Cambridge: Cambridge University Press, 1995), 1.
4. Ibid., 7.
5. Ibid., 15.
6. Ibid., 62-70.
7. Peter J. Taylor, "The State as Container: Territoriality in the Modern World-System," in *Progress in Human Geography* 18 (1994), 151-162.
8. Amongst others, please refer to Nancy Fraser, "Rethinking the Public Sphere: A Contribution to the Critique of Actually Existing Democracy" in *Justice Interruptus: Critical Reflections on the "Postsocialist" Condition* (New York and London: Routledge, 1997); Chantal Mouffe, "Feminism, Citizenship, and Radical Democratic Politics" in *Social Postmodernism*, eds. L. Nicholson and S. Seidman (Cambridge: Cambridge University Press, 1995); Bonnie Honig, "Difference, Dilemmas, and the Politics of Home" in *Democracy and Difference,* for examples of this feminist critique.
9. Benjamin Lee, "Peoples and Publics," *Public Culture* 10, no. 2 (1998), 371-394.
10. Tully, *Strange Multiplicity*, 100.
11. Ibid., 116
12. Holston explains that the U.S. Constitution serves this interactive principle a little better than other constitutions. The U.S. constitution has imprecise provisions and is very distrustful of the very institutions it creates. It is not designed to provide a fixed blueprint in a desire to legislate the future. It has seven articles only, and twenty-six amendments, "which establish a trust that future generations of citizens have the ability and the right to make their own histories by interpreting what the master plan means in light of their own experience." See James Holston, "Spaces of Insurgent Citizenship," *Planning Theory* 13 (1995), 43. The Canadian constitution, in contrast, includes very specific provisions and a complex formula for constitutional change.
13. Kirby, *Power/Resistance*, xiv.
14. T.H. Marshall, *Sociology at the Crossroads* (London: Heinemann Educational Books, 1963).
15. Bryan Turner, "Outline of a Theory of Citizenship" in *Dimensions of Radical Democracy: Pluralism, Citizenship, Community*, ed. Chantal Mouffe (London and New York: Verso), 35.
16. Jurgen Habermas, quoted in Will Kymlicka and Wayne Norman, "Return of the Citizen: A Survey of Recent Work on Citizenship Theory," *Ethics* 104 (1993-94), 284.
17. Kymlicka and Norman, "Return of the Citizen."
18. Daniel M. Weinstock, "La citoyenneté comme 'réponse' au problème du pluralisme des sociétés modernes" in *Les enjeux de la citoyenneté: Un bilan interdisciplinaire/A Multidisciplinary Approach*. Report of Immigration et Métropoles Research Group (Montreal, June 1998).
19. David Theo Goldberg, ed. *Multiculturalism: A Critical Reader* (Cambridge: Blackwell, 1994), 7.
20. Ibid., 9

21. Will Kymlicka, *Multicultural Citizenship: A Liberal Theory of Minority Rights* (Oxford: Oxford University Press, 1995).

22. Iris Marion Young, *Justice*, 119-120. See also Fraser, "Rethinking the Public Sphere."

23. Ibid., 184.

24. Ibid., 186.

25. For example, see Mouffe, "Feminism, Citizenship, and Radical," 325; William Connolly, *The Ethos of Pluralization* (Minneapolis, London: University of Minnesota Press, 1995), 125; Paul Barry Clarke, *Deep Citizenship* (London, Chicago: Pluto Press, 1996), 1.

26. Ernesto Laclau and Chantal Mouffe, *Hegemony and Socialist Strategy: Towards a Radical Democratic Politics* (London and New York: Verso, 1985).

27. Chantal Mouffe, "Democracy, Power, and the 'Political'" in *Democracy and Difference*.

28. Ibid., 250.

29. Mouffe, "Feminism, Citizenship, and Radical," 325.

30. Mouffe, "Democracy, Power, and the 'Political'," 252.

31. Goldberg, *Multiculturalism*, 9. See also Connolly, *The Ethos of Pluralization*, for a similar argument with the concepts of "agonistic respect" and "critical responsiveness" in what he calls the "ethos of pluralization."

32. Tully, *Strange Multiplicity*, 11, emphasis is original.

33. Kymlicka and Norman, "Return of the Citizen."

34. Mouffe, "Feminism, Citizenship, and Radical," 326.

35. Jurgen Habermas, "Three Normative Models of Democracy" in *Democracy and Difference*, 24.

36. Seyla Benhabib, "Toward a Deliberative Model of Democratic Legitimacy" in *Democracy and Difference*, 70.

37. Iris Marion Young, "Communication and the Other: Beyond Deliberative Democracy" in *Democracy and Difference*.

38. Honig, "Difference, Dilemmas."

39. K.A. Appiah, "Cosmopolitan Patriots" in *Cosmopolitics: Thinking and Feeling Beyond the Nation*, eds. P. Cheah and B. Robbins (Minneapolis: University of Minnesota Press, 1998), 95.

40. Ibid., 107.

41. B. Robbins, "Actually Existing Cosmopolitanism" in *Cosmopolitics*, 2.

42. Among many others, see Arjun Appadurai, *Modernity at Large: Cultural Dimensions of Globalization* (Minneapolis: University of Minnesota Press, 1996); M.E. Keck and K. Sikkink, *Activists Beyond Borders: Advocacy Networks in International Politics* (Ithaca and London: Cornell University Press, 1998); Soysal, *Limits of Citizenship*.

43. Saskia Sassen, *Losing Control? Sovereignty in an Age of Globalization* (New York: Columbia University Press, 1996), 94-95.

44. David Jacobson, *Rights Across Borders: Immigration and the Decline of Citizenship* (Baltimore: The Johns Hopkins University Press, 1996), 3.

45. Soysal, *Limits of Citizenship*.

46. Jacobson, *Rights Across Borders*, 39-40.

47. Soysal, *Limits of Citizenship*, 123-130. Unlike Goldberg discussed above, Soysal uses the notion of incorporation strictly in the legal sense.

48. H. Patrick Glenn, "La citoyenneté et le droit: un bilan" in *Les enjeux de la citoyenneté*, 43.
49. Soysal, *Limits of Citizenship*, chapter 8.
50. Holston and Appadurai, "Cities and Citizenship," 188.
51. Holston, "Spaces of Insurgent," 48.
52. Ibid., 49.
53. Ibid., 50.
54. Ibid., 44
55. M.-C. Caloz-Tschopp, ed. *Hannah Arendt, les sans-État et le "droit d'avoir des droits"* Vol. 1 (Paris: L'Harmattan, 1998).
56. Urs Marti, "Hannah Arendt et le monde d'aujourd'hui," in Caloz-Tschopp, *Hannah Arendt*, 24.
57. François Collin, "Hannah Arendt: droit et frontières," in Caloz-Tschopp, *Hannah Arendt*, 81.
58. Laclau and Mouffe, *Hegemony*; Mouffe, "Feminism, Citizenship, and Radical."
59. Simåin Laacher, Etat, immigration et délit d'hospitalité," in Caloz-Tschopp, *Hannah Arendt*, 134-150.
60. Holston, "Spaces of Insurgent," 47.
61. See Soysal, *Limits of Citizenship*, 127, for examples.
62. Young, *Justice*, 172.
63. Holston and Appadurai, "Cities and Citizenship," 197.
64. Raymond Rocco, "The Formation of Latino Citizenship in Southeast Los Angeles," *Citizenship Studies* 3, no. 2 (1999), 263.
65. Holston and Appadurai, "Cities and Citizenship," 199.
66. Murray Low, "Representation Unbound: Globalization and Democracy" in *Spaces of Globalization*; Jessop, "A Neo-Gramscian Approach."
67. Anthony Giddens, *The Constitution of Society: Outline of the Theory of Structuration* (Berkeley and Los Angeles: University of California Press, 1984).
68. Except in the cases of violence, war, or colonization.

CHAPTER 6

# PERFORMATIVE CITIZENSHIP AND CITIZENS FOR LOCAL DEMOCRACY

> Right now my main concern is seeing anger turning into apathy. As I have mentioned many times, the whole purpose of the neo-conservative agenda for amalgamating towns and cities is to silence dissent and create a condition that is ideal for political apathy. Keep on telling people that their efforts are useless and they will begin to believe it.[1]

They were no ordinary citizens; they were incredibly creative and passionate people who genuinely believed in democracy being essential for human flourishing. After all, they were Citizens for Local Democracy! From detailed analyses of neoliberalism to debates on the fiscal crisis, C4LD resisted political apathy and fought to give a voice to as many people as possible. According to them, the Progressive Conservative policies may be nonsense, but they have been in the workings for many years. As Ruth Cohen writes, the Tory victory of 1995 was "preceded in the short term by an accumulation of business school pseudo-scientific jargon, and at least 20 years of organized propaganda by right wing think tanks; in the medium term by political theorists who assumed a preordained hierarchical social order, and in the long term by the example of the tyrants of history, whose main purpose was to impose their will on the populations they sought to control."[2]

Citizens for Local Democracy fought for keeping citizen voices alive in this neoliberal climate. No taxes without representation, no state restructuring without consultation, no business-friendly climate without democracy, no global city without local communities, no circus without bread for all, no Megacity without quality of life, no boosterism without civility! "How about a Canada, an Ontario and a Toronto that is governed by Canadian citizens and not by the ideology of American experts?" asks Gary Morton in a document entitled "The Megacity & the Principles of Democracy," "How about a city democracy built for people—a place where citizens can live and be more than the well dressed props government wants to present to wealthy tourists?"[3] From constitutionalism to the rights of the city, Citizens for Local Democracy settled for resisting political apathy and foster performative citizenship.

### *The Performative Paradox of Liberal Democracy*

When a movement evolves at the local level, it can easily engage with actions both in civil society and in local institutions.[4] Citizens for Local Democracy was quite successful in developing interdependent relationships between local institutions and people in the city. It forced not only local councillors, but also provincial representatives, to engage in a dialogue with "citizens." They were able, in other words, to reassert the politics of everyday life in Toronto. The movement understood the importance of social mobilization not only to encourage participation in the "formal" channels of participation such as public hearings, elections, political pressure, or policy-making. But it also mobilized people for demonstrations, media campaigns, dissemination of alternative information, creating a sense of identity and "ownership" by the people:

> In all my efforts, both as volunteer and employed, I have focused on finding meaningful ways for citizens to seek involvement and build local ownership. Local ownership means people are highly motivated to sustain change over time.[5]

Developing a sense of identity and community in order to nurture control over daily life and participation in the "formal" state institutions illustrates C4LD's rationale for acting on both fronts, the state and civil society. Civil society and the state are intimately related and they evolve in relationship to one another. People make states; they do not only suffer them or use them. The state is not outside society. Politicians, bureaucrats, judges, and police officers also live a daily life in the city; they are part of civil society. Citizens for Local Democracy's involvement in municipal politics, with a foot in both civil society and the state, gave the movement a strategic standpoint. Participants in the movement were very conscious of this interdependent relationship, and the movement's role in shaping their contours. Much emphasis was put on political literacy, outreach, and education. "We do not need to reconstruct institutions—actually, we do," writes a participant, "But not before we reconstruct minds. Not before we reach ordinary (not stupid) people who hear nothing but claptrap."[6] Democracy, it is thought, cannot be achieved without first empowering people to become politically active. Despite a focus on what could be seen as a very technical question of municipal boundaries, C4LD never lost sight of the necessity to not only change the institutional structure of governance, but also to empower people to gain control over their daily lives. C4LD, in other words, was first and foremost concerned with giving meaning to democratic institutions in an attempt to resolve the "performative paradox" of liberal democracies. Put differently, they attempted to ease the tension between civic and political actions on the one hand, and the constitutional/legal/institutional democratic order on the other. They asserted that reality is far from being abstract enough to neatly fit into the "formal" channels of public participation of the representative democratic system.

C4LD was very concerned with the lack of democratic process in the Harris government's strategy to rush a large amount of restructuring legislation through the legislative assembly:

> My concern from the beginning of this horrible year 1997 has more generally been with the process you have employed in attempting to get that legislation passed. You have refused meaningful consultation with the citizens. You have ignored a legitimate referendum that expressed the will of the people. You have changed the rules of debate in the legislature so as to seriously curtail the ability of the opposition parties, the media and the public to understand the substance and impact of your bills."[7]

Not only did the government drastically re-engineered the municipal structure, it also modified the rules of procedure for debates in the legislature and with the public. C4LD resisted such an affront to major tools of political action. It highlighted many tactics employed by the Harris government to curtail the "chaos" of democracy. The government did not have an electoral mandate to amalgamate Toronto, they did not present a White Paper outlining government intentions and promoting public discussions before the bill was presented to the legislature. There was no explanatory document discussing how the legislation evolved. Moreover, the government employed the "time allocation motion" to restrict the time allowed for debate on the bill and the time allowed for public hearings.[8]

John Sewell questioned Bill 36, The Election Statue Amendment Act, introduced on June 9, 1998. The bill reduces the electoral campaign time from thirty-seven to twenty-eight days. "If one assumes that elections are about voters making intelligent choices between competing political visions and abilities," writes Sewell on his web page, "this change does not help voters—it gives a significant advantage to the incumbent party over other political voices. The shorter period also makes it more difficult for individual candidates in ridings to meet voters and deliver pamphlets."[9] Bill 36 also changes the regulation of campaign expenditures and contributions. It exempts research, polling, and travel from the legal definition of expenses, thus giving advantage to wealthier candidates who can now spend more than the expenditure limits by deducing these items from the tally. The bill further increases allowable spending by central party organization, again giving a significant advantage to party candidates over independent candidates. The limit of a donation to a party has increased from $4000 to $7500. Moreover, a donation for the purpose of a campaign is considered a "separate calendar year," thus increasing the amount of donation allowable. The bill also establishes a permanent voter's list, thus prejudicing people who move frequently (mostly tenants) over homeowners.

This form of government, many people in C4LD believe, is based on "resentment," "chaos," and "propaganda." There were long discussions on the forum e-mail list about the government's use of public opinion polls and referendums to legitimate its Common Sense Revolution. What was needed, many people suggested, is an electoral reform, not these halfway, dangerously manipulative "crack cocaine of democracy."[10] What kind of democracy did C4LD envision? What kind of structure was proposed to support and enhance democracy? I do not think we can talk about a unified vision for all C4LD participants. John Sewell and others believed in representative democracy, where elected representatives would be genuinely accountable to their constituents, not to their party leaders. Sewell said in a press release announcing his candidacy in a downtown Toronto riding as an independent for the 1999 provincial elections:

> Some people say you have to belong to a party to have any influence in government. I'm not sure. There are many backbenchers—and even frontbenchers—in the government parties at Queen's Park and Ottawa who have no influence at all with their leader. Because of the demand for party loyalty they are unable to

represent the opinions of the people of their riding. To these people I say: we need some fresh air. We need a return to representative democracy.[11]

Sewell did not necessarily argue against party politics all together. He believed nonetheless that his candidacy created a space for other candidates to speak out loud about urban issues. In his own words: "But if my campaign can bring focus to city issues, perhaps that will create enough room that other candidates will find ways of speaking up loudly and clearly for the city, and not have to wait in vain for the party leader to make a pronouncement."[12] Sewell's political strategy was very interesting. Like many of C4LD's political strategy, he focused on the "formal" political channels by seeking to be elected to the provincial legislature. But he did it with a firm foot in civil society. He talked about representing the constituents, not the party leaders. He talked about opening a space for public debate. He defined himself as a "citizen candidate."

Other participants in C4LD suggested to push for a system of proportional representation instead of parliamentarism as we know it today in Canada. Proportional representation would allow many more parties to be elected because seats would be distributed in proportion to the percentage of votes the party obtained province-wide, not only in the constituency. The party who received the largest percentage of votes would form the government. This system usually creates minority governments making alliance with other parties to create a majority. Under parliamentarism, the party who obtained the largest number of seats, which are won riding by riding, form the government. The government can have won a lower percentage of votes overall, but a larger number of seats because of the way the map of constituencies is defined.

Gary Morton suggested to elect a "People's Democracy Advocate" or Ombudsman that would review the entire process of municipal restructuring in terms of democratic compliance. "I am coming forward with this idea because it is possible to do without changing the Constitution, and because this is a democratic nation," writes Morton, a citizen active in C4LD, "We have representatives to protect human rights and other values. Why not have a special representative to protect democracy? A representative or body that would insure that government restructuring enhances democracy and is not a business deal?"[13]

Most of these proposals refer to a common rallying point for political mobilization among the progressive middle class, that is, a profound belief in liberal democracy. In this globalized world where uncertainty rules, and where the state is restructured, the argument is that by reinvigorating liberal democratic procedures through formal channels of participation such as public hearings, referendums, town hall meetings, or mechanisms to force accountability to the voters, state institutions would act hand in hand with their constituencies when representing them within the belly of the global monster. People would regain control over their lives by reinstating accountability for their representatives. Citizens for Local Democracy combined this strategy with an argument for local autonomy. With its vital involvement in urban and municipal politics, the genius of this combined strategy resulted in a "decentring" (or re-scaling) of representative democracy, to use Magnusson's expression.[14]

In the end, C4LD is a good inspiration for overcoming the performative paradox of national liberal democracy. If we recall the three elements brought forward through an urban critique of modern constitutionalism in the previous chapter (the fluidity of membership, intercultural constitutional dialogue and performative citizenship), we can identify in Citizens for Local Democracy a sensitivity to each of them, albeit to different degrees. With a focus on urban politics and liberal democratic principles, the movement integrated elements of fluidity in the understanding of membership, because local democracy inevitably entails taking non-citizen urban residents into consideration. But this was not the main concern of the movement. Central to C4LD's strategy was to emphasize the importance of re-scaling the state and interpret the constitution in terms of conventions more than strictly according to the text. Individual liberal democratic rights were thought to be protected at the local level when transposing them to the rights of the municipality. Finally, with their success in asserting the politics of everyday life, the movement clearly stated the importance of a performative understanding of citizenship.

### *The Fluidity of Membership*

As we have discussed in the previous chapter, urban critiques of modern constitutionalism lead to conceive citizenship as both a legal status and a political practice. Given that defining who is member of a polity and the rights and obligations attached to this membership is the primary function of citizenship, a focus on political practices, particularly in urban settings, brings a fluid conception of citizenship. Arendt pointed to the necessity to consider not only basic democratic rights in themselves, but also the people bearing (or not) these rights. She pleaded for a consideration of "the right to have rights," of the right to be there and become politically active regardless of one's legal status as a citizen or not. The presence of many non-citizens in cities and the central role urban politics plays in this globalized world call for a fluid understanding of citizenship, which would perhaps include residency as a criteria for membership.

On this issue, Citizens for Local Democracy mostly kept silent. Although participants were very vocal and passionate about democracy. People tended to use interchangeably "citizen" and "resident." Public hearings on Bill 103 provided the opportunity to reflect on these two terms. "Citizen" was understood as the legal definition of a status proper to the national level of government. "Resident" was understood as people living in a specific place, whether they are citizens or not. The first step towards the problematization of the two terms was the use of the term "citizen" as meaning what it literary means: "inhabitant of the city." This opened a more inclusive perspective with a consideration of people living in the city that are usually not recognized as citizens: immigrants, homeless people, the marginalized:

> I wish to speak to you as an ordinary citizen. Webster's dictionary defines a citizen as "an inhabitant of a city or town" before it mentions "country" or "nation." I find this appropriate, because the concept of the citizen was born in a city—somewhere in ancient Greece I believe. I want to talk about what local democracy means to me as a citizen, about some of the content of Bill 103 and its manner of implementation.[15]

During the hearings, "identification to a place" was more linked to the notion of "resident" than "citizen." This was the case in many deputations. Many persons presented themselves as "citizens," having the opportunity to speak to the government. Then they would elaborate on their personal story as "residents" on this or that city. From resident to citizen (inhabitant of the city), from an identification to a local place ("local ownership"), to the use of this sense of place to foster political activism, C4LD created a specific definition of local democracy which implicitly includes concepts of residency and citizenship. According to C4LD, local democracy is an accessible and educational form of democracy. C4LD insisted that local democracy is not specific to Toronto, but it is a vital principle underpinning liberal democracy. They defended the possibility of having control over the living space. This was particularly evident during the 1997 Federal elections. C4LD's strategy was to prompt a national debate of the issue of local democracy.

Moreover, in *The Globe and Mail*, John Barber addressed some concerns outside Toronto about the debate on Bill 103 in the provincial legislature, which was perceived by many outside the metropolis as a local issue that should not have been taking that much time at the provincial level:

> This column is addressed to all those good Ontarians who are not so blessed as to make their homes within the borders of Metro Toronto, and who might be feeling some resentment this week at seeing the Ontario Legislature transformed into a bigger and even crazier version of Toronto City Hall.[16]

Most of the time, however, Citizens for Local Democracy did not pause to reflect on the boundaries of membership and citizenship. Nevertheless, a very interesting thread developed on the e-mail list server when discussing the issue of direct democracy and referendums. The issue of the right to vote was raised by a non-citizen:

> A little-known side effect of all this is that those of us who, for whatever reason, have not taken out Canadian citizenship, are disadvantaged and disenfranchised, because we're not allowed to vote in municipal elections or referenda. I do not see why not—we live here, we pay taxes, we own property, we fulfil all the conditions of any reasonable voting requirement, and we're equally affected by the policies the winners put in place. But we're not allowed to participate.[17]

The right to have rights, the right to be politically active, the right to participate in city affairs and to have a say on everyday life, were asserted by this participant. Who has the right to participate in collective action depends on what counts as collective action. If a group of non-citizens gets together to prepare collective meals and to buy food not available in grocery stores, is this considered collective action? I would say so. And nobody with the minimum tolerance for different cultures will complain about that. But if the same group marches to Queen's Park to ask for food vouchers, then many will consider this form of collective action illegitimate because the people involved do not have the citizenship status. Who has the right and privilege to advocate for access, equity, and human rights? Who has the right to use the language of rights? The same participant further developed the idea of a residency criteria for the right to vote:

> Voting, especially at a local city level, is surely a right of residence, rather than citizenship. I live here. I pay taxes here. (I even go out and demonstrate here!) Why should I not have the chance to have a

> say about who governs my neighbourhood? After all, the logical follow-on your position is that I shouldn't be allowed to get involved in local politics either. And do not confuse a decision not to take out citizenship with a lack of commitment to a country or a society. There may be many reasons why a person might not want to, or be unable to, take out citizenship in a country, but that shouldn't make him or her less able to have a say in his society or her future.[18]

In Canada, to vote in Federal elections one must be a Canadian citizen and be 18 years old.[19] To vote in Ontarian provincial elections, one must be 18 years of age, hold the legal Canadian citizenship status, and have resided in Ontario six months prior to election day.[20] To vote in municipal elections in Ontario, a person must reside in the municipality, be the owner or tenant of land there or the spouse of such person, be a Canadian citizen, be at least 18 years old, and not prohibited by law from voting (prisoners, corporations, executors or trustees, and persons convicted of corruption in previous elections are prohibited to vote).[21] C4LD participant, Nigel Blumenthal, convincingly pointed out that the right to vote at the local level would legitimate his political activity. For him, membership is defined by solidarity and public involvement more than legal citizenship, for such status is not always available.

Membership in a polity, henceforth, could be conceived in a more flexible manner if one would emphasize political practices as well as voting rights. The right to have rights, according to Arendt, implies the right to membership based on the willingness to become politically active. Membership, therefore, is about interdependence. However, a participant on the C4LD e-mail list server pointed that:

> …a substantial majority of ordinary, decent people in this country do not believe in our interdependence. They do not believe in interdependence because it is inconsistent with what they consider to be the fundamentally "moral" position that we are individuals essentially in competition with one another and clothed with rights "against" all others in the community.[22]

Such a statement brings us back to the middle-class action space. Unfortunately, this C4LD participant indicated, mainstream middle-class people do not always believe in interdependence. Many C4LD adherents were conscious of the power of these mainstream individualistic ideas and sought to change them for more progressive and responsible values. Their position within the middle-class action space permitted to understand these mainstream ideas and not to underestimate their strength and the work needed to dislodge them. Indeed, another participant highlighted, fluidity in membership and the right to be politically active are very good ideas, but they are very difficult to implement:

> Sometimes the collective action succeeds and the workers'/citizens' lot improves. Certainly this is manifestly unfair for the outsider who happens to live outside the relevant boundaries: be they non-CAW workers or non-Canadian citizens. Tearing such borders down is a delightful idea. An absolute meritocracy is an equally lovely thought. However, none of these thoughts seem operative in today's society.[23]

*Intercultural Constitutional Dialogue*

Henceforth, struggles for a recognition of the fluidity of membership necessitate as well a constitutional and institutional framework that supports fluidity. Radical democrats such as Mouffe, insist on the necessity to leave open a space for the critique of the democratic rules and norms. Tully proposes more concretely to persistently stimulate an "intercultural constitutional dialogue." But this is not easy to implement, because the idea of a well-bounded sovereign territory as a basic condition for democracy is so entrenched. Nevertheless, Citizens for Local Democracy directly challenged this rigid division between different levels of government and asserted the importance of the municipal level in re-scaling the state.

Legal individual rights are not necessarily extended to non-citizen residents within this framework. Rather, local interests are to be protected by municipalities who themselves are entitled to rights of autonomy. Individual rights such as voting remain the privilege of citizens of the national state. The rationale behind the Citizens' Legal Challenge was that "citizens have got to be interested in their basic rights—whether a vote really means anything, whether something we vote for today can be turned over like that tomorrow by a provincial government."[24] The structure of governance was of major concern to C4LD, on the grounds that local autonomy is the only effective and genuine means to really implement liberal democratic principles. As mentioned previously, C4LD's thinking was very influenced by liberal thinkers such as Alexis de Tocqueville and John Stuart Mill, with some indirect insights from anarchists such as Bookchin and Biehl.[25] They saw in municipal governments possibilities for radical politics challenging other levels of government.

But this focus on the constitutional and institutional framework worried other C4LDers because it prioritizes formal channels of participation in the state such electoral reforms and rules of procedures over political activity in civil society:

> What worries me about suggestions for making fundamental changes to our institutions is that the changes all seem directed to the ballot box. They all seem directed to bringing majority opinion into line with electoral results. Recall is aimed at fine tuning the system so that ever-changing public opinion is more nearly reflected between elections. And referendums are a device for imposing majority views upon governments. None of the devices actually empowers people. All of these fixes are aimed at aligning a majority vote with the issue of the day. That's not what democracy is all about.[26]

> Democracy is NOT synonymous with a system that sees to it that the will of the majority prevails. Democracy is not an institutionalized system of governance. It is a concept. It is the concept that society consults widely amongst its members, ideally with every member, in reaching its communal decisions.[27]

> ...neither the forms of democratic process nor the institutions of the state are essential to democracy. What is essential, I think, is adherence to a principle which makes sense to each of us, a principle against which we can compare our expectations and (more often) our disillusion and find satisfactory reason for it.[28]

These quotes highlight the dangers of falling into the trap of the performative paradox when the understanding of democracy becomes too proceduralist and functionalist. Moreover, Isin adds that one way or the other, the institutional framework tends to be skirted by privatization, and that power resides elsewhere:

> Frankly, while important, the structure is not key to how power is exercised in the city and who exerts influence...there has been a massive shift from governing the city via government toward governing the city via regimes, agreements, alliances and non-governmental entities without any democratic control whatsoever. In other words, while we thought that democracy was slipping from our hands because of megacity, actually other trends are perhaps more important and hardly received our attention.[29]

*Performative Citizenship*

> The concept of Canadian democracy was born in this city. We had quasi-universal male suffrage almost from the beginning. Our suffrage was based on property ownership and we were a population of small-property owners.[30]

John Ralston Saul highlights fundamental democratic principles. During the struggle against amalgamation, he provided rich arguments on Toronto's thriving democratic culture. But legal citizenship remains a passive status. Active citizenship, in contrast, is a set of performative rights and moral obligations that are negotiated by residents of a specific place. Performative citizenship is also a device to foster a sense of belonging to a place, to develop a stake in the polity. "Performed" rights need to constantly be claimed and materialized in order to expand the framework of liberal rights. Affirming the importance of these rights and of creating space for claiming and materializing them is an important step. However, the difficulties of meeting, delivering, and monitoring them remains.

Citizens for Local Democracy successfully asserted the importance of active citizenship. Central to this conception was to foster a sense of "local ownership." Many members of C4LD believed in everyday politics, which highlights the tacit knowledge brought by people:

> To my mind, first principles must be about people and their place in Ontario. I like the idea of civic ownership by the people who live, work, love, play, and die here, not by some abstract conglomeration of foreign business masters nor the local 'elite' who pander to them. Now that MegaMel [for Mel Lastman, the mayor of Toronto] has downloaded the Harrisites' [from Harris] "Open for Business" motto for Toronto, the 21st century's premier NorthAm [for North American] City-State, it would be refreshing to see some reminder that our society has traditionally been made up of actual flesh-and-blood PEOPLE-WITH-SPINES rather than vanquished neoslaves.[31]

People make the city. And for C4LD, "civic ownership" is that feeling of belonging to the city and thus the motivation to be active in and on it, to perform the city in daily life. Amalgamation was threatening this feeling, developed over the years through Toronto's progressive political tradition:

> Since the beginning of amalgamated cities in the United States, the real cost of such political "reforms" has been the entrenchment of political apathy. Once you find that you cannot "fight city hall" your

> interest in municipal matters soon dissipates. When this occurs, a municipality can continue to look bright, clean and wonderfully maintained, but without the gritty genius that comes from the participation of all the people found in a community you can never really develop that subjective sense of "home" with a community. When this apathy takes hold the real cost of our recent events will become clear. We will all fully understand that the loss of real civic ownership of our communities will have more impact upon us than economics.[32]

"Small is Beautiful!" captures in a nutshell C4LD's views of the good society. The state, particularly the provincial state, was seen as disruptive of the ideal community life. Municipalities were seen as allies of communities because of their accessibility, small scale, and their responsibilities over matters of daily life (garbage pick-up, recreation, transportation, etc.). C4LD did not want a Megacity giant to disrupt the comfort of community life. As a citizen said to the hearing committee on Bill 103:

> Community psychologists find that a prime component of health and well-being is a sense of belonging and community that larger cities are not conducive to developing… the lack of community belonging is associated to powerlessness which then serves as a risk factor for the development of malaise, illness, and disease.[33]

But beyond the sense of civic ownership fostering performative citizenship, arguments for smaller scale communities also referred to questions of quality of life and efficient governance:

> As a system engineer, I know that if a system, or proposed city in this case, is too complex for people to comprehend or, in this case, manage, then the system will break down…I presume what the sentimentalists refer to as the neighbourhoods are these "vital, unique, intricate and interlocked details" of our city.[34]

Political agency is not hampered by the complexity of city life. Complexity does not prevent people from being politically active; to the contrary. And politicians who long for simple solutions, ready-made plans to govern the city, are doomed to fail because they do not correspond to the urban fabric:

> Lastman, through his words and actions, shows that he does not understand what a community is, and confuses buildings and streets for a neighbourhood. By failing to make a commitment to walking

> in the Gay Pride Day parade he shows that he does not understand the importance of that event, and the necessity for the leader of the city to show support through participation. Not only does this show that he really does not understand the day to day events that make up Metro Toronto, it also shows that he fears certain people that live in their community in this city.[35]

For C4LD, what is governance in the city? It has to do with democracy, access, participation, community, and urbanity. Political restructuring cannot, should not, result in political apathy. The Megacity saga was a very intense moment of insurgency in Toronto, and such a moment could not have occurred without some notion of performative citizenship.

### *Conclusion*

Citizens for Local Democracy played a leading role in mobilizing a broad constituency and attracting media attention in Toronto. It brought Toronto to the forefront of daily news all over Canada. People outside Toronto saw the Megacity saga as an intense moment of resistance. Toronto the peaceful was shouting out loud.

In thinking about citizenship, cities, and democracy, Toronto provides an important illustration of a "class struggle in space."[36] In this context of neoliberal globalization, in this context of sweeping economic and political restructuring, a struggle to use and shape the city is raging. On the one hand, boosterists and free market proponents are seeking to create a "business-friendly climate" and tame the "chaos" of democracy. On the other hand, the urban progressive middle class seeks to protect urban daily spaces, the "city of small spaces."[37] Middle-class urbanism is an important aspect of urban politics that is too often neglected in academic debates. However, the story of amalgamation in Toronto has illustrated the liveliness of this form of political mobilization. Most importantly, it has highlighted the importance of municipal politics within state re-scaling strategies and a shift from industrial-based mass mobilization to mobilization based on issues of quality of life and identity. Middle-class urbanism is not a revolutionary form of political mobilization, but rather a form of conservationism based on the will to enhance the liberal democratic process. In this sense, a reflection on democracy and citizenship ought to explore the sort of middle-class mobilization Toronto witnessed, for it illustrates the pitting of liberal democracy against globalization.

But reality cannot be so neatly dichotomized. Globalization does not automatically erase states and diminish democracy, it rather fosters re-scaling strategies. Citizens for Local Democracy was involved in the municipal aspect of this re-scaling. And this also brought to the forefront the issue of changes in the governance process, not only its structure. As Jessop noted, governing complexity is both a multi-scaling strategy and an interdependent relationship between state and civil society.[38] It becomes clear that the nation state does not have a monopoly over the use of legitimate violence and that its capacity to create order evolves on a different institutional terrain where other players such as supranational and local administrations operate. Globalization processes highlight the nation state as a terrain of social and political relations rather than as a container for politics. The Megacity saga has demonstrated that mechanical transformations of the state structure and the municipal boundaries cannot erase politics. Governing complexity entails thinking about co-ordination mechanisms much more than dividing a territory into hierarchical administrative units.

Indeed, the Tory provincial government was operating within the ideological terrain of neoliberalism and authoritarian populism. "Taming" politics to make room for economic development was the main goal. It conveyed the idea that nothing can be done to resist globalization, through the use of discursive strategies such as economism which defines the political field solely in instrumental economic terms, or the use of common sense and moral tropes to justify austere fiscal measures and political restructuring in a climate of fiscal panic. In order to take advantage of this new globalized context and to propel Ontario on this arena of economic prosperity, transformations in the organization of social management were necessary. Measures such as the privatization of service delivery, of decision-making powers and of management techniques are at the heart of the neoliberal political agenda. Nonetheless, beyond this ideological view on globalization, remains a very powerful economic, institutional, and social phenomenon with positive and negative impacts. The Megacity saga has illustrated the new Right's advance in addressing this new reality. Beyond the neoliberal ideological gloss, globalization is a reality that profoundly alters the terrain of politics.

Facing these restructuring policies and the forces of globalization, a number of resistance strategies have surfaced. The most visible is the increasingly transnational strength of progressive social movements clustering around issues such as environmental protection, human rights, peace, or feminism. Other strategies embrace the reality of globalization and focus on constructing transnational institutions to cope with the negative effects. The North American Commission for Labour Co-operation and its environmental counterpart are examples of this institutionalist response. Whereas other movements focus on consumption as a means to bring globalization back in the hands of the individual rooted in popular culture; for instance, campaigns against sweatshop or child labour, or the promotion of green products are part of this socio-economic response. For its part, Citizens for Local Democracy chose to focus on the safeguard and development of political accountability in the true spirit of liberal democracy.

Political liberalism and democratization institutionalize important values such as human rights, governance by the people, universal suffrage, freedom of speech and association, equality, and the rule of law. But the new terrain of politics created by globalization processes open a window of opportunity to critically assess state performance in enacting these principles.

Movements for democratization or for more accountability to citizens, offer a rallying point for much of the Left. In reaction to the trend of economism, this rallying point has the advantage of bringing politics back in. However, it may result in the Left's inability to address economic issues raised by the current phase of globalization. In reaction to the neoliberal mantra of efficiency and productivity, liberal democratic activism calls attention to the importance of the democratic process much more than the achievement of substantial outcomes such as transforming the class structure and eradicating inequalities. In these conditions, struggles for liberal democracy emphasize process over outcome, rational activity over equal conditions.[39] Reacting to neoliberal economism is one thing, but it should not result in dismissing political economic concerns with the material conditions sustaining the enactment of a fair and rational democratic process. I have tried to argue that C4LD's concern with the betterment of liberal democratic procedures relied on a middle-class action space, where inequalities were not that visible. But to genuinely extend these democratic procedures throughout society, it will necessitate explicit work to provide the substantive conditions (material, conventional, legal) to perform and participate in the democratic process.

In reaction to neoliberal globalization, a particular segment of the middle classes—the urban progressive middle class—struggles for the preservation of a civic space, a space for politics, a space to sustain their urban lifestyle. In promising moments of insurgency like the ones witnessed in Toronto in the 1990s, the urban progressive middle class is willing to take to the streets to defend the liberal democratic principles of equality, freedom, and access to a fair and ordered process of democratic decision-making. The goal is to shape the city with progressive values by keeping control over a major tool: local institutions. Middle-class activism is a very important element of resistance to globalization. It is an appealing rallying point for many resistance movements by virtue of its ordered, "rational," and legitimate position in the social power structure. The literature on social movements, on the one hand, tends to dismiss the importance of the urban progressive middle class as a collective actor. On the other hand, new democratic and citizenship theories rarely make the connection with middle-class activism and the political struggle for democratization.

What I have attempted to do here is to analyze the Megacity saga in light of a possible redefinition of democracy and citizenship in the context of economic, social, and institutional globalization. If democracy means bringing politics back on the public agenda, then it also means seeking political agency that goes beyond intermittent elections. Democracy, as I use it here, is not only a question of accountability and adequate representation, but rather a day-to-day practice of public debate located in every corners of society. Politics takes place in both the "formal" and the "informal" realms of politics, but also in everyday life, in the tiny actions that shape the city. Therefore, not only citizens, but also residents are political actors in the living sponge of the city. The city is a key sites of politics. However, it also takes place within a broader structural and conjunctural context that define new institutional arrangements and a new political terrain. The Megacity saga unfolded in an urban and globalized world where the national has been re-scaled and where neoliberalism still dominates the ideological landscape.

In light of Citizens for Local Democracy's importance as an illustration of middle-class activism and the use of liberal democratic principles to resist neoliberal globalization, how can we explain the Harris government's strategy for restructuring? Changes were cast within the framework of a "Common Sense Revolution." A revolution based on the idea that urgent transformations were necessary to adapt to the new global reality. The progressive urban middle class in Toronto and elsewhere in the province did not buy this. Democracy was not something that could be sacrificed for the purpose of enriching a small segment of the population at the expense of quality of life in the city. The glamorous title of a global city did not impress the urban progressive middle class who in fact saw it as a huge shadow endangering its lifeworld, its power, and its social democratic beliefs. The prospect of economic growth dangled by this strategy of "going global" did not fool the urban progressive middle class, who, contrary to what most class theories predicted, did not simply emulate the behaviour of the upper class. The government underestimated the strength of middle class belief in democracy. It underestimated its capacity to react, to organize, and to resist. Contrary to the ongoing welfare reform which attacks the very poor and the marginalized, in restructuring Toronto, the government was attacking a political tool used by progressive middle class people that had more resources to react. Moreover, the Harris government not only did not choose the right process to implement its reform, it did not choose the appropriate scale. However, the goal of this book was not to decide whether or not amalgamation is a good strategy for Toronto. Debates around the proper structure of governance in the metropolis have already produced very specific and valid policy-making recommendations especially since the GTA Task Force of 1996. This book explored instead the phenomenon of middle-class activism clustering around claims for a return to accountable and legitimate democracy. Why did issues of process and administrative boundaries raise so much anger? How can we account for the powerful voice raised by the urban progressive middle class in this era of neoliberal globalization? What does it mean when the "silent majority" gets angry? What does it mean for other "more radical" social movements?

## NOTES

1. Joseph Cooper, posted on the C4LD list server (November 12, 1997).
2. Ruth Cohen, *Alien Invasion: The Occupation of Ontario* (Coalition to Restore Democracy in Ontario: www.interlog/~free/one04.htm, 1998).
3. Gary Morton, *The Megacity & Principles of Democracy: Democracy Model Group Investigation* (www.interlog.com/~cjazz/studyto.htm, September 1998).
4. Magnusson, *The Search for Political Space*.
5. Liz Rykert, *Deputation to the hearing committee on Bill 103* (February 24, 1997).
6. John McLaren, posted on the C4LD list server (January 24, 1998).
7. Bronwyn Drainie, reported in Citizens for Local Democracy, *The Word on the Street: NO MEGACITY* Newsletter 19 (September 1997).
8. Citizens for Local Democracy, *Harris clams down*.
9. www.johnsewell.org
10. Joseph Cooper, posted on the C4LD list server (March 17, 1998).
11. John Sewell, "Announcement of Candidacy to the Provincial Elections," *John Sewell: Our Voice at Queen's Park* 1 (June 11, 1998).
12. Ibid.
13. www.interlog.com/~cjazz

14. Magnusson, *The Search for Political Space.*
15. Wally Brooker, *Deputation to the hearing committee on Bill 103* (February 17, 1997).
16. John Barber, "Struggle over megacity well worth to all of us," *Globe and Mail* (April 4, 1997), A10.
17. Nigel Blumenthal, posted on the C4LD list server (March 23, 1998).
18. Ibid.
19. cicnet.ci.gc.ca/english/newcomer
20. www.electionsontario.on.ca
21. www.nt.net/temagami_lakes/election/who.votes.htm
22. John McLaren, posted on the C4LD list server (February 4, 1998).
23. Birchwood, posted on the C4LD list server (November 25, 1997).
24. Reported in Bruce De Mara, "Citizens eye Megacity appeal," *Toronto Star* (July 27, 1997).
25. See Alexis de Tocqueville, *Democracy in America* (New York: Vintage Books, 1945); John Stuart Mill, *Utilitarianism, On Liberty* and *Considerations on Representative Government*, ed. H.B. Acton (London: Dent, 1972); Murray Bookchin, *Limits of the City*, Second revised edition (Montreal: Black Rose Books, 1986), *Urbanization Without Cities: The Rise and Decline of Citizenship* (Montreal: Black Rose Books, 1992); Janet Biehl, *Politics of Social Ecology: Libertarian Municipalism* (Montreal: Black Rose Books, 1998).
26. John McLaren, posted on the C4LD list server (February 10, 1998).
27. Paul Isaacs, posted on the C4LD list server (February 1998).
28. John McLaren, posted on the C4LD list server (February 23, 1998).
29. Engin Isin, Contribution to a special discussion organized by Citizens for Local Democracy, *After the Megacity: What Next?* (www.web.net/~citizens/megaw/aftermeg.html, May 11, 1998).
30. John Ralston Saul, "Toronto, the (Public) Good," *Toronto Star* (June 22, 1997), F6.
31. Donald McKinnon, posted on the C4LD list server (January 24, 1998).
32. Joseph Cooper, posted on the C4LD list server (November 13, 1997).
33. Dennis Raphael, *Deputation to the hearing committee on Bill 103* (March 3, 1997).
34. Eric Zhelka, *Deputation to the hearing committee on Bill 103* (March 6, 1997).
35. Joseph Cooper, posted on the C4LD list server (November 9, 1997). Lastman ultimately participated in the Gay Pride Day.
36. Kipfer, "Urban Politics in the 1990s."
37. John Friedmann, "The City of Small Spaces and the Problem of Representation," prepared for the conference on *Cities and Metropolis in the 21st Century: Breaking or Bridging?* (La Rochelle, October 19-21, 1998).
38. Jessop, "Capitalism and its Future" and "A Neo-Gramscian Approach."
39. Susan S. Fainstein, "Can We Make the Cities We Want?" in *The Urban Moment*, Sophie Body-Gendrot and Robert Beauregard, eds. (Thousand Oaks: Sage, 1999).

# APPENDIX A

## CHECKLIST FOR LOCAL DEMOCRACY A DOCUMENT DISTRIBUTED BY CITIZENS FOR LOCAL DEMOCRACY

*March 21, 1997*

The very idea of democracy arose in ancient cities, and in the centuries that have followed, has spread and been seen as the essence of reasonable governance in many cities and later in many countries. Democratic principles were embedded in political institutions in the Town of York before they were embodied in the governing of the province of Upper Canada. Democratic principles were assumed by the leaders who agreed on and enacted the British North America Act in 1867, to be the basis of governments in Canada. Since 1867, Ontario have become much more urbanized. Now, more than three quarters of Ontarians live in cities, compared to less than a quarter one hundred and thirty years ago. Accordingly, it is more important than ever that local governments be respected and be treated as partners with other governments in this province and in Canada.

This checklist gives voice to the salient aspects of local democracy that have underpinned local government in Ontario, even if those aspects have been rarely stated. We are not inventing these principles, but rather retrieving them from the lengthy practise of municipal government in Ontario at a time when it seems the provincial government wishes to forget them. These are the basic points that inform the system of local democracy practised in Ontario. Each statement is followed by a brief commentary on how the principle relates to the megacity amalgamation proposal of Bill 103, The City of Toronto Act, 1996.

*Preamble*

Municipalities are the first order of government within the Canadian political system, and exist to provide residents with control over a wide range of local matters, as well as being entrusted to discharge other duties. These principles describe the basis on which local democracy is maintained and enhanced. Section 92(8) of the British North America Act states that the Legislature may "exclusively make laws in relation to...municipal institutions," but nothing in the constitution gives a province the power to abolish municipalities or local governments against the will of those served by those governments. Nothing in the constitution says that municipalities are a "creature" of the provincial government which can be reshaped according to the whim of provincial politicians. It should be noted that the same section gives the Legislature power to make laws in relation to "property and civil rights"—and no one would suggest this means a province can abolish property or civil rights.

The Ontario government has no legal authority to abolish arbitrarily six local governments in Metro Toronto. It does not own local governments: those governments exist to provide local democracy for local residents.

*1. Municipal governments are elected by and accountable to their local citizens, therefore changes to the structure of municipal governments should require the consent of their citizens.*

Before any province can abolish a local government, it must obtain the general consent of local residents. A province has no right to run roughshod with a plan of restructuring when local residents are clearly in opposition to such a plan.

In the March 3 referendums, voters in Metro Toronto decisively rejected the restructuring plan proposed by the Ontario government. That should be an end to the matter: The legislation should be withdrawn without further discussion.

*2. Municipal government responsibilities are the exclusive authority of locally elected councils and cannot be suspended or assumed by provincial appointees.*

The provincial government has no moral authority or legal right to impose its appointees as the leaders of local government in place of those elected to do so (as it is trying to do with the Board of Trustees and the Transition Team). Except in extreme cases such as bankruptcy, imminent bankruptcy, or the break down of law and order, the province has neither moral nor legal right to push municipal government into trusteeship.

3. *Municipal governments, through their locally elected councils, have the exclusive authority to determine their internal administrative structures including the hiring, management and firing of staff and the manner of delivering services under their responsibility.*

The Ontario government has neither moral authority nor legal right to remove from locally elected councils the right to hire, manage and fire local staff, and to give those powers to its appointees (as it is trying to do with the Board of Trustees and the Transition Team.)

4. *Municipal governments, through their locally elected councils, have the exclusive authority to decide how to spend locally generated tax revenues.*

The provincial government has neither moral authority nor legal right to dictate or control—through appointees or others (as it is trying to do in Bill 103, both for the current budget year and in future years)—how locally generated revenues will be spent. These decisions rest entirely with locally elected leaders.

5. *Local governments have the authority and duty to manage public services and affairs under their responsibility and within their jurisdiction.*

The main reason for local government is to give people the opportunity to ensure that decisions made are appropriate to their needs and wishes. Those who wish to get involved in these decisions should participate in the local governing process. Other levels of government have neither right nor power to take away this decision-making ability, which is what the Ontario government is trying to do with Bill 103.

6. *The process for reviewing or developing proposals to restructure municipal government should involve citizens in a meaningful way. It should begin with a full and independent study of the problems with current structures, the opportunities restructuring presents, and the impacts of the different restructuring options.*

The Ontario government does not have a single study available which recommends the kind of restructuring it is proposing for

Metro Toronto. Not one study. And not a single study indicating the impact of these changes.

*7. These studies and any restructuring proposals should be publicized and made widely available to all citizens throughout the municipalities affected. A meaningful public consultation process should be undertaken to facilitate citizen debate and input. Any restructuring proposals should include a recommended process for public consultation and decision making on the details of the finally agreed-upon structure, such as ward systems and boundaries, council size, etc.*

The Ontario government has rushed its unfounded proposal through a legislative process which has been so speedy that there has been no opportunity for a broadly based discussion of alternatives, impacts, and opportunities. Worse, it has repeatedly indicated it will not be influenced by reasoned objections or alternative proposals.

Bill 103 states that the Minister of Municipal Affairs will decide on such things as ward boundaries and the size of council. These decisions are being proposed without any consultation, and through a process which is closed and private—totally in the control of the Minister. This approach offends the basic tenets of local democracy.

*8. Restructuring proposals should ensure the protection of reserve funds for local citizens, the protection of the financial interests of the citizens, and ensure that levels of service do not deteriorate.*

Reserve funds can be fully protected for the citizens of the municipalities in which they were generated by so stating in the restructuring proposal, and by making it clear they will not be used to meet the financial needs or desires of the provincial government. Bill 103 does neither of these things.

Bill 103 makes no provisions to ensure continuity of service, but attempts to guarantee a reduction in service after forced amalgamation.

*9. All organs of local democracy are subject to the rule of law and the supervision of the courts.*

Bill 103 attempts to set up a provincially controlled regime which is not subject to the rule of law or the direction of the courts. These provisions have no place in a democracy.

# APPENDIX B

## CIVIC PRIORITIES

Statement agreed to on September 15, 1997, at a meeting of Citizens for Local Democracy, after several months' consideration and debate.

*Principles*

Citizens for Local Democracy affirms these three principles:

- The new city must include at the local level strong, effective, and democratic decision-making structures similar to the six existing city councils.
- Those elected must be people who have shown they want to involve citizens and communities in decision-making at City Hall: They must be people who were against the idea of forced amalgamation in the first place, people who agree decisions should be made public by elected (not appointed) officials, on the basis of supporting evidence and justification that is publicly debated and evaluated before decisions are made.
- Those elected must implement programs which will better share money, power and resources among all people living in the new city, programs which respect local values and resist the effects of globalization.

*Actions*

Citizens for Local Democracy believes the following actions must be taken:

*Local democracy*

- Local government structures (such as community councils) must be shaped to reflect the same powers and financial responsibilities exercised by the present six municipalities. The current city halls must be retained as the sites of local governments.

- Effective local school boards must be re-established.

*Local control over municipal institutions*

- Community hospitals, community-based health facilities, and a strong local public health system must be supported as integral to a publicly-funded health care system.
- Libraries, arts, heritage and cultural bodies, community committees, and other local boards and advisory bodies, must be continued, and must receive at least 1996 levels of funding and support.

*Strong public services*

- Services in each municipality, including transit and education, must be maintained at no less than 1996 standards.
- Staffing levels and salaries of municipal workers must be protected and the provincially controlled arbitration process contained in Bill 136 must be avoided.
- Public services such as transit, water, sewage, refuse, recreation, social services, hydro, and health must not be privatized.

*Economic justice*

- Effective programs which create a more equitable and caring society must be implemented, including special attention to eradicate homelessness, creating more affordable housing, ending the plight of poor children, stopping workfare and other programs which stigmatize the poor, and meeting challenges facing immigrants.
- Social programs and services must not be downloaded by the province onto municipal property taxpayers, but should be funded through progressive income taxes.

*Fair property taxes*

- A fair property tax system must be studied, debated, widely understood, and agreed to by residents and commercial taxpayers before implementation

## APPENDIX C

# CITIZENS FOR LOCAL DEMOCRACY VALUES STATEMENT

*March 9, 1998*

Harris says he's making things better. So why are things getting worse?

---

*This is what we hear from our neighbours...What do you hear?*

- My mother's in hospital. There's no room for her in a nursing home. I can't look after her but I feel terrible that she's occupying a bed when others can't get care.
- Last year, we lost junior kindergarden and some ESL at my son's school. What will be left in two years for my youngest?
- My neighbour got downsized a year ago. Now they live in one of those motels for people without housing. I worry that it could happen to us.
- The government's been changing everything at once, no matter what we say. What happened to discussion and public debate?
- The Premier promised that downloading wouldn't cost us more. Why do we have to choose between rec centres and garbage pickup and road repair? We need them all.

---

*In our Ontario, we want politicians to work for*

- compassion and respect among people
- fairness and anti-discrimination
- safe and healthy homes, workplaces and communities
- diverse and inclusive communities
- adequate food and shelter
- accessible education and health care
- strong public services under public control
- public libraries, recreation and arts
- accessible children's services

Citizens for Local Democracy wants to find common ground based on values we can share. We believe that men and women in different communities, organizations and political parties can work together to build public policy that meets our needs.

---

*1. Democratic decision-making works.*

- We expect elected officials to provide full, honest information about what they are doing. Democracy cannot be built on lies and secrets.
- We expect enough time for public participation and discussion before votes. No more bulldozing.
- We need strong local councils and schools boards that make decisions public.
- We want local politicians who listen and are accountable to local residents.
- We want local councils and school boards with enough money to meet local needs.

---

*2. Strong public services build strong communities.*

- We need social policies that make sure all residents in Ontario, regardless of their means, are adequately fed and housed.
- We expect governments to honour their commitments to basic rights for all people.

- We expect full public financial support for resources like schooling, health care, libraries, recreation, arts and culture. We are more than just consumers.
- We expect our governments not to enter into agreements that sign away our power to shape our future.

---

*3. A strong economy shares resources and opportunities, and protects the natural environment.*

- We want an economy in which the gap between rich and poor gets smaller; where every woman and man can live in dignity without fear of poverty.
- We want a tax system that does not place the heaviest burden on those least able to pay.
- We need a regulatory system that conserves our natural resources and enhances the natural environment.

Let's find common ground. We encourage you and your community to work with us to assert our common values.
Here are some questions we are asking:

- What policies make communities safe and strong?
- How can communities be involved in democratic decision-making?
- How can we ensure that all communities have appropriate services that meet their needs?
- How can we reduce the gap between rich and poor?
- How can we protect the natural environment?

How can we elect a government that will act on the values that we stand for?

---

*Get involved*

To create change, everyone must take some action. Please let us know you are willing to:

[ ] distribute this pamphlet
[ ] help organize a meeting
[ ] be a contact point for your community

*Name* ..........................................................................
*Community* .................................................................
*Postal Code* ..............................
*Phone (......)*..............................
*Fax (......)*................................
*Email* .......................................

Please fax this page to (416) 977 5909 or mail it to 50 Baldwin St., Toronto, M5T 1L4 or email to citizens@web.net.

HOT LINE: (416) 977 8736

Our Web site is http://community.web.net/citizens

This brochure is produced by Citizens for Local Democracy, and is paid for by individual donations. C4LD meets every Monday night in downtown Toronto. Our Hot Line contains news, information, and action suggestions related to local democracy.

## APPENDIX D

# PRINCIPLES GOVERNING MUNICIPAL / PROVINCIAL FINANCIAL RELATIONSHIPS A DOCUMENT DISTRIBUTED BY CITIZENS FOR LOCAL DEMOCRACY

*March 20, 1997*

At a time when the province is proposing to alter radically its financial relationships with municipalities and particularly to download financial responsibilities, it is important to set out the principles which have governed these relationships. In past decades, provincial governments have generally recognized the separate nature of local government and have not acted unilaterally in the field of financial relationships, but have attempted to reach amicable agreement. The principles governing these relationships have not previously been set down, but have proceeded according to unwritten assumptions which we believe are fairly summarized below, followed by a brief commentary.

*Preamble*

Municipalities are the first order of government within the Canadian political system, and exist to provide residents control over a wide range of local matters as well as being entrusted to discharge other duties. The following statements describe the principles that have generally established the terms of the municipal/provincial financial relationships: Section 92(8) of the British North America states that the Legislature may 'exclusively make laws in relation to…municipal institutions,' but nothing in the constitution gives a province the power to abolish municipalities or local governments against the will of those served by those governments, or impose new responsibilities without their consent. Nothing in the constitution says that municipalities are a 'creature' of the provincial government to be reshaped according to the whim of provincial politicians. The Ontario government does not have the moral authority or legal power to force municipalities to assume responsibility for new program areas. For instance, nothing in the Canadian constitution permits the province to require municipalities to assume costs for universal program areas which are broadly social in nature.

*1. Municipal governments are elected by and accountable to their local citizens for the expenditure of locally generated tax revenues. Accordingly, changes to what services are funded by locally generated tax revenues require the agreement of municipal councils.*

For instance, if the Ontario provincial government wishes to re-organize how the costs of income redistribution programs are paid, it must first get the agreement of municipalities to these changes. The provincial government has no right to impose unilaterally new program expenditures on an unwilling partner.

*2. Property tax revenue is the major source of municipal revenue, and must remain in the control of municipalities. Property tax revenue may not be used as a revenue source by the provincial government.*

The proposals for changing education financing entirely violates this principle by assuming that the province will use property tax revenue from non-residential properties to pay for the costs of a provincially controlled education system.

*3. In general, universal programs addressing problems of health care and income distribution should be funded by sources of taxation that are progressive and based on ability to pay, such as income and corporate taxes, and should be spread across as broad a population base as possible.*

Some people believe there is a small degree of progressiveness in property taxes—more expensive properties pay more taxes in a system based on market values—but most people recognize that at best, property taxes are not very progressive, and are inappropriate for supporting universal social programs. Further, the costs of such programs are counter-cyclical, and are highest when a community's ability to pay is the lowest—which is why such costs should be spread as widely as possible. It is unacceptable to burden families and individuals with fixed incomes (such as senior citizens) with heavy social costs which will force them to sell their homes.

4. *The development of proposals to significantly change the municipal/provincial financial relationship should begin with the establishment of a process involving a wide range of interests led by locally elected representatives chosen by councils and municipal organizations, and representatives of service agencies and other interested groups and persons. The process should start with a full and independent study of problems, opportunities, alternatives and impacts.*

The changes being proposed by the Ontario provincial government are without any foundation; there is not a single report the government can point to which reviews problems, opportunities, alternatives or impacts. Not one single report. As a result, there can be no intelligent discussion.

5. *The study and any proposals to significantly change the municipal/provincial financial relationship should be publicized and made widely available to all affected municipalities and their citizens. A meaningful public consultation process should provide full opportunities for a full discussion by citizens, permit the securing of other information if needed, and encourage citizen input.*

To begin discussing how the proposed downloading relationship will be changed, the Ontario government has refused to provide any comprehensive report on its proposals. It has then carefully hand-picked a few elected councillors and friends who agree with its drift and direction, people do not represent the vast number of municipal councils, social agencies, community leaders, and others interested in this issue. They are unable to hold a legitimate and informed discussion about what a new relationship might be.

6. *In discussing changes to municipal/provincial financial relationships, care must be taken to protect public assets and the contractual interests of third parties.*

Some social programs contractually involve third parties—non-profit housing companies, for instance, have contractual relationships for the management and provision of social housing. Many employees have contractual arrangements securing terms of employment. Changes affecting these contractual obligations should only be made with the consent of such third parties.

Changes might also imply the disposal of public assets such as sewage and water facilities. Protections must be built into discussions to ensure the public interest is protected.

# Selected Bibliography


Ackelsberg, Martha A. "Communities, Resistance, and Women's Activism: Some Implications for a Democratic Polity." In *Women and the Politics of Empowerment*, edited by Ann Bookman and Sandra Morgen. Philadelphia: Temple University Press, 1988.

Amin, A., and N. Thrift, eds. *Globalization, Institutions, and Regional Development in Europe*. Oxford: Oxford University Press, 1994.

Andrew, C. "Provincial-municipal relations; or hyper-fractionalized quasi-subordination revisited." In *Canadian Metropolitics: Governing our Cities*, edited by J. Lightbody. Toronto: Copp Clark Ltd, 1995.

Appadurai, Arjun. *Modernity at Large: Cultural Dimensions of Globalization*. Minneapolis: University of Minnesota Press, 1996.

Appiah, K. A. "Cosmopolitan Patriots." In *Cosmopolitics: Thinking and Feeling Beyond the Nation*, edited by P. Cheah and B. Robbins. Minneapolis: University of Minnesota Press, 1998.

Appleby, Timothy. "Hall accepts her defeat with grace." *Globe and Mail*. (November 11, 1997): A13.

Badie, Bertrand. *La fin des territoires: Essai sur le désordre international et sur l'utilité sociale du respect*. Paris: Fayard, 1995.

Barber, John. "Experts joining throng of megacity bashers." *Globe and Mail*. (February 26, 1997): A2.

Barber, John. "Sending a message to King Mike." *Globe and Mail*. (March 4, 1997): A10.

Barber, John. "Struggle over megacity well worth to all of us." *Globe and Mail*. (April 4, 1997): A10.

Bartolini, Stefano. *Exit Options, Boundary Building, Political Restructuring*. EUI Working Paper SPS No. 98/1. Florence: European University Institute, 1998.

Beauregard, Robert. "The Politics of Urbanism: Mike Davis and the Neo-Conservatives."*Capitalism, Nature, Socialism*. (May 1999).

Benhabib, Seyla. "Toward a Deliberative Model of Democratic Legitimacy." In *Democracy and Difference: Contesting the Boundaries of the Political*, edited by Seyla Benhabib. Princeton: Princeton University Press, 1996.

Benzie, Robert. "Mel makes his biggest sale." *Toronto Sun*. (November 11, 1997): 5.

Biehl, Janet. *Politics of Social Ecology: Libertarian Municipalism*. Montreal: Black Rose Books, 1998.

Blatchford, Christie. "In the end, voters put their wallets first." *Toronto Sun*. (November 11, 1997): 5.

Blumer, Herbert. *Symbolic Interactionism*. Englewood Cliffs: Prentice Hall, 1969.

Bookchin, Murray. *Limits of the City*. Second revised edition. Montreal: Black Rose Books, 1986.

Bookchin, Murray. *Urbanization Without Cities: The Rise and Decline of Citizenship.* Montreal: Black Rose Books, 1992.

Bourdieu, Pierre. *La Distinction : Critique sociale du jugement.* Paris : Minuit, 1979.

Brenner, Neil. "Global cities, glocal states: Global city formation and state territorial restructuring in contemporary Europe." *Review of International Political Economy* 5, no. 1 (1998): 1-37.

Brooker, Wally. *Deputation to the hearing committee on Bill 103.* (February 17, 1997).

Browne, Paul Leduc. "Déjà Vu: Tatcherism in Ontario." In *Open for Business Closed to People*, edited by D. Ralph, A. Régimbald, and N. St-Amand. Halifax: Fernwood Publishing, 1997.

Butler, Tim, and Mike Savage, eds. *Social Change and the Middle Classes.* London: UCL Press, 1995.

Caloz-Tschopp, M.-C. ed. *Hannah Arendt, les sans-État et le "droit d'avoir des droits."* Vol. 1. Paris: L'Harmattan, 1998.

Calvino, Italo. *Les villes invisibles.* Paris: Éditions du Seuil, 1972.

Campbell, M., I. Ross, G. Abbate, and M. Grange. "Metro voters reject amalgamation." *Globe and Mail.* (March 4, 1997): A10.

Carey, Elaine. "Minorities set to be majority." *Toronto Star.* (June 7, 1998).

Castells, Manuel. *The Rise of the Network Society.* Cambridge: Blackwell, 1996.

Caulfield, Jon. *City Form and Everyday Life: Toronto's Gentrification and Critical Social Practice.* Toronto: University of Toronto Press, 1994.

Citizens for Local Democracy. *What's Going On Here?* Newsletter 1. (December 1996).

Citizens for Local Democracy. *Principles Governing Municipal/Provincial Financial Relationships.* (March 20, 1997).

Citizens for Local Democracy. *Checklist for Local Democracy.* (March 21, 1997).

Citizens for Local Democracy. *Local democracy is an issue across Canada.* Newsletter 11. (May 1997).

Citizens for Local Democracy. *The Word on the Street: NO MEGACITY.* Newsletter 19. (September 1997).

Citizens for Local Democracy. *Civic Priorities.* (September 15, 1997).

Citizens for Local Democracy. *First they took our city government, then our hospitals, now our schools, next* Newsletter 20. (November 1997).

Citizens for Local Democracy. *Harris clamps down: Should anyone be worried?* Newsletter 21. (December 1997).

Citizens for Local Democracy. *Citizens for Local Democracy Values Statement.* (March 9, 1998).

Citizens for Local Democracy. *After the Megacity: What Next?* www.web.net/~citizens/megaw/aftermeg.html. (May 11, 1998).

Citizens' Assembly Ward 19. *What Is The Citizens' Assembly?* webhome.idirect.com/~burp/what.htm.

City of Toronto. *Community Consultation: Options for Decision Making in the Megacity.* City of Toronto. (June 1997).

City of Toronto. "Facing Up to the City's Future Challenges." *Toronto Plan* 2 (October 1999).

City of Toronto. *Toronto City Council's Strategic Plan–Part 1.* Toronto: Strategic & Corporate Policy Division, Chief Administrator's Office, City of Toronto. (November 1999).

Clarke, Paul Barry. *Deep Citizenship.* London: Pluto Press, 1996.

Clarke, Susan E., and Gary L. Gaile. *The Work of Cities.* Minneapolis: University of Minnesota Press, 1998.

Clement, Wallace, and John Myles. *Relations of Ruling: Class and Gender in Postindustrial Societies.* Montreal and Kingston: McGill-Queen's University Press, 1994.

Cohen, Ruth. *Deputation to the hearing committee on Bill 103.* (February 3, 1997).

Cohen, Ruth. *Alien Invasion: The Occupation of Ontario.* Coalition to Restore Democracy in Ontario: www.interlog/~free/one04.htm, 1998.

Colton, Timothy J. *Big Daddy: Frederick G. Gardiner and the Building of Metropolitan Toronto.* Toronto: University of Toronto Press, 1980.

Committee for the Province of Toronto. www.interlog.com/~cjazz/prov-t.htm.

Community Social Planning Council of Toronto. "An Act for the new Millenium?" *Sound Bite* 15. (January 18, 2000).

Connolly, William. *The Ethos of Pluralization.* Minneapolis: University of Minnesota Press, 1995.

Conway, Janet. "Knowledge, Power, Organization: Social Justice Coalitions at a Crossroads." *Community Social Planing Council of Toronto*. Occasional Paper 1 (Fall 1999).

Conway, Janet. "Knowledge, Power, Organization: Social Justice Coalitions at Crossroads." *Studies in Political Economy* 62 (Summer 2000): 43-70.

Cooly, Glenn. "Citizen Insurrection: How to Use the Timeless Art of Civil Disobedience to Upend the Tories." *Now Magazine.* (February 8-14, 1996): 16-20.

Cooper, R. "Municipal law, delegated legislation and democracy." *Canadian Public Administration* 39, no. 3 (1996): 290-313.

Cox, Kevin, ed. *Spaces of globalization: Reasserting the Power of the Local.* New York: Guilford Press, 1997.

Davis, Mike. *City of Quartz: Excavating the Future of Los Angeles.* New York: Verso, 1990.

De Mara, Bruce. "Citizens eye Megacity appeal." *Toronto Star.* (July 27, 1997).

DiManno, Rosie. "Give our city a slogan." *Toronto Star.* (December 21, 1997): A1.

DiManno, Rosie. "Binoculars in order for this council." *Toronto Star.* (January 7, 1998): B1.

Donzelot, Jacques. "La nouvelle question urbaine." *Esprit* 258 (novembre 1999): 87-114.

Eder, Klaus. *The New Politics of Class: Social Movements and Cultural Dynamics in Advanced Societies.* London: Sage, 1993.

Etter, Janice. *The Death of a Thousand Cuts.* community.web.net/citizens. (April 1, 1997).

Fahrig, Kristen. *Deputation to the hearing committee on Bill 103.* (February 10, 1997).

Fainstein, Susan S. "Can We Make the Cities We Want?" In *The Urban Moment*, edited by Sophie Body-Gendrot and Robert Beauregard. Thousand Oaks: Sage, 1999.

Farrant, David. *Deputation to the hearing committee on Bill 103.* (February 12, 1997).

Faubert, Frank, Barbara Hall, Doug Holyday, Mel Lastman, Frances Nunziata, and Michael Prue. *Change For the Better: A vision for the future of our communities, A framework for restructuring local government.* www.city.toronto.on.ca/3wrd/change.htm, 1997.

Filion, Pierre. "Rupture or Continuity? Modern and Postmodern Planning in Toronto." *International Journal of Urban and Regional Research* 23, no. 3 (1999): 421-445.

Fraser, Nancy. "Rethinking the Public Sphere: A Contribution to the Critique of Actually Existing Democracy." In *Justice Interruptus: Critical Reflections on the "Postsocialist" Condition.* London: Routledge, 1997.

Friedmann, John. "The World City Hypothesis." *Development and Change* 17, no. 1 (1986): 68-84.

Friedmann, John. "The City of Small Spaces and the Problem of Representation." Prepared for the conference on *Cities and Metropolis in the 21st Century: Breaking or Bridging?* La Rochelle. (October 19-21, 1998).

Frisken, Frances. "Planning and Servicing the Greater Toronto Area: The interplay of provincial and municipal interests." In *Metropolitan Governance: American/ Canadian Intergovernmental Perspectives*,. Edited by David Rothblatt and Andrew Sancton. Berkeley, CA: Institute of Governmental Studies Press, 1993.

Ghomeshi, Jian. *no mega-cd [no – megacity]*. Toronto: Protest Boy Record, 1997.

Giddens, Anthony. *The Constitution of Society: Outline of the Theory of Structuration.* Los Angeles: University of California Press, 1984.

Glenn, H. Patrick. "La citoyenneté et le droit: un bilan." In *Les enjeux de la citoyenneté: Un bilan interdisciplinaire/A Multidisciplinary Approach*. Report of Immigration et Métropoles Research Group. Montreal. (June 1998).

Globe and Mail Editorial. "What's good for Toronto is good for Ontario." *Globe and Mail.* (January 21, 1997).

Globe and Mail Editorial. "Four steps to Toronto." *Globe and Mail.* (April 23, 1997).

Globe and Mail. "Lastman makes megacity history." *Globe and Mail.* (November 11, 1997): A1.

Goldberg, David Theo, ed. *Multiculturalism: A Critical Reader.* Cambridge: Blackwell, 1994.

Graham, K. A., and S. D. Phillips. ""Who Does What" in Ontario: the process of provincial-municipal disentanglement." *Canadian Public Administration* 41, no. 2 (1998): 175-209.

Grange, M. "Amalgamation follows Tories' philosophy." *Globe and Mail.* (December 18, 1996).

Greater Toronto Area Task Force. *Report of the GTA Task Force.* Toronto: Publications Ontario, 1996.

Greenwald, Roger. *Deputation to the hearing committee on Bill 103.* (February 12, 1997).

Gwyn, Richard. "Lastman catches attention on city-state." *Toronto Star.* (November 26, 1999).

Habermas, Jurgen. "Three Normative Models of Democracy" In *Democracy and Difference: Contesting the Boundaries of the Political*, edited by Seyla Benhabib. Princeton: Princeton University Press, 1996.

Hajer, Maarten A. *The Politics of Environmental Discourse.* Oxford: Clarendon Press, 1995.

Hall, Stuart et al. *Policing the Crisis: Mugging, the State and Law and Order.* London: Verso, 1978.

Hall, Stuart. *The Hard Road to Renewal: Tatcherism and the Crisis of the Left.* London: Verso, 1988.

Haraway, Donna. "The Promises of Monsters: A Regenerative Politics for Inappropriate/d Others" In *Cultural Studies.* Edited by L. Grossberg, C. Nelson, and P. Treichler. London: Routledge, 1992.

Hardt, Michael, and Antonio Negri. "Postmodern Law and the Withering of Civil Society." In *Labor of Dionysos: A critique of the state-form.* Minneapolis: University of Minnesota Press, 1994.

Harvey, David. *Justice, Nature & the Geography of Difference.* Oxford: Blackwell, 1996.

Held, David. *Democracy and the Global Order: From the Modern State to Cosmopolitan Governance.* Stanford: Stanford University Press, 1995.

Herman, Edward S., and Noam Chomsky. *Manufacturing Consent: The Political Economy of the Mass Media.* New York: Pantheon Books, 1988.

Hirschman, Albert. *Exit, Voice, and Loyalty: Responses to Decline in Firms, Organizations, and States.* Cambridge: Cambridge University Press, 1970.

Hollett, Michael. "Oh What A Night." *Now Magazine.* (March 6-12, 1997): 17.

Holston, James. "Spaces of Insurgent Citizenship." *Planning Theory* 13 (1995): 35-51.

Holston, James, and Arjun Appadurai. "Cities and Citizenship." *Public Culture* 8, no. 2 (1996): 187-204.

Honig, Bonnie. "Difference, Dilemmas, and the Politics of Home." In *Democracy and Difference Contesting the Boundaries of the Political*, edited by Seyla Benhabib. Princeton: Princeton University Press, 1996.

Hume, Christopher. "The city that Jane helped build." *Toronto Star.* (October 12, 1997): F5.

Isin, Engin. *Cities Without Citizens.* Montreal: Black Rose Books, 1992.

Isin, Engin. "Governing Toronto Without Government: Liberalism and Neoliberalism." *Studies in Political Economy* 56 (1998): 169-191.

Isin, Engin. "Rights to the City." Prepared for the International Symposium on *The Rights to the City: Citizenship, Democracy, and Cities in a Global Age.* York University. (June 26-28, 1998).

Isin, Engin. "Citizenship, Class and the Global City." *Citizenship Studies* 3, no. 2 (1999): 267-283.

Isin, Engin, and Joanne Wolfson. *The Making of the Toronto Megacity: An Introduction.* Working Paper no. 21. Toronto: Urban Studies Programme, York University, 1999.

Jacobs, Jane. *The Death and Life of Great American Cities.* New York: Vintage Books, 1961.

Jacobs, Jane. *Deputation to the Standing Committee on General Government conducting hearings on The City of Toronto Act – Bill 103.* (February 3, 1997).

Jacobson, David. *Rights Across Borders: Immigration and the Decline of Citizenship.* Baltimore: The Johns Hopkins University Press, 1996.

Jessop, Bob. "A Neo-Gramscian Approach to the Regulation of Urban Regimes: Accumulation Strategies, Hegemonic Projects, and Governance." In *Reconstructing Urban Regime theory: Regulating Urban Politics in a Global Economy*, edited by Mickey Lauria. Thousand Oaks: Sage, 1997.

Jessop, Bob. "Capitalism and its Future: Remarks on Regulation, Government and Governance." *Review of International Political Economy* 4, no. 3 (1997): 561-581.

Keating, Michael. "Les régions constituent-elles un niveau de gouvernement en Europe?" In *Les paradoxes des régions en Europe*, edited by P. Le Galès and C. Lequesne. Paris: Éditions La Découverte, 1997.

Keating, Michael. "Megacity: not big enough, not small enough." *Globe and Mail.* (February 4, 1997).

Keck, M. E., and K. Sikkink. *Activists Beyond Borders: Advocacy Networks in International Politics.* Ithaca and London: Cornell University Press, 1998.

Keil, Roger. "Globalization makes states: perspectives of local governance in the age of the world city." *Review of International Political Economy* 5, no. 4 (1998): 616-646.

Keil, Roger. "Toronto in the 1990s: Dissociated Governance?" *Studies in Political Economy* 56 (1998): 151-167.

Keil, Roger. *Los Angeles: Globalization, Urbanization and Social Struggles.* Chichester: John Wiley & Sons, 1998.

Kipfer, Stefan. "Global-city politics in the 1990s: Facing the dilemmas of oppositional politics in Toronto." Prepared for the Annual Meeting of the Research Committee 21 of the *International Sociological Association.* Berlin. (July 21-23, 1997).

Kipfer, Stefan. "Urban Politics in the 1990s: Notes on Toronto," In *Possible Urban Worlds*, edited by Inura Zurich. Zurich: ETH, 1998.

Kipfer, Stefan. "Whose City Is It? Global Politics in the Mega-City." *Cityscope*. Newsletter of the Community Social Planning Council of Toronto. (Winter 1999-2000).

Kipfer, Stefan, and Karen Wirsig. "Politics and Possibilities: Re-Living the Suburban Paradox in the New Toronto." *Inura Bulletin* 17 (Fall 1999).

Kipfer, Stefan, and Roger Keil. "Still Planning to be Different? Toronto at the turn of the millennium." *DISP* 140 (2000): 28-36.

Kirby, Andrew. *Power/Resistance local politics and the chaotic state*. Indianapolis: Indiana University Press, 1993.

KPMG. *Fresh Start: An Estimate of Potential Savings And Costs From The Creation of a Single-Tier Local Government for Toronto, Executive Summary*. www.kpmg.ca/centre/vl/cg_gta.htm. (January 27, 1997).

Kymlicka, Will. *Multicultural Citizenship: A Liberal Theory of Minority Rights*. Oxford: Oxford University Press, 1995.

Kymlicka, Will, and Wayne Norman. "Return of the Citizen: A Survey of Recent Work on Citizenship Theory." *Ethics* 104 (1993-94): 352-381.

Laclau, Ernesto, and Chantal Mouffe. *Hegemony and Socialist Strategy: Towards a Radical Democratic Politics*. London: Verso, 1985.

Leach, Al. "A Note From the Minister, Municipal Affairs and Housing." In *A Guide to Municipal Restructuring*, edited by Ministry of Municipal Affairs and Housing. Toronto: Publications Ontario, August 1996.

Leach, Al. *Statement to the Legislature by The Honourable Al Leach, Minister Of Municipal Affairs and Housing On Who Does What*. www.mmah.gov.ca/inthnews/backgrnd/970113e.htm. (January 13, 1997).

Lee, Benjamin. "Peoples and Publics." *Public Culture* 10, no. 2 (1998): 371-394.

Lefebvre, Henri. *The Production of Space*. Oxford: Blackwell, 1991.

Lefebvre, Henri. *Writings on Cities*. Translated and edited by Eleonore Kofman and Elizabeth Lebas. Oxford: Blackwell, 1996.

Lefèvre, Christian. "Metropolitan Government and Governance in Western Countries: A Critical Review." *International Journal of Urban and Regional Research* 22, no. 1 (1998): 9-25.

Legislative Assembly. *The City of Toronto Act: Third Reading*. Toronto: Publications Ontario, 1997.

Lévy, Jacques. "Urbanité: à inventer." *Annales de la recherche urbaine* 64 (1994): 11-16.

Ley, David. *The New Middle Class and the Remaking of the Central City*. Oxford: Oxford University Press, 1996.

Leys, Colin. "Neo-Conservatism and the Organic Crisis in Britain." *Studies in Political Economy* 4 (1980): 41-63.

Liczyk, W. A. *Building a New City: A Blueprint for the Political and Administrative and Organization Structure*. City of North York. (June 27, 1997).

Lofsky, Arthur. *Deputation to the hearing committee on Bill 103*. (February 3, 1997).

Logan, J. R., and H. L. Molotch. *Urban Fortunes: the political economy of place*. Los Angeles: University of California Press, 1987.

Lorinc, John. "Making of the Megacity: An Epic Tale of a Political Founding." *Toronto Life* 32, no. 17 (November 1998).

Low, Murray. "Representation Unbound: Globalization and Democracy." In *Spaces of Globalization: Reasserting the Power of the Local*, edited by Kevin Cox. New York: Guilford Press, 1997.

Lustiger-Thaler, Henri. "New Social Movement Discourse: The Unsolved Democracy." In *Organizing Dissent: Contemporary Social Movements in Theory and Practice*, edited by W.K. Carroll. Toronto: Garamond Press, 1992.

Magnusson, Warren. "Toronto." In *City Politics in Canada*, edited by Warren Magnusson and Andrew Sancton. Toronto: University of Toronto Press, 1983.

Magnusson, Warren. "Bourgeois Theories of Local Government." *Political Studies* XXXIV (1986): 1-18.

Magnusson, Warren. *The Search for Political Space: Globalization, Social Movements, and the Urban Political Experience*. Toronto: University of Toronto Press, 1996.

Mann, Michael. "The Autonomous Power of the State." *European Journal of Sociology* 25 (1984): 185-213.

Marshall, T. H. *Sociology at the Crossroads*. London: Heinemann Educational Books, 1963.

Mays, John Bentley. "Monitoring Toronto's pulse." *Globe and Mail*. (March 5, 1997).

McAdam, D., J. D. McCarthy, and M. N. Zald, eds. *Comparative Perspectives on Social Movements*. Cambridge: Cambridge University Press, 1996.

McCarthy, J. D., and M. N. Zald. "Resource Mobilization and Social Movements: A Partial Theory." *American Journal of Sociology* 82, no. 6 (1977): 1212-1241.

Mihvec, Joe. *Deputation to the hearing committee on Bill 103*. (February 25, 1997).

Mill, John Stuart. *Utilitarianism*, *On Liberty* and *Considerations on Representative Government*, edited by H.B. Acton. London: Dent, 1972.

Milroy, Beth Moore. "Toronto's Legal Challenge to Amalgamation." In *Urban Affairs: Is it Back on the Policy Agenda? / Les affaires urbaines: sont-elles de nouveau à l'ordre du jour?*, edited by C. Andrew, K. Graham, and S. Phillips. Montreal and Kingston: McGill-Queen's University Press, 2000 (forthcoming).

Ministry of Municipal Affairs and Housing. *Fewer Politicians, Lower Taxes More to do in the City of Toronto*. Press Release (December 2, 1999).

Mittelstaedt, Martin. "Shutdown of Toronto would make history." *Globe and Mail*. (October 19, 1996): A1, A4.

Morton, Gary. *The Megacity & Principles of Democracy: Democracy Model Group Investigation*. www.interlog.com/~cjazz/studyto.htm, September 1998.

Mouffe, Chantal. "Feminism, Citizenship, and Radical Democratic Politics." In *Social Postmodernism*, edited by L. Nicholson and S. Seidman. Cambridge: Cambridge University Press, 1995.

MovingTo. "Toronto Spells Home." *Moving To and Around: The Greater Toronto Area* 26, no. 4 (1999-2000).

O'Brien, Richard. *Global Financial Integration: The End of Geography*. London: Pinter Publishers, 1992.

Ohmae, Kenichi. *The End of the Nation State*. New York: Free Press, 1995.

Olsen, Bob. *Deputation to the hearing committee on Bill 103*. (February 5, 1997).

Panitch, Leo. "Globalization and the State." In *Socialist Register 1994*, edited by R. Miliband and L. Panitch. London: Merlin Press, 1994: 60-93.

Peirce, Neal R. *Citistates: How Urban America Can Prosper in a Competitive World*, with Curtis W. Johnson and John Stuart Hall. Washington, DC: Seven Locks Press, 1993.

Peterson, Eric."William Lyon MacKenzie Lives!" Address to the Monday night meeting (January 20, 1997). Recorded on *no mega-cd [no – megacity]*. Toronto: Protest Boy Record, 1997.

Phillips, Ann. "Dealing with Difference: A Politics of Ideas, or a Politics of Presence?" In *Democracy and Difference: Contesting the Boundaries of the Political*, edited by Seyla Benhabib. Princeton: Princeton University Press, 1996.

Polanyi, Karl. *La grande transformation: Aux origines politiques et économiques de notre temps*. Translated by Catherine Malamoud. Paris: Éditions Gallimard, [1944] 1988.

Prescod, Elaine. *Deputation to the hearing committee on Bill 103*. (February 20, 1997).

Raphael, Dennis. *Deputation to the hearing committee on Bill 103*. (March 3, 1997).

Richardson, M., J. Sherman, and M. Gismondi. *Winning back the words: Confronting experts in an environmental public hearing*. Toronto: Garamond Press, 1993.

Robins, Kevin. "Prisoners of the City: Whatever Could a Postmodern City Be?" in *Space and Place Theories of Identity and Location*, edited by E. Carter, J. Donald, and J. Squires. London: Lawrence & Wishart, 1993.

Rocco, Raymond. "The Formation of Latino Citizenship in Southeast Los Angeles." *Citizenship Studies* 3, no. 2 (1999): 253-266.

Ross, Ijeoma. "Neighbours rally to fight amalgamation in Metro Toronto." *Globe and Mail*. (February 1, 1997): A6.

Ross, Ijeoma. "Business favours megacity, poll finds." *Globe and Mail*. (March 3, 1997): A3.

Rusk, David. *Cities Without Suburbs*. Second Edition. Washington, DC: The Woodrow Wilson Center Press, 1995.

Rusk, James, and Ijeoma Ross. "Tories' megacity bill now law." *Globe and Mail*. (April 22, 1997): A3.

Rykert, Liz. *Deputation to the hearing committee on Bill 103*. (February 24, 1997).

Sack, Robert David. *Human Territoriality: Its theory and history*. Cambridge: Cambridge University Press, 1986.

Sassen, Saskia. *Cities in a World Economy*. Thousand Oaks: Pine Forge Press, 1994.

Sassen, Saskia. *Losing Control? Sovereignty in an Age of Globalization*. New York: Columbia University Press, 1996.

Saul, John Ralston. "Address to the Monday night meeting, January 27, 1997." Recorded on *no mega-cd [no – megacity]*. Toronto: Protest Boy Records, 1997.

Saul, John Ralston. "John Ralston Saul: On false populism and the Harris Tories." *Globe and Mail*. (January 30, 1997).

Saul, John Ralston. "Toronto, the (Public) Good." *Toronto Star*. (June 22, 1997): F6.

Scott, Allen. *Regions and the World Economy: The Coming Shape of Global Production, Competition, and Political Order*. Oxford: Oxford University Press, 1998.

Sennett, Richard. *The Fall of Public Man*. New York, London: W.W. Norton & Company, 1974.

Sewell, John. *Deputation to the hearing committee on Bill 103*. (February 13, 1997).

Sewell, John. "The fight was for democracy." *Globe and Mail*. (April 26, 1997).

Sewell, John. "The mourning after." *Now Magazine*. (November 13-19, 1997): 16.

Sewell, John. *Local Government and the future of Canada*. Presentation the Municipal Governance Institute, Vancouver. Posted on C4LD list server (June 20, 1997).

Sewell, John. "Announcement of Candidacy to the Provincial Elections." *John Sewell: Our Voice at Queen's Park* 1 (June 11, 1998).

Sewell, John. "Democracy in Toronto." Prepared for the International Symposium on *The Rights to the City: Citizenship, Democracy, and Cities in a Global Age*. York University. (June 26-28, 1998).

Sewell, John. "Welcome to the Year of the Slingshot." *Eye*. (December 30, 1999).

Sewell, John. *Local Self Government–Bulletin no. 3*. www.localselfgovt.com. (January 2000).

Sharpe, L. J., ed. *The Government of World Cities: The Future of the Metro Model*. New York: John Wiley and Sons, 1995.

Soysal, Yasemin. *Limits of Citizenship: Migrants and Postnational Membership in Europe.* Chicago: University of Chicago Press, 1994.

Spears, John. "Voters set clear goals for super city." *Toronto Star.* (September 15, 1997): A1.

Spears, John. "Your vision for region: Caring, safe, affordable." *Toronto Star.* (September 15, 1997): B1.

Spears, John, and Gail Swainson. "Lastman leads new unified city." *Toronto Star.* (November 11, 1997): A1.

Spring, Lyba. *Deputation to the hearing committee on Bill 103.* (February 12, 1997).

Stein, David Lewis. "Lastman faces wild ride with left-leaning council." *Toronto Star.* (November 11, 1997): B1, B4.

Stodart, A. B. "Letter to the Editor." *Now Magazine.* (March 6-12, 1997): 10.

Storper, Michael.*The Regional World: Territorial Development in a Global Economy.* New York: Guilford Press, 1997.

Stratton, Jocelyn. *Deputation to the hearing committee on Bill 103.* (February 5, 1997).

Swanstrom, Todd. "Beyond Economism: Urban Political Economy and the Postmodern Challenge." *Journal of Urban Affairs* 15, no. 1 (1993): 55-78.

Tarrow, Sidney. *Power in Movement: Social Movements and Contentious Politics.* Second Edition. Cambridge: Cambridge University Press, 1998.

Task Force on Community Access and Equity. *Consultation Guide.* City of Toronto. (June 1998).

Taylor, Peter J. "The State as Container: Territoriality in the Modern World-System." *Progress in Human Geography* 18 (1994): 151-162.

Tiebout, Charles. "A Pure Theory of Local Expenditures." *Journal of Political Economy* 64 (1956): 416-424.

Tindal, Richard, and Susan Nobes Tindal. *Local Government in Canada.* Fourth Edition. Toronto: McGraw-Hill Ryerson Limited, 1995.

Tocqueville, Alexis de. *Democracy in America.* New York: Vintage Books, 1945.

Todd, Graham. "'Going global' in the semi-periphery: world cities as political projects. The case of Toronto." In *World Cities in a World-System,* edited by Paul L. Knox and Peter J. Taylor. Cambridge: Cambridge University Press, 1995.

Todd, Graham. "Megacity: Globalization and Governance in Toronto." *Studies in Political Economy* 56 (1998): 193-216.

Toronto Star Editorial. "What Toronto needs from new mayor." *Toronto Star.* (October 12, 1997): F2.

Toronto Star Editorial. "There's method in Mel's madness." *Toronto Star.* (November 24, 1999).

Toronto Star. "Birth of a City." *Toronto Star.* (November 11, 1997): B1.

Touraine, Alain. "An Introduction to the Study of Social Movements." *Social Research* 52, no. 4 (1985): 749-787.

Tourism Toronto. *Toronto 1998 Visitors Guide.* Toronto: Tourism Toronto, 1998.

Transition Team. *New City New Opportunities.* Toronto. (December 1997).

Tully, James. *Strange Multiplicity: Constitutionalism in an age of diversity.* Cambridge: Cambridge University Press, 1995.

Turner, Bryan. "Outline of a Theory of Citizenship." In *Dimensions of Radical Democracy: Pluralism, Citizenship, Community*, edited by Chantal Mouffe. London: Verso.

Urry, John. *Consuming Places.* London: Routledge, 1995.

Van, Sandra. "Getting to the Root of the Matter?" *Cityscope,* Newsletter of the Community Social Planning Council of Toronto (Winter 1999-2000).

Vaughan, Colin. "Ratepayers' groups gear up for megacity." *Globe and Mail.* (February 3, 1997): A3.

Vaughan, Colin. "Developers support megacity for bureaucratic neatness." *Globe and Mail.* (February 24, 1997).

Vaughan, Colin. "Toronto can learn much from German city-states." *Toronto Star.* (November 8, 1999).

Walker, Michael. *Secession of the City of Toronto from the Province of Ontario: "Let the People Decide."* Notice of Motion. Toronto City Council. (December 15-16, 1999).

Walker, William. "Harris calls big megacity meeting." *Toronto Star.* (March 20, 1997).

Walker, William. "Queen's Park on 're' alert: MPPs ready for megacity trouble." *Toronto Star.* (March 31, 1997).

Weinstock, Daniel M. "La citoyenneté comme 'réponse' au problème du pluralisme des sociétés modernes." In *Les enjeux de la citoyenneté: Un bilan interdisciplinaire/A Multidisciplinary Approach.* Report of Immigration et Métropoles Research Group. Montreal. (June 1998).

Wendell Cox Consultancy. *Local and Regional Governance in the Greater Toronto Area: A Review of Alternatives.* www.city.toronto.on.ca/3wrd/cox.htm, January 10, 1997.

Workman, Thom. *Banking on Deception The Discourse of Fiscal Crisis.* Halifax: Fernwood Publishing, 1996.

World Bank. *The State in a Changing World: World Development Report 1997.* Oxford: Oxford University Press, 1997.

Wright, Erik Olin.*Class Counts: Comparative Studies in Class Analysis.* Cambridge: Cambridge University Press, 1997.

Wright, Lisa. "Tension builds at Legislature." *Toronto Star.* (April 2, 1997).

Young, Don. *Deputation to the hearing committee on Bill 103.* (February 12, 1997).

Young, Iris Marion. *Justice and the Politics of Difference.* Princeton: Princeton University Press, 1990.

Young, Iris Marion. "Communication and the Other: Beyond Deliberative Democracy" In *Democracy and Difference: Contesting the Boundaries of the Political*, edited by Seyla Benhabib. Princeton: Princeton University Press, 1996.

Young, Nelly Auster. *Deputation to the hearing committee on Bill 103.* (February 12, 1997).

Zhelka, Eric. *Deputation to the hearing committee on Bill 103.* (March 6, 1997).

Zukin, Sharon. *Landscapes of Power: From Detroit to Disney World.* Los Angeles: University of California Press, 1991.

Zukin, Sharon. *The Cultures of Cities.* Oxford: Blackwell, 1995.

# INDEX

Access and equity, 42, 43, 51, 52, 58, 59, 105, 161, 167; Task Force on, 27, 51
Accountability, 68, 157, 159, 170, 171
Amalgamation, xi, 6, 7, 11, 13, 17, 34n38
Appiah, K. A., 141-2
Arendt, Hannah, 145-6, 159-60
Authoritarian populism, 91, 125, 168
Autonomy, xii, xiv, 16, 30, 54, 134, 159, 163

Benhabib, Seyla, 140
Bill 103, xi, 6, 7, 11, 13, 17, 34n38
Board of Trade, 9, 12
Board of Trustees, 6, 10, 13, 14, 62
Boosterism, 95, 96, 97, 114, 155, 167
Brenner, Neil, 92-3, 102

Caulfield, Jon, 42, 115
Centrality, 110-1, 115
Citizens' Assembly, 25-6
Citizens' Legal Challenge, 16, 18, 163
Citizenship, 69, 129, 130; legal status, 131, 143, 161-2, 165
City of Toronto Act, xi, 6,7,11, 13,17, 34n38
City-state, 30, 105, 165; Province of Toronto, 31
Civic commitment, 40
Civic space, 71-2, 119
Civility, 110-1, 115, 155
Class struggle in space, 47-8, 68, 114, 116, 167
Colton, Timothy, 96
Common Sense Revolution, 5, 9, 37, 74, 84, 157, 170
Community control (needs, preferences), 20-21, 42, 49, 55, 56, 58, 64, 100
Community councils, 24, 25, 56
Conservatism, 62-3, 65
Cosmopolitanism, 110-1, 141-3
Crombie, David, 6, 8, 12

Deliberative democracy, 140-1
Democratic process, 10, 11, 15, 18, 23, 47, 49, 52, 54, 169-70
Disentanglement, 6, 11, 34n29
Downloading (offloading), 15, 17, 28, 34n37, 71, 93, 104

Economism, 85-6, 168, 169
Eder, Klaus, 45-46, 63, 120-1
Election: municipal, 7, 8, 18, 19-24, 31, 48, 56, 70; provincial, 5, 66-9, 74, 117-8, 123, 124; federal, 69, 160
Enclosure, 103, 105
Essentialism, 137-8

Filion, Pierre, 94-5
Fiscal crisis, 39, 88-9, 154, 168
Formal realm of politics, 57, 58, 59, 60, 68, 70, 73, 77, 155, 158, 170
Friedmann, John, 93, 167

Giddens, Anthony, 149-50
Global city, 3, 13, 27, 30, 32, 58, 70, 84, 85, 93-5, 112, 114, 123, 170
Globalization, xii, 47, 84, 106n18; adaptation policies, xii, 86, 94, 95, 114, 122, 124, 170, 171
Goldberg, David Theo, 136-9
Governance of complexity, 103, 105, 113, 148, 168
Greater Toronto Area Task Force, 7-8, 95-6, 122, 123, 125-6, 171

Habermas, Jurgen, 135, 140
Hall, Barbara, 13, 21-4, 48
Hall, Stuart, 91
Harris, Mike, xi, 5, 9, 11, 12, 14, 18, 23, 28, 29, 30, 33n17, 38, 68, 71, 76, 78, 79, 86, 89, 114, 123-4,
Harvey, David, xiv, 88

Holston, James, 144-146, 151n12; and Arjun Appadurai, 101, 144, 147
Human rights, 51, 142-3, 168
Informal realm of politics, 59, 73, 155, 170
Intercultural constitutional dialogue, 148, 151n12, 163
Isin, Engin, 43, 48, 55, 89-90, 99-100, 119, 122, 164; and Joanne Wolfson, 2-5, 7, 10, 122, 124
Jacobs, Jane, 30, 41, 42, 59, 64, 104, 110
Jessop, Bob, 93, 103, 113, 168
Keating, Michael, 123, 125
Keil, Roger, xii, 80, 86, 87, 95, 97, 100, 101, 102, 105
Kipfer, Stefan, xii, 27, 47, 114, 120, 167; and Roger Keil, 2, 3, 32, 95; and Karen Wirsig, 126
Kymlicka, Will, 136, 139; and Wayne Norman, 135, 139
Lastman, Mel, ix, 21-4, 28, 29, 30, 33n17, 47, 48, 104, 165, 166
Leach, Al, 6, 8, 11, 13, 14, 15, 60, 84, 86, 114
Lefebvre, Henri, 74-5, 111-2, 146
Levels of government: hierarchy, 100, 102, 113, 119, 134, 168; balance of power, xii, 2, 55; changing relationship between, xiii, 15, 34n29, 55, 79, 99, 104, 163
Liberal democracy, 54, 58, 159, 167, 169-70; political liberalism, 52, 58, 80n13, 130, 137-8, 169
Local (civic) ownership, 74, 75, 113, 155, 160, 165
Local democracy, 20-1, 26, 38, 50, 69; threats to, 10, 13, 47; training ground for democracy, 98-9, 160
Local nature of individual rights, 54, 163
Local self-government (self-determination), 30, 55
Losing one's lifeworld, 64, 171
MacKenzie, William Lyon, 14, 72-3
Magnusson, Warren, x-xi, 101-3, 104, 114, 155, 159
Marshall, T. H., 135
Membership, 129, 141, 143, 145-7, 162-3
Metro Network for Social Justice, 4, 7, 76
Middle-class: urbanism, 42, 45, 47, 49, 167; radicalism (activism), 45, 63, 76, 80, 121, 122, 170, 171; urban progressive, x, xii, 22, 37-8, 43, 49, 52, 84, 86, 102, 105, 115, 121, 124, 167, 169; action space, 45-6, 49, 51, 52, 54, 57, 58, 59, 72, 74, 162, 169
Mill, John Stuart, 54, 55, 98, 163
Mobilization, ix, 1, 13, 16, 26, 46, 49, 50, 71, 77, 119, 167; sites of, 75
Modern constitutionalism, 132-3
Moment of insurgency, 77, 122, 167, 169
Mouffe, Chantal, 137-139, 163
Multiculturalism, 131, 135-9
Municipal (local) boundaries, xi, 5, 25, 49, 84, 101, 104-5, 156, 167
Municipal politics: accessibility, 64, 65; as a tool, 43, 80, 115, 122, 170-1; at the juncture of the state and civil society, xi, 54, 101, 103, 105, 125, 155; urban politics, 101-2
Neighbourhood committees, 7, 25
Neoliberalism, xi, 9, 37, 50, 56, 85, 88, 89, 91, 92, 95, 123, 131, 154, 167, 168, 170
Offloading (downloading), 15, 17, 28, 34n37, 71, 93, 104
Ohmae, Kenishi, 107
Participation (citizen, public, political), 20, 25, 26, 38, 45, 54, 55, 65, 131, 140, 167
Party line system, 2, 68, 157-8
Performative citizenship, 119, 131, 147-8, 155, 165-6
Performative paradox, 133, 135, 136, 139, 140, 147, 156, 159, 164
Phillips, Ann, 61
Place-construction, 87-88, 112
Political liberalism, 52, 58, 80n13, 130, 137-8, 169; liberal democracy, 54, 58, 159, 167, 169-70

Political opportunity structure, 121
Politics of everyday life, x, 75, 101, 103, 109, 111, 114, 119, 122, 124, 125-6, 144, 155, 159, 161, 165; impact of amalgamation on, 57, 64, 120
Politics of presence, 60-1, 70
Popular sovereignty, 54-5,
Producing space, 74-5, 112-3
Progressive regime (Toronto), 4, 12, 24-5, 37, 43, 47, 50, 52, 55, 56, 116-7, 165
Property taxes: increases, 12, 21, 51; reform, 28, 56, 71; local control over, 8, 29, 55; freeze, 48; no taxes ideology, 29, 49, 51; in Toronto, 95
Protest culture, 45-6, 49; differing, 76

Quality of life: against globalization, xii, 115, 170; against amalgamation, 12, 38, 50, 55, 58, 63, 119, 155, 166; as a competitive advantage, 32, 98; as a social movement, 43, 45, 47, 49-50, 105, 167

Radical action, 58, 76-7
Radical democracy, 137-9
Rawls, John, 137-8
Referendum, 14-5, 40, 60, 119
Reform movement, 9, 10, 32, 42-3, 65, 88, 94-5, 100, 114-5
Regionalism, 125; in Toronto, 125-6
Representative democracy, 11, 157, 159
Residency, 131, 142, 145-7, 160, 170; non-citizens, 21, 161, 163
Restructuring, xiii, 6, 13, 79; municipal, x, 2, 22, 45, 46, 48, 50, 61, 91
Revenue-neutrality, 28
Right to have rights, 145-6, 161
Rights of the city (rights of the municipality), 52, 55, 122, 159, 163
Rights to the city, 16, 122, 130, 146, 148

Sassen, Saskia, 95-6, 142-3
Saul, John Ralston, 1, 11, 41, 165
Secession, 30
Sennett, Richard, 110-1
Sense of community, 40, 69, 155, 166
Sense of place, 65, 75, 105, 147
Sewell, John, 1, 5, 10, 13, 14, 18, 22, 31, 39, 42, 58, 59, 63, 65, 68, 71, 77, 114, 116, 157-8
Social management, 89-90, 168
Social movements, 16, 39, 43, 45, 49, 70, 77-8, 101, 120, 125, 168, 170
Soysal, Yasemin, 101, 143
State re-scaling, xii, 92-3, 101, 102, 104, 105, 159, 163, 168, 170
Strategic voting, 68
Swanstrom, Todd, 86

Taking to the streets 20, 72
Tindal Susan Nobes, 99-100
Tindal, Richard, 99-100
Tocqueville, Alexis de, 54, 55, 98, 163
Todd, Graham, 59, 93-4
Transition Team, 6, 10, 18, 24, 25, 26, 97
Tully, James, 132-4, 139

Urban politics, 101-2
Urban/suburban contrast, xii, 22-3, 25, 47-8, 68, 102, 110, 116, 126
Urbanity, 12, 110-2, 115-6, 122, 167

Voice, 61, 64, 78, 124, 154
Voting right, 131, 147, 161-2

Who Does What Panel, 6, 8, 12
Withering away of the state, 91, 92, 106n21, 144
Workman, Thom, 88-9

Young, Iris Marion, 110-1, 136-7, 138, 139, 141, 147

Zukin, Sharon, 87

ALSO PUBLISHED BY

BLACK ROSE BOOKS

PUBLIC PLACE

*Citizen Participation in the Neighbourhood and the City*

*Dimitrios I. Roussopoulos*

Drawing on his experience in community journalism, Roussopoulos writes on a broad range of issues that affect the daily life of neighbourhoods and cities, using *The Public Place* as a source of citizen participation.

> *The lessons to be learned are invaluable...topics well chosen...succeeds in making citizens conscious of their role in the community, and how they too can make significant change.* —*Canadian Content Online*

208 pages, bibliography, index
Paperback ISBN: 1-55164-156-9 $19.99
Hardcover ISBN: 1-55164-157-7 $48.99

LOCAL PLACES

*In the Age of the Global City*

*Roger Keil, Gerda R. Wekerle, David V.J. Bell, editors*

Looks at the complex social, economic and political contexts of cities in the 1990s. Contributors include: Jane Jenson, Gardner Church, Franz Hartmann, Prabha Khosla, Engin F. Isin, Susan Ruddick, Edmond P. Fowler, Michael Hough, Roger Keil, Gerda R. Wekerle, and David V.J. Bell.

272 pages, index
Paperback ISBN: 1-55164-046-5 $19.99
Hardcover ISBN: 1-55164-047-3 $48.99

CITIES WITHOUT CITIZENS

*Modernity of the City as a Corporation*

*Engin F. Isin*

Traces how cities evolved from autonomous entities with citizens to modern corporations without citizens.

> *...a remarkable book...explains the origins of modern Canadian cities as corporations.* —*Imprint*

245 pages, index, appendices
Paperback ISBN: 1-895431-26-3 $19.99
Hardcover ISBN: 1-895431-27-1 $48.99

BOOKS OF RELATED INTEREST BY

BLACK ROSE BOOKS

Canadian City, *by Kent Gerecke*
City and Radical Social Change, *by Dimitrios Roussopoulos, editor*
Conquest of Bread, *by Peter Kropotkin*
Designing Utopia, *by Michael Lang*
Evolution and Environment, *by Peter Kropotkin*
Humanity, Society and Commitment, *by Kenneth McRobbie*
Humerous Sceptic, *by N.Anthony Bonaparte*
Green Cities, *by David Gordon, editor*
Killing Hope, *by William Blum*
Manufacturing Consent, *by Mark Achbar*
Philosophy of Social Ecology, *by Murray Bookchin*
Military in Greek Politics, *by Thanos Veremis*
Mind Abuse, *by Rose Dyson*
Montréal, *by Jean-Hugues Roy, Brendan Weston, editors*
Other Mexico, *by John Warnock*
People, Potholes and City Politics, *by Karen Herland*
Perspectives on Power, *by Noam Chomsky*
Pirates and Emperors, *by Noam Chomsky*
Political Arrangements, *by Henri Lustiger-Thaler, editor*
Private Interest, Public Spending, *by William Scheuerman, Sidney Plotkin*
Shelter, Housing and Homes, *by Arnold Bennett*

send for a free catalogue of all our titles
BLACK ROSE BOOKS
C.P. 1258, Succ. Place du Parc
Montréal, Québec
H3W 2R3 Canada

or visit our web site at: http://www.web.net/blackrosebooks

To order books in North America:
(phone) 1-800-565-9523 (fax) 1-800-221-9985
In the UK & Europe: (phone) 44 (0) 20 8986-4854 (fax) 44 (0) 20 8533-5821

Printed by the workers of
MARC VEILLEUX IMPRIMEUR INC.
Boucherville, Québec
for Black Rose Books Ltd.